CONSTITUENT ASSEMBLY OF INDIA

CONSTITUENT ASSEMBLY OF INDIA

N. GANGULEE

GYAN

Published by

GYAN

Gyan Publishing House
5, Ansari Road
Daryaganj, New Delhi-110002
Phone: 011-47034999, 9811692060
E-mail: books@gyanbooks.com

Distribution Network
gyanbooks.com
India, USA, Canada, UK, Australia

ISBN: 978-93-7169-051-5 (PB)

First Published, 1942

2nd Impression 2025

Printed at: Gyan Press, Delhi.

CONSTITUENT ASSEMBLY OF INDIA
Author: N. GANGULEE

Freedom to achieve Freedom

CONSTITUENT ASSEMBLY *for* INDIA

by

N. GANGULEE

Formerly Professor, University of Calcutta, Ex-member of the Royal Commission on Agriculture in India and of Imperial Research Council, New Delhi

"Ah, Ricci, the form of Government is not eternal; we shall march with the times"

(*King Carlo Alberto to Count Giuseppe Ricci*)

London

GEORGE ALLEN AND UNWIN LTD

CONTENTS

INTRODUCTION

I

The demand of the Indian National Congress, India's foremost political organization, is no longer vague and vacillating. It no longer thinks in terms of an abstract polity. The President, in his address before the Congress held at Haripur (1937), declared: "The time has come for us to raise the issue of *Swaraj* (independence) and submit our National Demand to the British Government in the form of an ultimatum. The time is long past when we could have adopted a passive attitude and waited for the Federal Scheme to be imposed on us." That acceptance of the Government of India Act (1935) would only perpetuate the stranglehold of British Imperialism was fully realized by the Congress, which warned India not to expose herself to further delusions. Meanwhile the Act itself broke down, and the Government reverted to the form of bureaucratic dictatorship.

Those who ask us to appreciate the ideal of partnership with Britain do not realize that there is no bond other than that of freedom which could make that ideal realizable. They point to the Federal constitution framed by the British Parliament as a decisive step towards that freedom, but we know that constitutional bonds based upon "special responsibilities," "reserved powers" and safeguards innumerable are not only unsubstantial, but brittle. Legal and constitutional forms, notwithstanding their liberal appearance, do not contain the essential elements of independence, and it is clearly evident that, while the Imperial Government have sought to pacify Indian aspirations by yielding on non-essentials, they have taken adequate measures to strengthen their grip on those essentials whose maintenance perpetuates the British sovereignty in India.

The demand for a Constituent Assembly, elected by the people, to frame the constitution of India, with full safeguards for the protection of rights and interests of minority communities, has been repeatedly put forward by the Congress since 1934; but as it raises the fundamental issue of the location of sovereignty in the Indian people, it is ignored by the British Government. The result is the present constitutional *impasse*, the continuance of which should convince the leaders of the united national movement that India's freedom cannot be gained by "the war of words." The vague declarations as to "Dominion Status for India" after the termination of the present war are irrelevant, because they do not satisfy India's unequivocal demand for political freedom. But the case for India's freedom is unanswerable. Only under the conditions of political freedom can India adjust the relations between the main elements in her national life.

The basis of our national demand is therefore the inalienable sovereignty of India. It is not a question of better government or even of self-government; nor are we concerned with the minute details of a constitutional edifice in the preparation of whose "blue-print" the Imperial Government spent eight years. The concrete demand of the Indian National Congress is to convoke a Constituent Assembly in order to frame a constitution that would confer an independent sovereign status on India.

It is often asked, what is the status of the Indian National Congress which justifies its claim to be in the forefront as an organized exponent of Indian national sovereignty, and to what extent does this political organization represent the spirit of Indian nationalism? We must answer these questions, because even some of the sympathetic observers of the West do not see in the organized expression of Indian nationalism anything but a complex pattern of competing forces emanating from numerous religious faiths. They question the basis of unity among our diverse peoples, which is a *sine qua non* of freedom, and lay stress upon the achievement of the political unity of India by British rule. It does not occur to them that the unity consequent upon the operation of what Mr. Winston Churchill describes as "technical and administrative apparatus" is the unity of servitude and that the organic cohesion of a nation develops only in the atmosphere of independent national sovereignty. What is surprising is that India has never lost sight of the ideal of fundamental unity transcending "the innumerable diversities of blood, colour, language, dress, manners and sect." The survival of the basic elements of Indian culture, the growth of the National Congress and the response to the demand for freedom are some of the examples of that living ideal and we firmly believe that it will increasingly find expression in our national life once India is free from being a servile State.

The aim of Indian nationalism is to achieve national unity and independence. It does not endanger the peace of the world, for it has no aggressive spirit; it does not aim at subjugating others; it has no "heavenly mission" to fulfil in the world nor does it dream of building an empire. It wants India's freedom—the freedom to foster the spirit of nationality within her own territories and among her own diverse peoples. It seeks to be free from the domination of what Seeley calls the "inorganic" state originating from British conquest and it sets as its goal the creation of that form of State which would establish an independent status for India in the comity of nations. Only then can India have a share in the political and cultural movements of the new epoch.

While we deprecate the growth of aggressive Nationalism, it is necessary for us to stress the feeling that the country is in the possession of an alien power and to instil into the soul of the people that political tutelage under its yoke impoverishes the national well-being and causes a spiritual exhaustion. Once a foreign visitor asked pupils of a secondary school in Bengal, "To whom does India belong?" "England" was the prompt reply. It is not generally realized that this feeling reacts upon the spirit of service for commonweal; because the amount of sacrifice people will willingly undergo in their own interests is certainly greater than what they would be prepared to adopt at the dictation of a foreign Government which assumes the ultimate responsibility of their country's welfare. Lack of voluntary social service in India—that distinctive feature of a free country—may be explained by this psychological reaction to a foreign rule. As Benedetto Croce put it, "To love the State is to work with the State, to put into the State and to pour into political life which is best in us, our feelings, the truths we think, that is, our active faith, our ideals; and it is this participation which, in other words, is called Freedom. This Freedom is not opposition to the State, an offence to its majesty, but is the very life of the State itself—unless we are ready to suppose that the blood circulating and renewing itself continually in our veins is lawless agitation against the sovereign claim of our physiological organism. Nor is freedom conceivable in the State unless it be political freedom to co-operate with its life. . . ." But political affiliations with an alien state cannot evoke in the people that enthusiasm for service which the country needs. Consequently when we apply ourselves to any task of reconstruction, our efforts becomes imitative rather than creative.

Without our independent political sovereignty we cannot rehabilitate the economic and social structure of the country to suit our own ideals of life. Our efforts in this direction would not have been so barren if the choice of spontaneously developing such forms of organization as are required to meet the changing circumstances of our life and labour were left to us. The system of local self-government, for example, introduced by the Imperial Government towards the end of the nineteenth century was so devised that it succeeded in killing local initiative and exterminated the status of the village commune which, like the Russian Mir, might have furnished us with a basis of democratic government. It is indeed one of our chief concerns that the system of the village councils should be revived so that they may be found, to quote Sidney Webb, "exercising actually the greater part of that share of the people's income which is administered collectively, appointing and controlling the majority of all the salaried servants of the community, and even enacting . . . the greater volume of the laws that the people obey."[1] The institutions developed within the system of village government were not the product of bureaucracy. As Hegel truly remarked, what is best in human personality comes from the individual's organic membership in the community. The government of a centralized alien bureaucracy have destroyed this relationship and have seriously disturbed the pattern of our socio-economic life. The process by which the initiative of the people was stifled was deliberately pursued in order to consolidate its rule. It realized that the development of corporate life among the various classes of the population through their traditional forms of local organization would make the task of consolidation difficult. Even the indigenous schools were therefore swept away.

It is for this reason that the task of rural reconstruction has become extremely complicated, and those of us who have had some experience in this field realize that the regeneration of

[1] Sidney Webb in Preface to *Village Government in British India*, by John Mathai (1915).

village communities is not possible so long as the impact of British imperialism in India controls her destiny.

To-day a state of chaos and confusion prevails in the machinery of local self-government introduced by the Government in the place of indigenous organizations. Some years ago the late Lord Sinha (the first Indian raised to the peerage) introduced certain modifications in the Bengal Self-government Act of 1885 in the hope of creating effective village unions, but such attempts bore no fruitful results. The pious hope expressed in the Report of the Commission on Agriculture in India that "the people must be organized to help themselves and their local organizations must be grouped into larger unions" cannot be fulfilled without political freedom.

Again, take the case of education. Here is a problem which profoundly affects the development of all other phases of our national life. But in its solution we have had no free hand. The educational policy was shaped by our rulers without any comprehension of our needs and aspirations. Thus the system of education imposed on us has not only failed but has done great injury to the soul of India. After a century and half of British rule, only 0·78 per cent of our population is literate in English and less than 8·1 per cent of the total population is literate according to the census standard. Two-thirds of our seven hundred thousand villages have no schools at all. Under such conditions of illiteracy, it is not surprising that the majority of our people cling tenaciously to those worn-out traditions and customs which handicap progress. One of the urgent problems before us is the widespread illiteracy which impedes to a great extent the growth of political and social consciousness among the masses. The Congress has undertaken to remedy this fatal weakness with all the resources at its command. The literacy campaign has already made a mark in the national movement and the psychological reflex of this campaign upon the educated youth augurs well for the Congress itself.

But it is not merely the question of the quantitative factor of education that concerns us. Education through an alien bureaucracy is largely responsible for misunderstanding of ourselves; it has kept us ignorant of the significance of Indian culture; it has no "vital spark" and that is why India's reactions to contact with the modern world have been so disappointing. If the West is still "a living world of mind," as Rabindranath Tagore tells us, our access to that world has not been free, easy and constant.

Then, there is the fundamental question of the material condition of the people. The crisis in agricultural production is chronic in India because the means of production and distribution are controlled by a formidable chain of vested interests. "Within the protective shell of imperialist domination and exploitation has grown up a host of subsidiary parasitism dependent on and integral to the whole system," writes a recent author[1] in his survey of the Indian agrarian problem. The ending of that system is the goal of Indian nationalism.

The aim of Indian nationalism is not incompatible with internationalism. We regard a Nationalism which seeks to rob any nation of its freedom as mischievous and as one that can only be maintained by force. Our goal is *Purna Swaraj*, that is, conquest of inalienable rights to control our national destiny without interference and to co-operate freely with nations.

Indeed, constitutional independence is a necessity for India if she is to establish international relations. For long India remained "outside the arena of living and creative history" and it is this fatality that has resulted in the atrophy of her own national life. Not only does our political bondage restrict our free participation in international life but it chokes the normal channel of our cultural intercourse with the civilized world. What sort of a place is assigned to a nation without political sovereignty is shown by India's position in the League of Nations. She has never been permitted to hold a seat on the League Council because of her status as a *dependency* of Britain. Article One of the Covenant stipulates that "a member of the League must be a community that can contract international obligations and be responsible for them," and it is argued that "India was not admitted to the League by the League under Article One."[2] Her delegates are no more than mere spokesmen of the British Government as India is denied the right of autonomy in external affairs. Indeed, her anomalous position in the League could never be rectified without constitutional freedom. Without an independent political status, India can neither restore her prestige in the international world nor contribute her due share in the

[1] R. Palme Dutt, *India To-day*.

[2] E. R. Phelan, *Problems of Peace*; The League of Nations Series, Vol. VI.

remaking of Asia. Her struggle for freedom is therefore not unrelated to Asia's preparation to defend the future of the Asiatic races.

The issue is clear: India is determined to assert the sovereignty of the people by demanding her inalienable right to frame a constitution by a democratically elected Constituent Assembly. The Indian National Congress, the Indian States' Peoples Association, the All-India Kisan Sabha (Peasant Leagues), the Trade Unions and other organized national institutions throughout the country recognize that democracy in India must be "that form of government and of society which is inspired above every other with the feeling and consciousness of the dignity of man."[1] The growth of the Indian National Congress is by itself an expression of that consciousness. Only the imperial jingoes regard Indian nationalism as being of a "spurious brand" and "not primarily love of country but love of racial caste and personal prestige." In a recent publication entitled *India and Democracy*[2] the authors ridicule Congress, sneering at it as "a collection of almost every conceivable interest and type of personality," and describe its annual sessions as "in atmosphere part gipsy encampment, part football match, part parish bazaar," paralleled in their view only by the Nuremberg rallies of the National Socialists of Nazi Germany. Seeking to besmirch Congress with the pitch of Nazi-ism, they seem to make it a matter of reproach that the party of Indian freedom should be an all-embracing union of "millionaires, mill-workers, landlords, peasants, saints, gangsters, professors, experts in international affairs, parochialists, liberals, anarchists, communists, ascetics, fanatical Moslems, and fanatical Hindus. . . ." Does it not rather follow that this unity of diverse elements in India's national life is proof positive of a united struggle by her people to achieve freedom?

II

This book is an attempt to present the problem of the Constituent Assembly as an instrument through which peoples have gained, or made efforts to gain, their constitutional independence. Although our situation in India is extremely complicated, not

[1] Thomas Mann (Winner of Nobel Prize for literature).

[2] Sir George Schuster and Guy Wint, *India and Democracy*, 1941.

only by reason of the presence of a strong alien bureaucracy, but also because of the vastness of the country and its population, with all its varied characteristics, we can certainly draw some lessons from the struggles of other races and civilizations for independence. What concerns us, however, is not the political theories underlying the concept of Constituent Assembly, but rather the manner in which it has functioned under varying circumstances in determining the location of sovereignty in response to the peoples' demand.

The book opens with a chapter dealing with origins of the Constituent Assembly, and in the two following chapters I have given an account of constitutional struggles in the United States of America and in France. Since the political theories underlying the concept of the Constituent Assembly are supposed to have been applied to the framing of the Dominion constitutions, I have briefly outlined these developments, showing how constitutional changes have been effected in Canada, South Africa and Australia. Since the history of Ireland's struggles for constitutional independence falls into a special category, I have had to devote a separate chapter to it.

Within the limit of a single chapter I have sought to bring together certain material for the study of political changes in those countries in which national efforts gathered momentum, either by internal revolution, or in consequence of the Great War of 1914–1918. The narrative is intersting, and it is, I believe, possible to gain from its study an understanding of the principles that have determined the success of political revolutions—as in the case, for example, of the Union of Soviet Socialist Republics—or of the causes of their tragic failure, as in republican Spain.

The second part of the book begins with a chapter enumerating certain features of India's opposition to the Federal scheme elaborated in the Government of India Act, 1935. The leader of that opposition is the Indian National Congress: this vast organization, with its five millions of members, is no longer what our rulers used to regard as "a microscopic minority." Although the tempo of Indian political conflict has been intermittent, and reminiscent of an eddy rather than a steady current, this conflict has never abandoned its goal of freedom. The *will* to win freedom for India is manifest in Indian mass movements, and in recent years the National Congress has shown enough political competence to bring the struggle to a final issue. Indeed, the national struggle for the liberation of India has responded to the reactions against the dominance of an alien bureaucracy—reactions which must eventually free the peoples of India from the tutelage of their rulers.

But the struggle will be long and arduous. It involves freedom from the yoke of British imperialism, so deeply entrenched in the country; it means bold and persistent attack upon the numerous evils that become domesticated when a nation remains for long under servitude; and it has to liquidate the unholy alliance of all the reactionary forces within the country with those of imperialism.

Mustafa Kemal, who restored "the sick man of Europe" to exuberant health and vitality, once said: "Sovereignty is never yielded through reason and arguments; it is taken by force and violence." India, however, aspires to reach her goal by non-violent revolution. Her demands are not backed by physical force, and therefore they do not attract much attention from our rulers or from the world at large. Since we cannot face aggression with armed revolution, we have become, as it were, "an outcast in the pantheon of humanity." By a policy of non-violence the Indian National Congress has therefore assumed responsibility, not only for the success of our own struggle, but for the demonstration of the truth that revolution—which, to quote Bergson, "is a process of adjustment"—cannot *really* be effective if its strength is derived from violence.

The question may be asked whether it will ever be possible to bring about an adjustment between the claims of Indian nationalism and those of a powerful imperial bureaucracy. I have given an account of the stalemate in the Indian political controversy, so that the reader may appreciate the situation and form his own conclusion.

In a final chapter I have attempted a brief discussion of the lessons which we can draw from the experiences of those Constituent Assemblies to which reference has been made in the earlier chapters. I have not ventured to discuss those decisive steps which must *now* be taken in India with a view to preparing the ground for a Constituent Assembly. Obviously these tasks should be left to those who occupy the front rank in India's struggle for national liberation. If there still appears to be a good deal of rather nebulous thinking as to the conception, the purpose, and the method of a Constituent Assembly for India, they alone can clarify the issue by drawing up such programmes of action as are necessary to make the Indian national demand effective. My own feeling in writing this book may be aptly expressed by an extract from the introductory preface to Gerald Winstanley's *The Law of Freedom in a Platform*, addressed to Oliver Cromwell, Lord Protector of the Commonwealth:

> "And now I have set the candle at your door, for you have power in your hand, in this other added opportunity, to Act for Common Freedom if you will; I have no power.
>
> "It may be here are some things inserted which you may not like, yet other things you may like, therefore I pray you read it, and be as the industrious bee, suck out the honey and cast away the weeds.
>
> "Though this Platform be like a piece of timber rough hewd, yet the discreet workman may take it, and frame a handsome building out of it.
>
> "It is like a poor man that comes clothed to your door in a torn country garment, who is unacquainted with the learned citizens' unsettled forms and fashions; take off the clownish language, for under that you may see beauty."

I must confess to have written this book from a viewpoint somewhat different from that which I held in the past. As a student of agricultural research, I came to believe that India's economic life could be improved by the application of science to the problem of livelihood. What was necessary was an enlightened policy of reforms in the economic and social structures, and I was inclined to be content, provided the execution of the organized plan were effected by the existing administrative machinery.

But now, after spending nearly a decade in Europe, and having devoted much time to the study of various plans for agricultural and rural development, I am convinced that the basic problem of a nation cannot be solved without the essential prerequisite of political rights and freedom. It is the lack of this freedom, inherent in the conception of popular sovereignty, that creates the naïve and complacent type of nationalism. Only when the assertion of national independence against a foreign rule or against a system of government incompatible with the democratic ideal becomes effective does the medley of contradictions in which the reformist ideas are entangled disappear. India's struggle for freedom must therefore be placed in the forefront of all her national endeavours.

The Indian National Congress must shoulder the inevitable responsibility of preparing the ground for a Constituent Assembly. It must now actively collaborate with the Indian State Peoples' Association, with the ever increasing numbers of Peasant Leagues, and with the Trade Unions. The conditions prerequisite for the convocation of a Constituent Assembly can be brought about only by a closer co-ordination of the Indian mass-movements. Only then will there be an impregnable front against imperialism, the reactionary Indian feudal princes, and the equally reactionary bourgeoisie. And the economic and social rehabilitation of the masses can be a reality only when they themselves secure political power.

In conclusion, I trust that this book may be of some use to those who are now determined to assert India's right to independence, and I hope that the day is not far when they may address the author as Henry IV greeted the tardy Crillon after a great battle had been won: "Hang yourself, brave Crillon! We fought at Argues, and you were not there."

It is now my pleasant duty to express my gratitude to all those who have generously helped me in my work. Thanks are especially due to Mr. Bernard Miall for reading the entire book in manuscript; to Mr. Christopher Steel for giving me valuable guidance in writing the first three chapters; to Mr. Howard Drake for similar assistance in regard to chapter four; and to Miss Eleanor Willson for preparing the manuscript for the press.

N. GANGULEE

LONDON *1941*

Part One

THE CONSTITUENT ASSEMBLY: ITS HISTORY AND DEVELOPMENT

Chapter One

THE ORIGINS OF A CONSTITUENT ASSEMBLY

I

The term "Constituent Assembly or Convention" may be defined as signifying a representative body chosen for the purpose of considering, and either adopting or proposing, a new constitution, or changes in an existing constitution. In the former case such a body is inherently illegal, or rather, extra-legal, since it arises in times of national stress and can be justified only by the modern theory that Sovereignty resides, in the last resort, in the people. It is an emergency body, set up without legal precedent, to deal with a political explosion, while in the second case the Sovereignty of the people has been deliberately written into the Constitution, and the Constituent Assembly is merely a political device or safety-valve designed to allow of unforeseen changes being carried out in an essentially orderly and legal manner.

We may inquire what is the relation between the State as supreme coercive power and the Constituent Assembly as defender of the Rights of Man. The State, the Government and the people are three independent units, but the State itself is neither the people nor the Government nor the Constitution. The State and Government are by no means the same thing. The State becomes a *body-politic* only when a community desires or acquiesces in bringing into existence political authorities upon whom it can rely for its welfare. Just as the Constitution of any object is the *sum* of all its parts, so the Constitution of a State should include all the elements that are essential for the development of Statehood.

But we should remember that there are several types of State, because political institutions follow no generally fixed order of development. If we assume, with Marx, that the State is merely the coercive framework of the governing class, the means whereby those in power retain that power unchallenged, then we have to explain how it is that a governing class has from time to time, by means of Charters, Bills of Right, Grand Remonstrances, or what you will, been forced to admit that certain natural rights of man are inviolable; and by setting these out at length the class in power has definitely promised to set bounds to the exercise of its unlimited authority.

Clearly a governing class cannot limit its power in this way and yet remain sovereign. Each one of these landmarks, then, represents a transition, great or small, in the location of Sovereignty. By Magna Carta the King abdicates to his great nobles; by Habeas Corpus a resuscitated monarchy yields primarily to a landed oligarchy; by the Parliament Act of 1911 the House of Lords resigns its shadowy claim to obstruct the Commons without limit.

But a basic assumption of the Marxist theory is the necessity for the proletariat to destroy the existing bourgeois state as soon as it wins power, and forthwith to build up its own representative and protective organization. How, then, on this theory, can we find any room for such a body as a Constituent Assembly, since once the proletariat has destroyed the existing framework of society, and substituted its own, the State as such, the machinery *for the oppression of class by class, begins to wither away, and* vanishes entirely with the disappearance of the disgruntled remnant of the bourgeois rump?

The Constituent Assembly comes into existence to protect the bourgeois class against disruption. By offering machinery for supposed protection against unanticipated ills the bourgeoisie appears to be making a striking and generous gesture of trust in the people. Closer analysis, however, reveals the inconspicuous fact that the normal State machinery of Government possesses precisely similar electoral qualifications to those required for the Constitutional Conventions. In other words, the reforms and alterations gained by a Constitutional Convention are hardly likely to be more than skin-deep, since the nature of the electorate for the two bodies is identical. Only where the bourgeoisie is strongly entrenched, without having, as yet, aroused a virile proletariat opposition, can two rival sections of the governing class afford the luxury of a fight to determine which shall enforce its own sectional interests. A study of the various Amendments to the Federal Constitution of the United States bears out this point. The first Amendments, forming a virtual Bill of Rights, were the price of ratification exacted by a number of the original thirteen members. In the 1860's, after the Confederates' attempt at Secession had been defeated, the luxury of the Slave Amendments was possible, because the vast continent had even then hardly begun to develop industrially on a national scale. But the later Amendments are of fifth-rate quality, dealing with comparative trifles such as the levying of a Federal Income Tax, the reconstitution of the system of election for Federal Senators (by substituting direct for indirect election), and the imposition and subsequent cancellation of Prohibition. Whatever be the future development of the United States, it is certain that a socialization of any of the key industries, such as Banking, Armaments, Transport and Oil, will not come by way of peaceful Amendments to the Federal Constitution.

The government of mankind has passed through various stages of development. So far as Europe—the cradle of modern political thought—is concerned the original form is in every case that of a monarchy based on conquest. In order to raise into eminence so naked a title, the Crown was, in every case, speedily draped with an air of mystery and religious inspiration, based on divine authority, with the deliberate idea of rendering practically impossible any questioning of political origins.[1]

The early monarchies, however, soon hardened into despotisms. The uneven balance of the feudal structure, in which the Crown is but the apex of a steadily broadening series of ever-diminishing land tenures, led directly to disintegration, as those immediately below the king, and possessed of almost as vast landed estates as their feudal lord, tended to regard him merely as *primus inter pares*. Military service being the one obligation of feudal tenure, the possessors of vast landed estates, who could bring almost as many troops into the field as the king himself, refused to be bound by any concrete ties of inferiority. In Poland, for instance,

[1] Witness the tactics of William I, who claimed the English Crown in 1066, *inter alia* on a basis of papal support.

this was carried to its logical conclusion: the nobles were powerful enough to keep the Crown elective, while a single veto in an otherwise unanimous assembly was sufficient to wreck a decision. The result of this aristocratic anarchy led to the disappearance of Poland as an independent entity in the eighteenth century; devoured, like post-war Czechoslovakia, by partitions between Russia, Prussia and Austria

The Crown, therefore, in order to preserve its authority, had to subdue its immediate feudal dependants, the great landlords. This was effected by an alliance with the earliest merchant interests of the towns, which were prepared to finance the Crown in exchange for exemptions from feudal exactions. In most European countries, such as Habsburg Spain and monarchical France, the necessary rudiments of Parliamentary government (the *Cortes* and the *Trois États*), which the townsmen had been able to exact as the price of royal existence, were allowed to wither away, and the power of the executive moved steadily in the direction of uncontrolled absolutism. In England alone Parliamentary institutions did manage to survive, though it is not generally realized how, under the Tudors, the House of Commons, well-nigh defunct as a result of the baronial civil war of the fifteenth century, was revived and shamelessly packed as an instrument for carrying out the arbitrary designs of the Crown. The "murmuring" Parliaments of Queen Elizabeth belong definitely to the end of her reign, after the great triumph over Spain in 1588 had given the still feeble middle class sufficient confidence in itself to push forward unafraid.

The birth of a democracy proper in England was largely due to the invention of printing, which enabled every educated man to read and study the Bible in his mother tongue. The rising nationalism of Henry VIII, who effected the substitution of himself for the international autocracy of the Papacy, in order to assume control of the rich revenues of the Church, was reflected in a literal application of the doctrines of the Holy Canon to everyday affairs, and left-wing Puritans arose to question the right of the Crown to govern the lives of the Saints. At the same time the new bureaucracy of the Tudors was settling down into the germ of the modern çapitalist class. The scramble for Church lands led to a general move in the direction of enclosures of hitherto "common" lands in the interests of the big landlords, thus tending to develop large-scale farming. The consequent shift of population towards the larger towns tended to foster the growth of the various Puritan sects, and the City of London especially becomes famous as a centre of Puritan money-getting.[1] Thus it was that Puritan members were continually returned for the House of Commons all through the reign of Elizabeth, and the fact that democracy was able to survive at all, albeit tainted with a strong capitalist bias, was largely due to this feeble spark of Parliamentary life, kept glowing throughout the Tudor period by the Puritan members.

As the history of France shows, absolute government may succeed for over a century, instead of being overcome, as in England, and yet fail to prevent the final emergence of democracy; but its form in England would have been very different, and more violent, if Parliament had withered away, as happened in other lands. The religious socialism of the Puritans, although perpetually harried by the executive, was to keep alive in the House of Commons the spirit of democratic freedom; and though landed capitalism, under the Commonwealth, was able to suppress the rude Communism of the Levellers and Diggers, there was a sufficient democratic leaven to prevent upheaval until the worst excesses of an unfettered capitalist exploitation gave rise to the abortive rising of the Chartists.

A brief reference to the Chartist movement may be of interest to us. The invention of the Spinning Jenny by Hargreaves in 1764 may be taken as a convenient date from which to trace these industrial conditions that led directly to the demand for the Workers' Charter in 1839. Hours were so long and wages so low in the early factories that the working class could exist only by the deliberate propagation of as many children as possible, in order to obtain by their labour some pitifully inadequate but essential additions to an otherwise starvation wage.

Against such intolerable conditions of labour as were imposed by the relentless forces of the nascent capitalism the first reaction of the new-born proletariat was one of blind hostility to the new inhumanity. The machines, instead of the system, were mistakenly held to blame, and the reactionary destruction of these instruments of capitalism was widespread in the wave of despair

[1] See Ben Jonson, *Bartholomew Fair;* Thos. Middleton, *A Chaste Maid in Cheapside,* and numerous other Jacobean comedies of the early seventeenth century.

known as the Luddite Riots. The political acumen of the English working class, however, soon asserted itself, and in 1792 the London Corresponding Society was founded for political discussion. It at once entered into relations with the United Irishmen and the French Convention, and was suppressed by Act of Parliament in 1799. Universal Suffrage and the Rights of Labour continued to be hotly discussed by an indignant working class, and the earliest modern strikes occur in the cotton and mining industries in 1810, although the Trade Unions had been illegal since 1800. In 1824 the Combination Acts were repealed by the governing class, deeply influenced by the Radical tailor, Francis Place, who mistakenly supposed that the legalization of Trade Unionism would see the end of strike action. In 1829 and 1830 Hunger Riots were general, and the desperate working class lent its aid to the powerful English bourgeoisie in its successful struggle to wrest power from the landed proprietors by the Reform Act of 1832. Their reward was the incredible inhumanity of the reformed Poor Law, and in the universal disillusion a wave of Anarcho-Syndicalism threatened to engulf the Labour movement. It was this which doomed to failure the great movement for the Workers' Charter, which was hopelessly split between advocates of physical force and moral suasion. Moreover, the increasing commercial supremacy of the British capitalist class—at this time possessed of practically a world monopoly—enabled it to afford tardy concessions in the shape of the first social services—the long series of Factory Acts—while the great gold discoveries in California and Australia ushered in a period of general prosperity in which higher wages could be conceded without undue discomfort. The British Trade Union movement turned inward, and began to concentrate on a policy of gradualism, and though the tumultuous Year of Revolutions, 1848, was sympathetically greeted by the British working class, yet the Communist Manifesto of Karl Marx, published in that year, fell upon barren ground, although translated into English by the Chartist Harvey. The birth of scientific socialism passed almost unnoticed by the English working class, decimated and exhausted as it had been by over two generations of fierce revolutionary struggle.

So much is clear: arbitrary government, representing solely the class interests of a small oligarchy, albeit, as in the case of eighteenth-century England, an oligarchy penetrable by and available to the money of the East Indian "nabob" and the Lancashire mill owner, must lead inevitably to such exploitation and misery for those who have no share in the government that revolt must follow, unless, as in the early nineteenth-century England, a safety-valve is opened in the shape of Factory Acts and other forms of ameliorative social legislation. Whether the rebels are strong enough to succeed or not is beside the point: the slave legions of Spartacus were starved into surrender, while the rising commercial bourgeoisie of England, securely based upon the wealthiest sections of the country, conquered and executed Charles I. The permanence of this victory is marked by the very first act of the reactionary Government that succeeded Cromwell, which was nevertheless forced to recognize that feudalism had been overthrown and could not be restored: amid the deliberate and thorough expunging of all the Commonwealth's reforms the Cavalier Parliament passed a bill abolishing Knight Service as a real estate tenure in England. Sooner or later there comes a point when conditions have worsened so far that men will continue in the old way no longer, and in desperation they exclaim: "Give us liberty or give us death."

Now this passionate cry for liberty signifies that the inherent dignity and worth of man cannot tolerate circumstances which repress his capacities. It means that equality of opportunity is the birthright of mankind, and it implies the necessity of a structure of social relationships which recognizes the individual. Liberty has been defined by Thomas Mann as the preservation of the fundamental concepts of freedom, justice and truth; but these concepts cannot in fact be preserved unless *every* member of the community has the opportunity for sufficient self-development to understand and fight for this heritage. It may be that in the past, and even to-day, such a pure unfettered ideal has not yet been attained: this offers no excuse for a failure to sustain the rights of mankind in the face of possible individual unworthiness. To-day, when the concept of authoritarian rule seeks to overwhelm the rights of the individual beneath the sovereign power of a State, which, in accordance with the ideas of Hobbes, represents the Monarchy of to-day in Big Business, it is especially important that we should preserve this concept inviolate.

But arbitrary power is everywhere the earliest form of civilized government. Politics originated in the family, and an aggregation of families, as we see in the case of the Trobrianders and other Melanesian and Polynesian peoples to-day,[1] can live a communal life without any arbitrary power whatever. There is, to be sure, a complex and all-powerful system of taboos, but this system of early laws is enforced by the community at large against *all* its members. Senior members of the community possess larger privileges, certainly, but there are well-defined bounds marked out for them as well as for everyone else.

Rousseau, then, was far nearer than he realized in drawing his artificial and fanciful picture of the noble savage. Though he was unaware of it, there was a rude rule of law, omnipotent and all-embracing. How comes it, then, that whole systems of political philosophy, from Machiavelli and Hobbes down to Treitschke, and the apologists of the totalitarian State, have been erected upon the opposite rule of force?

The reason is to be found in the fact that all European civilization is based, historically speaking, upon conquest, and so, in the last resort, upon force. To the vast majority of men, whatever is, is right, simply because they can conceive of no other alternative, not being themselves politically conscious, and the power of prescription is such that to many a government founded upon a bad title is preferable to no government at all.

It is easy to understand the success that attended Hobbes in the creation of his imaginary Social Contract. Life in the natural State being assumed to be "nasty, brutish and short," men were so thankful to find a power, mysteriously existing *in vacuo*, which held out promises of protection against the existing anarchy, that in return they were supposed to have willed away all their natural rights to the Sovereign Power. The inherent contradiction in this theory was not at first perceived, for English political writers in the main much prefer rule-of-thumb empiricism to abstract theory, and the logical conclusion, in favour of unfettered absolutism, was not drawn. The reason for this is probably to be found in historical fact: at a time when the people had beheaded one king only the most incorrigible optimism could have baldly stated that they had agreed to surrender themselves unconditionally to his successor. Hobbes was

[1] B. Malinowski, *Sexual Life of Savages*; Tom Harrison, *Savage Civilization*.

not at once accepted as the official apologist of monarchy, because he derived the absolute power of the Sovereign from a human contract, instead of basing it upon a divine precept drawn from the Old Testament. Herein lies the service of Hobbes to posterity. Vicious and rotten though his political philosophy may be, yet he did strike a very necessary blow against the unthinking basis of superstition which had formerly prevailed. Before him it had been blasphemy to question the divine right of kings. His popularization of the idea of a Social Contract led directly to the divine right of majorities.

Why, then, must we assume that all men are equal? Simply because any other assumption leads to a justification of slavery, and the rule of force. This is the ultimate axiom of politics, enshrined in the American Declaration of Independence and the French Declaration of the Rights of Man. Man is born free, cried Rousseau, and everywhere he is in chains. These tremendous words found an echo in two continents, and formed the basis of the first two modern democracies. We hold these truths to be self-evident, asserted the founders of the American Republic, in the preamble to the Declaration of Independence, and it is not possible to discover any fundamentals that go deeper than these. To-day, when Democracy is on trial, it is right that these words should be remembered and acted upon; for as Mr. John Foot has recently observed: "The Dictators have declared war not only upon Marx and the Communist Theory, but upon Milton, Rousseau, Fox and Tom Paine, upon the Bill of Rights and the American Declaration of Independence."[1]

II

The eighteenth century was remarkable for the awakening of peoples to political consciousness, but it was an awakening restricted to a portion only of the community. In Puritan New England, a century earlier, the influence of the Netherlands had led to the most advanced political development of the day, the New England Town Meeting, in which the assembled congregation met together to administer local affairs. But though the

[1] Quotation from speech by Mr. John Foot at a Liberal Party Organization dinner given to Sir Archibald Sinclair (November 1, 1938).

personnel was largely the same in both secular and religious capacities, the Town Meeting remained secular, one might almost say anti-clerical, in its relation to the Church. Men who had voluntarily left England because of the persecution of a State Church, and had reinforced their ardour by a first-hand experience of the liberal institutions of the Dutch, were not likely to submit themselves to the control of even their own Church in non-spiritual matters.[1]

The great struggle between King and Parliament in seventeenth-century England led to the emergence of the new middle-class trader, standing upon the ruins of a feudalism whose increasing poverty insured its ever more rapid decline. The reason why Cromwell failed to consolidate his victory was two-fold. In the first place, the shackles of the past lay heavy upon him. He himself was a freeholder, pre-eminently a man who farmed his own land, while the class of traders, though growing yearly more powerful, was not yet fully developed, in spite of the fact that the great Trading Companies, such as the Muscovy, the Turkey and, above all, the East India Company, date from the end of Elizabeth's reign. It is true that under James I we meet with the constitutional landmark of Bates's Case, in which the commercial nature of the class struggle is well exemplified, as the point at issue was the validity or otherwise of the executive's attempt to levy an arbitrary duty on currants. The outbreak of the Civil War, however, led to a sharp division in the middle class. Men whose grandsons were to form the Whig party of Bank of England and East India Company merchants were now fighting for the King. The majority of the Parliamentary army came from the germs of the working class, the journeymen and small masters. These men, deeply religious, and forming a military democracy based on a literal interpretation of the English Bible, formed the group known as the Independents, opposed to the Presbyterians, who came in the main from the landed squires who supplied the membership of the House of Commons. The Independents were the backbone of Cromwell's army: their military democracy, which included the election of officers, and the provision, under the name of "agitators," of political commissars, was never again equalled until the

[1] See, on the whole question of Puritan development, D. Campbell, *The Puritan in Britain, Holland and America.*

advent of the modern Russian army and the troops of the Spanish Republic.

Secondly, Cromwell possessed no coherent theory of government. Circumstances had forced him to take over the post of chief executive, but his whole upbringing and sympathy were hostile to the pure democracy of the Diggers and Levellers, whom he suppressed by force of arms. Nevertheless, in the crude proposals of Gerald Winstanley we have the origins of real democracy. The logic of his statements is undeniable, though they fell upon sterile ground.

"You, Cromwell," he says, "have cast out the successors of William the Conqueror by the aid, and only by the aid, of the Commons of England: you must therefore restore to the Commons that freedom which was filched from them by the forcible conquest of the Bastard and give them back their right to the land untroubled."[1]

A few years before this, in 1647, Ireton and others had urged that power ought to depend on property. Colonel Rainsborough at once retorted: "The poorest He that is in England hath a life to live as well as the greatest He; and therefore . . . every man that is to live under a government ought first, by his own consent, to put himself under that government." Ireton logically replied that if the Law of Nature were to permit each a "right" to elect his governor there must follow the "right" to self-preservation, i.e. to food, clothes and land. But this would mean an end to private property, and it was precisely this that Ireton and Cromwell could not concede, for they represented a government of landowners, whose religious beliefs happened to be hostile to a State-controlled Church, and whose revenues were swollen by the continuous sale of the estates of "malignant" Cavaliers. The "Diggers" who essayed to cultivate common land on a communal basis at St. George's, Weybridge, were forcibly dispersed, and their leaders imprisoned.

It was only when James II, endeavouring by his bigoted support of Catholic Emancipation to reassert the divine right of kings, provoked the reaction of the landowning oligarchy, that political theory advanced another step.

The successful expulsion of James II and the Parliamentary title of William III—conveniently supported by the blood rela-

[1] G. Winstanley, *The Law of Freedom in a Platform.*

tionship of Mary, his wife, to the rejected king, who was her father—led of necessity to a complete revolution in political thought. It was, in a way, a more awe-inspiring event than the execution of Charles I. For the death of that king did not interfere with the well-established legal position that the heir automatically succeeded on the death of the father, and the reign of Charles II was accordingly dated from 1649, and not from his actual restoration eleven years later. But here the proprietary notion of kingship was successfully challenged, and the throne, having been forcibly removed from one individual, in defiance of the apparently established rights of his infant son, was successfully offered to a comparative stranger in blood,[1] who preserved a decent fiction of continuity solely by the fact that his wife was a daughter of the rejected monarch.

How was this to be explained away? The Convention of 1689 might pass a Bill declaring itself to be a Parliament, but this arrogation of Sovereignty cannot have proved convincing even to the most enthusiastic Whig. Accordingly, we find in Locke the apologist *par excellence* of the Revolution of 1688. The purport of his *Two Treatises of Civil Government* was to answer and confute Sir Robert Filmer, who sought to justify monarchy by a divine descent from Adam. No one remembers Filmer to-day, but Locke's discussion of the State and Political Power remains of the utmost importance.

Not only did he contrive to give, in modern terms, a sorely-needed ideology to the Whig revolutionaries, but his influence was profound throughout the following century. His conclusions were generally received as valid throughout the British settlements in North America, and they profoundly influenced the whole political thought of the American Revolution, while Rousseau, deriving from the Englishman the central concept of his "Social Contract," reacted in turn upon the American colonists, and served once again to strengthen the ideology of colonial revolt.

Locke was predominantly the spokesman of the landed aristocracy, which in England particularly has always had the

[1] William III was the son of James II's sister, Mary, who had married the Prince of Orange. He had, therefore, been reared as a Dutchman, and even throughout his English reign was regarded as a pure foreigner. His title to the English Crown was secured by Parliament exclusively through his wife, Mary, who was James II's daughter.

good sense to recruit and revitalize itself from below. As the possession of land was a prerequisite for the franchise, the rising bourgeoisie, now beginning to lay the foundations of its power by the first of a series of colonial wars with European rivals[1] for the right to exploit the people of India and the East Indies, naturally turned towards the country gentry, and though the antagonism of Whig and Tory, or country squire and moneyed interest, was a general fact for two generations,[2] a rapid fusion tended to occur, due primarily to the necessity of obtaining political power. The corruption of English public life in the eighteenth century may be traced to this ever more powerful body of moneyed men, who openly purchased rotten boroughs as being cheaper and more convenient to control than the uncertain votes of a restricted and bribe-ridden electorate.

Land had always been the great basis of Society, until the Industrial Revolution arose to modify this fact, and concentrate attention upon a new aspect of the old concept of the means of production. Feudalism was based upon a military tenure of the land, and while free land existed, in the shape of the commons of the old manors, industrialization was impossible.[3] Thus in England the small class of landowners set itself steadfastly to augment its power by a long series of Enclosure Acts, whereby, under colour of Parliamentary authority, the small yeomen and copyholders were steadily dispossessed of their rights in the common land, in order that large-scale agriculture might become possible. Similarly, in the United States of America, the existence of the open frontier, with its consequence of unlimited free land, retarded the development of a true industrial proletariat, until that frontier was closed. This may be said to have occurred about 1925.[4]

It is the supersession of the old blind superstition which based

[1] The Dutch in the seventeenth century, the French a century later.

[2] See the character of Squire Western, *passim*, in Fielding's *Tom Jones*, published about 1740.

[3] A non-agricultural, nomadic people has no tie to hold it stationary, so that political institutions may have time to germinate. In the Middle Ages the landless man is viewed with hostility as being difficult to control. The English Grand Jury arises from the necessity of Government, which forced local inhabitants (whose possession of land insured their reliability) to "present" such persons as appeared to be suspicious characters for investigation by the King's Justices in Eyre. A man possessing neither land nor lord was automatically a subject of suspicion.

[4] *Vide* H. L. Mencken, *Americana*, note on the State of Oklahoma.

government upon divine right, by the new realization of the importance of the land, that is the greatest contribution of the English political philosophers of the seventeenth century. Harrington, whose *Oceana* was somewhat whimsically dedicated to Cromwell in 1653, was the first to realize this fact, and to state categorically that the preservation of a State depends on the possession by the ruling class of an adequate proportion of the land. This truth was realized and developed by Locke, but Harrington's ideas, based upon a sympathetic study and approval of the constitutions of the Netherlands and of Venice, were too uncompromisingly republican to have any major influence in England. In the American colonies, especially in New England, it was otherwise, and Harrington was there studied and assimilated.

Locke, then, was the apologist of 1688. He had, therefore, to explain and justify the expulsion of James II. The supporters of James based themselves solely on the divine right of kings. This was a position that could not be logically defended, save by a blind act of faith, since it gave the Crown a complete right of ownership in the people. But this arbitrary power was indistinguishable from that of the slave-owner over his human chattels. Nevertheless, the undeniable fact of kingship remained. If the king is not an arbitrary slave-owner, how comes he to exist? asks Locke. The answer can only be, owing to some form of election; and hence the whole of Locke's system is based upon an imaginary social contract. "Every man," says Locke, "has a 'property' in his own person and in the labour arising therefrom." "The grass my horse has bit, the turfs my servant has cut, and the ore I have digged in any place, where I have a right to them in common with others, becomes my property without the assignation or consent of anybody." Again, "as much as anyone can make use of to any advantage of life before it spoils, so much he may by his labour fix a property in."

Life in the natural state, however, is very uncertain. Men therefore agree together to form a government for no other end but the preservation of their property. This basic idea, the preservation of property at all costs, appears again and again in Locke, and is always declared to be the sole basis and reason of Society. "Whenever, therefore, any number of men so unite into one society as to quit every one his executive power of the law of Nature,[1] and to assign it to the public, there and there only is a political or civil society. And this is done whenever any number of men, in the state of Nature, enter into Society to make one people one body politic under one supreme government: or else when anyone joins himself to, and incorporates with any government already made." Again, "that which begins and actually constitutes any political society is nothing but the consent of any number of free men capable of a majority[2] to unite and incorporate into such a society." But, "the people alone can appoint the form of the commonwealth, which is by constituting the legislative, and appointing in whose hands that shall be." It follows therefore—and here is the vital thrust at monarchical government—that what the people have delegated they may at pleasure resume, provided the conditions on which the original delegation was made have been violated. "When any one, or more, shall take upon them to make laws whom the people have not appointed so to do, they make laws without authority, which the people are not therefore bound to obey, by which means they come again out of subjection, and may constitute themselves a new legislature, as they think best, being in full liberty to resist the force of those who, without authority, would impose anything upon them."

Locke's problem, then, is the legalization of illegality in terms of real estate.[3] He has to demarcate the bounds of public interference with private affairs. By proving that rebellion was not only justified, but was indeed the lawful defence of men threatened by arbitrary force, he turned the tables upon his opponents. The squires of England, who hailed him as the defender of their estates against the confiscations of the executive, did not see that his argument proved too much for their liking. At the time when Locke wrote, the American colonies were not sufficiently developed in point of numbers to render an application of these doctrines against the mother-country practical. Economic war against Ireland, however, due to the short-sighted greed of Locke's

[1] Elsewhere defined as the right, in the natural state, to self-preservation and exaction of reparation for injury done.

[2] Presumably signifying any number above two.

[3] So great was the sanctity of the idea of property that Locke could argue that the right of conquest extended only to the lives of the conquered, not to their estates. This in face of the historical facts of Acts of Attainder, Impeachment and the whole theory of Deodand.

contemporaries, the rising commercial class at home, resulted in an immense flow of Scottish-Irish emigrants across the Atlantic. These men were all politically conscious of their destiny, and inflamed with a hatred of England, owing to the wrongs which they had suffered in respect of their economic interests and their religion. They were joined by an equally powerful stream of French, Dutch, German and Scandinavian immigrants, all of whom were serious men of good education, and it was to these, the pick of Europe's democrats, rather than to the big landowners and slave-masters of the South, that the theories of Locke proved a godsend. It was here that they found a rich quarry to provide them with unanswerable dialectical weapons to justify the colonial struggles which began after the conclusion of the Seven Years' War in 1763.

III

Rousseau was primarily an emotional cataclysm. He felt injustice with all the passionate sincerity of a neurotic, and he possessed an uncanny genius for voicing the indignation of humanity in unforgettable and burning phrases; but his constructive proposals were muddled, incoherent, and by no means free from mutual contradiction. Far more valuable theories are to be found in the writings of the Quaker, Thomas Paine, whose *Common Sense*, dealing with the American Revolution, and more especially his *Rights of Man*, written in defence of the French Convention against the attacks of Edmund Burke, the apologist of Conservatism, carry the theories of Locke to a logical conclusion.

Rousseau finally concluded that only in the small, compact and self-contained city-state, such as his own Geneva, or ancient Greek community, could a pure democracy exist. It has been well said of him that he leaves the mind in love with an object, without describing the means of possessing it. Paine, on the other hand, writing with the example of American federation before him, stated the modern problem concisely.

The end of all political associations, says Paine, is the preservation of the natural and imprescriptible rights of man; and these rights are liberty, property, security, and resistance to oppression. Civil rights derive solely from natural rights, being indeed the sum of all those natural rights which cannot usefully be enforced by the individual; and civil power cannot be applied to invade those natural rights retained by the individual, such as the right to intellectual freedom and all that this implies. Governments arise either out of the people, by their consent, or over the people, in which latter case the people, having no concern with such methods of rule, are bound only by force, and will therefore disown them as soon as practicable.

The problem which so eluded Rousseau, with his shadowy distinction between the *volonté générale*, in which true Sovereignty was held to reside, and the *volonté de tous*, or simple majority vote, is how to distinguish between legislative power involving civil rights (in Paine's phrasing)—the ordinary day-to-day task of government—and legislative power which extends its action to natural rights. It has been solved largely by setting out in a written constitution certain principles which cannot be improved or varied save by a specially laborious procedure. In this procedure is found the *raison d'être* of a Constituent Assembly, an extraordinary session of a specially created body, deliberately designed to consider one or more specific points. Man is fallible, and it is recognized that hasty action may lead to a real tyranny of the majority at the expense of a minority. The purpose of the Constituent Assembly is therefore seen to be the provision of machinery whereby the citizens may be forced to consider and debate with extra care any given subject. It is really another facet of the referendum, which is the logical and proper democratic development of it, and is itself closely allied to the device of the constitutional initiative, whereby citizens of a State which is fully developed politically may force their elected representatives to consider one specific subject, provided a sufficient number of citizens deem it of sufficient urgency to vote specifically for this course.

In the next two chapters we shall consider the first attempts of eighteenth-century America and France to solve this problem of reconciling the two opposites, stability and fluidity. Any written constitution is *ipso facto* inclined to stability, with the consequent danger of ossification. The Constitution of the United States is to-day so ill-adapted to modern conditions that large portions of President Franklin Roosevelt's "New Deal" were invalidated by the Supreme Court as unconstitutional. In Britain, on the other hand, the Constitution is unwritten in the sense that, apart from conventional practice, it is only to be found in certain ancient Acts of Parliament, any of which is theoretically at the mercy of any party possessing a bare majority. Thus an unwritten constitution is exposed to the danger—to most people a danger so serious as to render it unsuitable for use—of disappearance overnight in the face of a compact and resolute assault. That written constitutions will eventually become the rule for every nation we believe to be certain, since the protection of individual freedom is essential if democracy—which means government in accordance with the wishes of the greatest number of individuals—is to survive.

Democracy, paradoxically, is threatened everywhere to-day because it is not, and never has been, fully democratic. With the exception of Soviet Russia, which has been entirely rebuilt from the foundations, democracy has always been uneasily wedded to capitalism, and it is the increasing decline of this system of haphazard production for individual profit that has brought democratic institutions into disrepute. As it has been truly said, "Democracy implies universal suffrage, and that has never been easy to obtain when the ruling class has always tended to qualify the suffrage by making the possession of a landed interest an essential condition for the vote."[1] And even where adult suffrage has been won, the disproportionate economic power given by a capitalist system to its chief exponents renders a man like the late Lord Stamp (a director of the Bank of England and President of the London, Midland and Scottish Railway, the biggest British transport system) capable of exerting an influence equal to that of forty thousand of the two million unemployed of Great Britain. As Woodward says,[2] "Capitalism has a government of its own outside the sphere of politics. Its opposition to democracy is instinctive and inevitable for the reason that democracy rests on human values while capitalism rests on property values. There can be no reconciliation between capitalism and democracy; one of them must capture the other and hold the victim in bondage."

The first steps of the eighteenth-century pioneers were taken largely under the direction of capitalist guidance by the "respectable" landed interests of America and France. This is why

[1] Woodward, *A New American History*.
[2] See Woodward, op. cit.

these two revolutions were primarily bourgeois in character, emancipating the prosperous middle class, and not proletarian, since the proletariat, which had nothing but numbers and intellect on its side, was not yet sufficiently developed to claim power with any prospect of success. Nevertheless, ideas change so slowly that the first experiments of these pioneers are deserving of careful study, for this will at least reveal errors that may to-day be avoided. Though largely obsolete, these experiments are still in being, old-fashioned and restrictive, like the outworn shell of some giant crustacean. The crustacean is slowly shedding the old, inadequate armour, but only in Russia has the process reached a successful conclusion. And just as the crab is singularly vulnerable while he is shedding his old armour, so the peoples of the Western democracies stir uneasily as they pass through the dangerous growing-pains that herald the disruption of an outworn economic system.

Chapter Two

THE CONSTITUTIONAL CONVENTION IN NORTH AMERICA

I

The birth and consummation of the American Revolution may be regarded as one of the most significant political events of the eighteenth century. In a sense, it was largely a continuation of the rebellion in England under Cromwell. The settlement of North America grew largely out of the enterprises of capitalist trading companies, and it was the growth of a new middle class which brought about the Revolution. Although there emerged from this Revolution a great nation-State of heterogeneous peoples who had won their independence, its influence upon political theory and practice was not as striking as that of the French Revolution. But here we are not concerned so much with political theories; our purpose is to study the framing of the American Constitution, and to note what means and methods have been resorted to in order to revise it in accordance with changing conditions.

European colonial settlements upon the long eastern seaboard of North America had existed for a full century and a half in 1763. In that year the Peace of Paris brought to an end the disastrous Seven Years' War, which marked the end of the first French colonial empire. The war fell into two distinct halves. There was the usual European struggle, this time mainly in Western Germany, between Prussia, financed by England, and France, while a bitter colonial rivalry between France and Britain was fought out in America and in India, ending in favour of Britain, thanks to her superiority in sea power.

We are not here concerned with the struggle in India between two rival European nations, which fought under the guise of two jealous commercial competitors. The two nations were never formally at war in India. Two rival trading companies were perpetually fighting each other for the right to win trading concessions in the sub-continent, and their methods involved the raising of large Indian forces, officered by Europeans, and the hiring of these forces now to one Indian ruler, now to his rival, according to the ever-increasing "rights" which any particular nominee would grant to his European backers.

Similar tactics were pursued in North America among the various tribes of Red Indians. The civilization of that continent, however, being far below that of India—indeed, practically non-existent—and the climate being more temperate than that of Southern Asia, European exploitation, though still largely availing itself of the Chartered Company as the typical basis of development, assumed a very different form. Mass settlement was carried out, following, as a rule, the grant by the Crown to a selected number of individuals of the "right," under Royal Charter, to administer a given territory as part of the King's Dominions. The capitalist nature of the enterprise, however, was not concealed. Even from the time of James I the ruling motive was the expectation of profits, to be declared in the form of dividends upon the varying amounts of cash subscribed by the shareholders.

It is common knowledge, however, that the Atlantic coast settlements of the British were very diverse in character. The southern settlements, of which Virginia, as being the oldest and largest, may be taken as the prototype, almost at once based their economic life upon the cultivation of tobacco, indigo and rice, and later of cotton, by means of negro slave labour. In 1606 the London Company was chartered for the purpose of exploiting the resources of Virginia through a landowning class, but before long the charter had to be annulled, and the colony became a royal province. It is interesting to note that in the course of their struggles with the Company the landowners had set up "the House of Burgesses" in order to strengthen their case against undue interference from England. The more northern group of New England colonies, however, comprising Connecticut, Rhode Island, New Hampshire, and, above all, the powerful and politically adult Massachusetts, had a strong religious bias, which differentiated them sharply from the more capitalist communities of the South. Nevertheless, it must be realized that even in New England the influence of the Chartered Company, the business corporation as such, remained supreme throughout the history of the region. The hard-headed business ability of the Yankees, as the inhabitants of North-Eastern America came to be called, was a direct inheritance from those Pilgrim Fathers who landed from the *Mayflower* to seek religious freedom from the edicts of James I.

This is hardly surprising when we remember that the central concept of Calvinism is a complete and utter control over the life of every member of the congregation, not only in matters of religious doctrine, but also in every aspect of his secular life. A literal interpretation of the New Testament leads to a thoroughgoing democracy, if not to a completely religious communism, in which every member of the congregation, being *ipso facto* one of the Elect, the chosen of God, must therefore have a full right to be heard on any question that comes before the community. The New England Town Meeting, as already stated, was a vital part of the Puritan movement. It was an assembled church congregation, met together to discuss secular affairs, just as the early New England Town was, in at least one case,[1] an actual transplantation of an English Parish direct from London to America.

The fact that these men sincerely believed that any line they might take in mundane affairs, although purely a matter of business, nevertheless enjoyed the specific approval of the Deity, required, as a necessary corollary, that each member of the Elect must specifically bind himself, at one time or another, to associate with, and be ruled by, a majority of his fellow Puritans. This explains the existence of the many Solemn Leagues and Covenants in seventeenth-century England, such as the "Agreement of the People," a document composed in 1648 by Ireton and Lilburne, but emanating in essence from the rank and file of the Cromwellian Army, which was, to quote its own words, "to be tendered to the people in all parts, to be subscribed by those that are willing." The basic idea of this document was the establishment of a supreme law (a "fundamental"), *placed beyond the reach of Parliament*, defining the powers of that body, and expressly declaring the rights which the nation reserved to itself, and which no authority might touch with impunity. As above stated, provision was made for popular ratification. Although

[1] The town of New Haven, Connecticut, derived its origin directly from the Parish of St. Stephen, Coleman Street, London, which possessed the unique right of *electing* its Vicar.

this never advanced beyond the stage of a mere project, it may be claimed as the first step towards a written British Constitution.

Again, that notable Republican, Sir Henry Vane the Younger, who had been an early Governor of Massachusetts Bay, in 1656, during Cromwell's Protectorate, proposed a convention "chosen for that purpose by the free consent of the whole body" and designed "not properly to exercise the legislative power but only to debate freely and agree upon the particulars (i.e. details) . . . the nature of the convention wherein they are made, which is of the People represented in their highest state of sovereignty, as they have the sword in their hands unsubjected unto the rules of civil government, but what (*i.e. except that which*) *themselves*, orderly assembled for that purpose, do think fit to make."

New England was thus composed of a number of religious organizations, united by such specific covenants as those above referred to, on which was superimposed the character of a business corporation. And though, as among the individual members, there was proper democratic equality, yet, by the very doctrine of Election—that is, of divine predestined equality among the congregation—the freemen of the Corporation alone were eligible to enact the laws of any given community. By this means Capitalism was able to survive and increase in power even in the apparently hothouse atmosphere of democratic New England. True democracy in New England may be said to have had a very short life. There was direct popular legislation in Rhode Island in the seventeenth century, and in 1639 the "Fundamental Orders" of Connecticut formed the first written and popularly ratified American constitution, but when we come to the period of the War of Independence we find that the principles of pure democracy have been considerably diluted. Why this should have been so it is now necessary to inquire.

II

The seventeenth century, in European history, belongs unquestionably to the Dutch, despite the great significance of the Puritan Revolution in England. It is therefore not surprising that the territory of what is now New York should at this period have been settled by the Dutch, under the name of New Amsterdam, so that it formed an effective dividing point between the northern and southern British settlements in North America. In the latter half of the century, however, the rising power of France, under the youthful Louis XIV, dragging in its train the willingly subservient England of Charles II, applied itself to breaking the commercial supremacy of the Dutch, who possessed a rich empire in the spice islands of the East Indies, and had captured the carrying trade of the world. The rival imperialisms of England and Holland had indeed clashed in open warfare under Cromwell, whose blind political instincts had led him, in the first place, to continue the old Elizabethan struggle with the now decadent Spanish Empire. Accordingly, he captured Jamaica, the natural capital of the West Indies, from Spain, and he also expelled the Spaniards from the important Channel port of Dunkirk. But economic motives overcame his natural religious bias in favour of the Dutch, and the first Imperialist war of Britain was waged between two republics which might have been expected to be firmly cemented in a close and natural alliance.

It would be difficult to find more convincing evidence of the gulf between the political ideas of Cromwell and the pure Communism of Winstanley and the Diggers and Levellers.[1] If economic forces could thus overrule the natural alliance of religious and democratic forces, it will not be hard to understand why Charles II was willing to continue the war with the Netherlands, the ever-open refuge of his political opponents, thereby obtaining the cession of New Amsterdam, henceforth renamed New York in honour of his brother, the future James II.

We thus come to the third type of North American settlement, the middle colonies of New York, New Jersey, Maryland, Delaware and Pennsylvania. These were primarily royalist in origin, in some cases spiritually governed by the Church of England, but in all cases politically modelled on the English pattern more closely than was the case in New England. A Governor and two Houses existed, together with a stringent property qualification for the franchise, and the colonial charters of this period were extensively remodelled in the interests of the Crown. The fact that Maryland began as an officially Roman Catholic colony was due to the revival of that religion under the two post-Restoration kings, while the predominance of Quakers in Penn-

[1] See Chapter I, pp. 23 and 29.

sylvania was due to the great influence of the colony's founder, William Penn, with the later Stuarts.

It is thus not surprising that the Loyalist or Tory party in the American colonies should have found perhaps its strongest support in the colony of New York, which, unlike the New England colonies, owed its origin to the active support of the late Stuart sovereigns. The English inhabitants of the colony were among the staunchest supporters of the Mother Country, and the Republican movement was drawn largely from the earlier Dutch and French elements among the governing class, together with the germ of the later proletariat, the "Mechanicks in Union" as they styled themselves, who were barred from the franchise by a heavy property qualification.

The French arrived late upon the scene in North America. The Atlantic seaboard was already settled by the English, and the French, who came primarily not to settle but to trade, perforce confined themselves to the rich Newfoundland fisheries, and later to the valuable fur trade of the St. Lawrence basin. The mercantilist theory of economics, at this time paramount in Europe, regarded the obtaining of as much specie as possible as the chief end of government, and it is for this reason that the French, though possessing throughout the seventeenth and eighteenth centuries a far larger population at home than the British, did not set out definitely to colonize Canada—a term at this period restricted to the modern Province of Quebec—but primarily to exploit it without the settlement of a large permanent French population.

Nevertheless, a brilliant succession of French explorers and administrators rapidly discovered the existence of the vast system of waterways which lead from the St. Lawrence River, by way of the Great Lakes, to the mighty Mississippi, which in turn flows into the Gulf of Mexico. True, the mouth of that river lay in Spanish territory, but this was a minor difficulty which could be, and in fact was, overcome, and the City of New Orleans to-day bears witness, by its name, to the ambitious scheme of confining the English colonists to the Atlantic seaboard.

Though in fact doomed to failure, primarily because of insufficient man power for the control of so vast an area, this grandiose French scheme had two apparently powerful points in its favour. The existence of the Appallachian and Alleghany mountains, which form a natural barrier to internal expansion from the eastern coast, might excusably be thought to offer a delaying, if not an insuperable obstacle to a westward expansion of the British, while the French technique in dealing with the aboriginal inhabitants was far more sympathetic than that of the British colonists, greedy for new homesteads, and therefore automatically at war with the natives, and the French generally succeeded in enlisting their support. The incredible westward pressure of the thirteen colonies cannot be traced solely to the British: the rapid rise in the population, which naturally sought an outlet along the line of least resistance, was due to the fact that during the century that preceded the Seven Years' War there was not only a natural increase of population, but also an extensive political immigration from Ireland, from Germany (at this time a collection of petty principalities, each oppressing its inhabitants) and even from France, where the unwise revocation of the Edict of Nantes, the Charter of the Huguenots or French Protestants, caused an extensive emigration of some of the most valuable and sturdy French stocks, who were to become the bitter enemies of the Bourbons, instead of the loyal subjects which they might have been under a more enlightened religious policy.

III

With the removal of the French menace in 1763, therefore, the colonists felt free to develop, but they were already split into various sections. Racially they were predominantly, but by no means exclusively, British. Socially they had already split up into the well-to-do and the poor, but the poor had then the tremendous advantage of being able to seek a new life on the ever-receding western frontier. This perpetual development of the American frontier, which attracted all the most virile elements in the population, must never be overlooked. Pioneers of Dutch, German, French, Scottish, Irish, and British colonial stock, they ceaselessly poured through the rifts in the mountain chain, building log cabins, tilling the soil, floating down the Ohio in rude boats, hewn on the spot with the axe out of virgin timber. Geographical factors gave this invading flood a twist to the South-West, and the new, sturdy, independent democrats flowed effortlessly over the artificial State boundaries, plotted vaguely along parallels of latitude, and took the aristocratic, slave-owning Southern colonies in the rear. In what is now Kentucky and Tennessee the settlers pushed forward in such numbers that they could set up their own short-lived State of Franklin, without asking leave of anybody. It is from men such as these, the flower of two hemispheres, that two of the greatest of America's Presidents were drawn—Andrew Jackson and Abraham Lincoln, who won their way to the White House when the first generation of aristocratic founders of the United States had passed away.

But there was yet a further difference of interest between the thirteen colonies, which was to grow even more rapidly than the colonists themselves. Even as early as the beginning of the eighteenth century New England was maritime and commercial, famed for ships and crews second to none. She traded primarily with the West Indies, in rum, molasses and negroes, transhipping these products to the rich tobacco States of the South, which, in their turn, shipped their produce direct to Bristol, then the chief port of England.[1] The North-East was thus destined to become a high-tariff, protectionist area, while the South, and still more the ever-growing West, was to clamour for free trade, or at least a reasonably low tariff that would not totally prohibit the import of those manufactures essential to the pioneers of the Mississippi. With the invention of the cotton-gin and the rapid spread of intensive cotton cultivation in the South this diversity of interest became still more marked, as New England took over the spinning of the South's cotton, and successfully lobbied for a prohibitive tariff.

The *Mercantilist theory steadily drained the colonists of specie* and the Southern plantations existed literally upon a tobacco currency. The invention of paper money, the principles of which no one attempted to understand, naturally tended, after a brief respite, to make matters far worse, as extensive depreciation set in. The full effect of paper money was not to be seen until after Independence had been declared, when fourteen separate governments (thirteen States and one loose central authority), joyously competed in the unrestricted manufacture of currency.

[1] Slavery is not mentioned in the Federal Constitution, except by inference in Article 1, Section 9, clause 1, which enacts that import of slaves shall not be forbidden before 1808, but may be subjected to a poll tax not exceeding $10 per head.

It may be doubted whether, in any case, the thirteen colonies could have been retained much longer within an imperial system which tended more and more to regard them as inferior objects of exploitation, but there is no doubt that the Home Government set about the hazardous task of "making the colonies pay" as obtusely as possible. Under the Navigation Acts, a political measure originating with Cromwell, and directed against the Dutch, all colonial produce had first to be shipped to England in a British ship before it could be consigned to a foreign port, a principle which may once have been justified on political grounds, but which could not be successfully applied to three million people living along a thousand-mile seaboard. At this period the American colonies, as we have seen, traded primarily with the West Indies, and their systematic disregard of this regulation—for they traded impartially with Danish, Dutch, French, Spanish and British possessions—had hitherto been regarded with a blind eye. They had benefited by the total neglect by the Home Government during the first half of the eighteenth century, but with the advent of George III, who sought to break the Whig oligarchy that had ruled for over forty years, a different line of policy was adopted.

This Whig oligarchy had tended to leave the American colonies alone. The increasing corruption of the governing class, however, together with the shift in population due to the beginnings of the Industrial Revolution, and the consequent development of the rotten boroughs, forced the young king to fight the Whig junta with its own weapon of corruption, and the rise of the new party of King's Friends required financial backing. At this time the chief tax was one on land, but as this hit the Squirearchy hard, it was not a practical expedient for a king who sought to rally round him the Tory country gentlemen, hitherto the blind followers of the fallen Stuart cause.

Across the Atlantic, however, there appeared to lie a rich field ready for exploitation. Accordingly, George III's first administration, under Lord Grenville, applied the famous Stamp Act in 1765. This was accompanied by a general tightening-up of revenue administration, and an endeavour to extend the jurisdiction of Admiralty Courts, to the exclusion of the jury system. Colonial opposition at once reacted, on a scale entirely unexpected at home; nine colonies met in protest at New York, but their policy was purely one of opposition to a tax which was admitted to be constitutional but unfair. Only in Virginia, which had no representative at the New York meeting, did Patrick Henry, one of the few real democrats produced in the period of Independence, give utterance to a new view by tendering a resolution in the Lower House "that the General Assembly of this Colony have the only sole and exclusive right and power to lay taxes and impositions upon the inhabitants of this Colony." At this period, however, his was a lone voice, far in advance of general opinion, which was not prepared to endorse so radical a view.

Hence we can understand why the whole question of American taxation quickly provoked a civil war within the Empire rather than a colonial revolt pure and simple. The Whig opposition at home, finding a mouthpiece in Edmund Burke, at once took the line that such taxation was primarily inexpedient rather than unconstitutional. In 1766 Rockingham, Burke's patron, duly repealed the Stamp Act, the repeal being consequent on a change of ministry, but there had been little talk of independence. The Colonists' representative, Benjamin Franklin, could tell the House of Commons in that year that it was the general American opinion that England could control trade and levy incidental duties, but that internal taxation belonged to the colonists alone. The position, in fact, was precisely that now recognized by the Statute of Westminster (1931). The colonists admitted the paramount supremacy of the Crown, but not that of the House of Commons. In exchange for the protection of the Royal Navy the right of the Crown to recoup itself by means of duties levied on the colonists' external trade was conceded as a natural right, just as to-day the basic bond of the British Empire is, in the last resort, that of Debt. The services of the British Navy are supposed to be paid for by the provision of interest and sinking-fund charges on English loans.

The necessities of the Crown, however, overbore the good sense of Edmund Burke. Rockingham died, and the royalist ministry that succeeded him decided to set up an American Civil List, to be financed by the celebrated Townshend Duties, imposed in 1767. The motive behind these Duties, which is quite clear, disposes for good of the argument often advanced—that there was an element of justice in taxing the Americans, since it was but reasonable that they should contribute towards the cost of the Seven Years' War. As a matter of fact, the colonies had made a free grant-in-aid toward the financing of the war, besides raising a considerable force to fight the French in Canada, which took part in the capture of the important strategic outpost of Fort Duquesne, renamed Pittsburg in honour of the English Prime Minister, and to-day the centre of the great American steel industry.

Careful analysis suggests that at this date American Independence may be said to have been born, although the actual Declaration of Independence[1] was not issued for another nine years. The Massachusetts Assembly, after declaring the Townshend Duties to be unconstitutional, was dissolved by the Governor, but nevertheless continued to sit as a Convention. The period of constitutional opposition may be said to have closed.

In 1769 the Home Government repealed all the duties except that on tea, but it was now too late. In 1771 the Crown's right to levy duties of any kind was challenged by Massachusetts, always the most politically active of the colonies. Samuel Adams was skilfully using the mainly unfranchised body of artisans as shock troops in the agitation against English control, and this culminated in the famous Boston Tea Party of 1773, when the landing of the detested cargo of tea was prevented, the chests being thrown overboard into the harbour.

This was followed by the arbitrary closing of the port of Boston to all shipping, but the skill of Samuel Adams checkmated this attempt by the English to isolate his province: he was mainly responsible for the calling of the First Continental Congress of all the colonies in 1774.

The absence of political theory, as opposed to skilful propaganda against the English, was throughout very apparent. Samuel Adams, and the extremist party as a whole, continued to exhibit remarkable ability in adapting the forms of constitutional regularity to essentially unconstitutional purposes, but no coherent theory of government was advanced. Politically speaking, men lived from hand to mouth. Any argument that would justify the colonies' refusal to be taxed by England was gladly seized upon, but nobody seems to have had a sufficiently detached vision to realize the goal to which matters were tending, and to provide

[1] Appendix II.

a reasoned political theory that would justify the new departure. The Americans were content to regard their struggle as a mere recapitulation of the conflict between King and Parliament in England more than a century earlier.

The First Continental Congress possessed no executive functions whatever. It was a purely consultative body set up by thirteen governments that still considered themselves to be British colonies. It met, talked, and dispersed. Even in the following year Patrick Henry's cry, "We must fight," was far in advance of general opinion. The incredible folly of the English, who at this period conducted themselves like the notorious "Black and Tans" in post-war Ireland, provoked the colonists to further steps. A second Continental Congress met in 1775, after the battle of Lexington, in a far different temper from that of the previous year. Appeals were issued to Jamaica and to Ireland; the fact of a United Confederation was assumed; an army was raised and paid in paper, with Washington in command, while the crowning folly of the English, the hiring of German mercenaries to put down the rebellion, did much to weaken the Tory—or Loyalist—cause, and to sway towards Independence that vast unsettled body of moderate opinion which had been frightened out of its life by the popular demonstrations of Samuel Adams and his "Sons of Liberty."

Nevertheless, it required an Englishman to point the way to American freedom. In May 1776 the third annual Continental Congress met and adopted Jefferson's sonorous Declaration of Independence. Shortly afterwards Tom Paine published his *Common Sense*, in which the whole assumption of monarchy was denied. In a series of essays he set forth the case for American independence with extraordinary clarity. Avoiding the legal and political intricacies of the Colonial dispute with England, he presented the problem in a coherent form, and thus posed the question with such clear-cut, if perhaps misleading, simplicity that none could fail to understand the issue. This publication did more than any other single factor to convince the vast majority of Americans of the necessity for independence, and provided a political textbook on which they could base their arguments. Paine realized that the strength of American freedom must lie in a strong bond of union between the State governments, and suggested "a continental charter." We shall presently refer to the Federal Convention which completed the American Constitution in 1787.

It is not necessary to examine the progress of the war in detail. The British, with their command of the sea, could have overcome the revolt within three months had intelligent use been made of this advantage. Instead of profiting by their naval mobility, however, they preferred to send an army from New York up the Hudson valley to effect a junction with the Government troops in Canada. Eighteenth-century professional armies were not suited to campaigning in the wilderness, and the defeat of Burgoyne at Saratoga in the autumn of 1777 led directly to French intervention six months later. The command of the sea was lost, and with it all hope of a British victory. After a further resounding defeat in the South at Yorktown, peace was made in 1782 on a basis of full sovereign independence.

IV

How had the thirteen States been existing since 1776? In general, the old colonial constitution was taken over with as few alterations as possible. In 1753 Franklin had drawn up a scheme of Colonial Federation in North America, but this was inspired solely by fear of the French. With the destruction of French rivalry in the Continent after the Seven Years' War the whole purpose of federation was nullified, and the largely immature colonies relapsed into their normal state of sectionalism. It was not until after Independence had actually been declared and war had begun that the citizens of the various States were granted reciprocal rights. The war acted as a great forcing-house of political development: some of the colonies were still in a state of political infancy in 1775. Georgia, for instance, had been founded only during the reign of George II, and in 1776 there was no way of submitting any proposed draft to the people for their opinion. In South Carolina and Virginia it was definitely stated that a constitution was a mere act of the legislature, and similar views appear to have been held in New Jersey, Pennsylvania, Maryland and North Carolina. Only in Delaware were delegates expressly elected for the purpose of drawing up a new constitution, and there is no trace of evidence that the result was submitted for popular ratification. New England, however, provided an important exception. In Massachusetts popular ratification did occur, but on the basis of a restricted franchise. Here a politically conscious people insisted on a special constitutional convention, in the teeth of the opinion of the General Court, as the ordinary representative assembly was termed. The people angrily refused a plan offered by the General Court in 1778, and in 1780 ratified by a two-thirds majority the handiwork of their State Convention. The people of New Hampshire, too, insisted on a share in the drafting of their State Constitution. In 1779 they repudiated the work of a special constitutional convention, and ratified an entirely new draft, submitted in 1781, only on condition that certain alterations were made; and it was only in 1783 that the State Constitution of New Hampshire was ratified in its entirety.

Political necessity may be regarded as the main reason for this general refusal to submit directly to the opinion of the people, although the contrary theory that certainly the State Convention, and perhaps even the ordinary legislature, possessed sufficient power of itself to carry out such a reform, was far more widely held. It is, indeed, a logical development of the restricted franchise: if only a portion of the citizens can pronounce on public affairs there is much reason in the contention that their elected representatives have full authority to deal with any matters that may arise, that the full sum of political power has been delegated through the ballot box. This theory was widely held right up to the 1850's, and was extinguished only by the War of Secession and the consequent victory of the Federal Government. The large number of Loyalists, amounting perhaps to over one half of the population in New York, Georgia and South Carolina, together with the aristocratic influence of the age, rendered it unsafe, in the view of the Republicans, to submit to a majority vote. Revolutions have always been the act of a resolute minority, and these early State Constitutions were generally regarded as mere temporary makeshifts, ordinary legislative acts, created as a stopgap until more settled times would admit of more regular procedure.

As to any Federal authority, at this period, strictly speaking, there was none at all. In 1777 Articles of Confederation and Perpetual Union were drawn up, and were ratified by eight States in the following year. By 1781, when Maryland at last signed in agreement, all were bound, but the nature of the bond was of the slightest. It more nearly resembled the Covenant of the modern League of Nations than any true Federal agreement. Each State possessed one vote. The loose central authority could deal with the States alone, and that, in practice, solely by a recommendation unbacked by any coercive power. There was no Federal code, either of civil or of criminal law. Each State had its own tariff and its own depreciated paper currency. Under these circumstances it is not surpring that by 1787 the Confederation was on the brink of disintegration. The only remarkable fact is that it was able to make some little contribution to the foundations of a future national citizenship, such as the mutual recognition of a common citizenship by each of the State Governments, together with co-operation in the matter of criminal extradition and the recognition of one another's judicial proceedings and records.

Montesquieu observed: "The three powers of government must be kept separate in order that liberty may be preserved. When the legislative and executive powers are united in the same person, there can be no liberty, because apprehensions may arise lest the same monarch enact tyrannical laws, to exercise them in a tyrannical manner." But there was no threefold division of powers in the Confederation, on the model of Montesquieu's *Esprit des Lois*. Judicial powers did not exist at all, as there was no Federal judiciary. Legislative and executive powers, such as they were, were vested in Congress, which possessed only a few rudimentary departments, such as the Post Office and the four secretaryships of War, Foreign Affairs, Finance and the Navy.

In 1787, therefore, a Federal Convention assembled with specific instructions to *amend* the Articles of Confederation, generally considered to be almost unworkable. The ex-colonists were now outside the framework of the British Empire, which was therefore using to the full all the weapons of commercial prohibition to ruin the victorious Americans by barring their access to the British West Indies. In addition to this trade war, the thirteen sovereign States incessantly fought and quarrelled among themselves. Those with large claims to the hinterland were with difficulty brought to assign their rights to the central authority. Tariff wars broke out between neighbours; in the case of Connecticut and Pennsylvania a squabble over the Wyoming valley actually led to armed conflict. Some central authority that really could govern was clearly needed: but what was it to be?

V

The Convention which met at Philadelphia was to consist of 73 delegates, from every State except Rhode Island, which throughout refused to have anything to do with the others, and was with difficulty coerced into entering the Union in 1790 by the threat of being treated as a foreign country, and accordingly fenced in by a ring of Federal customs posts. Of these 73 delegates, 18 never appeared; 42 were present all through the deliberations and 39 actually signed the new Constitution. Woodward's description of these signatories is worth quoting. He writes: "Thirty-nine gentlemen in knee breeches, silk stockings and ruffled shirts signed the document one by one and stood around in leavetaking conversational groups, bowing ceremoniously and sniffing pinches of snuff from tiny boxes of gold and enamel." Sessions were in secret, and it was decided that seven States should form a quorum. Delegates might voice any opinion without committing their States, whose vote was cast on any specific issue after the particular representatives who were present had consulted together and agreed upon the line to be taken.

These delegates were all aristocrats, with a lively loathing for the common people, and appointed either by the State Governors or by the State Legislatures. Hot though the inter-State jealousies were, the guiding principle was a determination to make the nation safe FROM Democracy. The assertion of Roger Sherman, a delegate, that "the people should have as little to do as may be with Government" represents the unmistakable tone of the Convention. The revolutionary fire-eaters, the men behind the "Sons of Liberty," were conspicuous by their absence. Patrick Henry, Samuel Adams, Christopher Gadsden, the organizers of the "mechanicks," as they were called, were missing. Their supporters were by now nearly all excluded from the various State franchises by property qualifications. Just as fifty years later in England the Great Reform Bill, emancipating the middle class, was passed largely by the agitation of the working class, who received from it precisely nothing, so, in America, most of the men who fought in the Revolutionary Army were speedily disfranchised by the new State Constitutions, and had nothing whatever to do with the new Federal Constitution when it came to be ratified by the various States.

The economic struggle behind the founding of the Federal Constitution forms the key to the origins of the American Commonwealth. As Professor Beard very acutely observes: " . . . it (i.e. the Federal Constitution) was an economic document drawn with superb skill by men whose property interests were immediately at stake; and as such it appealed directly and unerringly to identical interests in the country at large."[1] The battle was really won even before the first session of the Convention was held. The "right people" had been successfully nominated in advance by the conservative, property-owning State legislatures, and the victory of Capital over Land was inevitable.

It was to prove a triumph for personalty, as against the agrarian interest of the small farmers, the men who stood to gain by the depreciation of the various paper currencies, and who actually rose in armed rebellion under Shayes in Massachusetts against the usurious exactions of the supporters of stable money. "The movement for the Constitution of the United States," writes Professor Beard, "was originated and carried through principally by four groups of personalty interests which had been adversely affected under the Articles of Confederation; money, public securities, manufactures, and trade and shipping." Of the delegates who attended the Convention 23 represented holders of Public Securities; 14 were speculators in the Western lands ceded by the various States to the central authority; 24 stood for Money at Loan, and therefore were against a continuation of a regime of widely fluctuating paper currencies; 11 represented commercial and shipping interests; and 15 were primarily slave-owners. In a word, it was Personalty against levelling Democracy, with all the cards stacked against Democracy. So we find that the new Constitution forbids paper money and specifically preserves the sanctity of contracts: the fundamental rights of private property are deliberately placed over and beyond the reach of chance popular majorities.

Modern Wall Street and those citadels of private profit, the

[1] C. A. Beard, *Economic Interpretation of the Constitution of the United States*. 1925.

American Public Utility Companies, owe their existence directly to the success of the financiers and the log-rolling tariff lobbyists, and to the land-speculators who freely bought up the paper pay-warrants of the veterans of Independence. In fact, the Constitution can best be understood in terms of the Stock Market. The first and greatest "Bear Raid" in American history was staged before ever the Wall Street Stock Exchange was founded. Government securities were at a heavy discount, artificially stimulated by the men of capital, scarcely one of whom had clean hands in the founding of the Constitution. Using their inside knowledge, the Fathers of American Democracy proceeded to effect the biggest coup in the history of Capitalism, and America suddenly discovered that she possessed the stabilizing influence of a National Debt!

The Convention had thus been made safe for the bourgeoisie, but there still remained the lively fear of the smaller States that they would be swallowed up by the four big States of North Carolina, Virginia, Pennsylvania and Massachusetts, if any strong Federal form were to be approved. The Constitution as we have it is therefore a compromise between the desire for a strong, centralized authority and an equally powerful demand for the preservation of State Rights. For this reason the excellent pattern of the new Massachusetts Constitution, which otherwise, very possibly, would have been copied with the minimum of alteration, was severely mutilated in deference to the wishes of the smaller States, who were determined to preserve their individuality as far as possible. The New England idea that the Sovereign People itself establishes the Constitution, and that the Constitutional Convention is merely a drafting committee, was destined to be overborne by the nervousness of the smaller States. Popular rule only began to make general headway after the war of 1812, and it required the constitutional explosion of the Civil War before popular sovereignty was definitely established as unquestionably superior to any legislative act.

In the last one hundred and fifty years Federal power has steadily increased, owing to the doctrine of "implied powers" enunciated by Chief Justice Marshall in the Supreme Court, but even to-day the traces of the protection demanded by the smaller States before they would consent to enter the Union remain plainly for all to see.

Quite early in the proceedings the two conflicting viewpoints were stated. Randolph of Virginia tabled the proposals of the large States, desirous of a strong central authority, while Paterson of New Jersey submitted the views of the small States, determined at all costs to protect State Rights. The final document[1] was a compromise leaning rather towards the centralized demands, although the small States, who fought hard for some guarantee of their individuality, obtained notable concessions.

Of these the most striking relate to the provisions for proposing and ratifying amendments. The proposal for amendment, having passed both Houses by a two-thirds majority, has then to be ratified by three-quarters of the States in order to become effective. By this means it is to-day theoretically possible for 6 million people, in the 13 smallest States, to cast a vote more than equal to that of 116 millions in the remaining 35 States.

No particular benefit can be derived, therefore, from following the precedent of the United States. A simple referendum, perhaps protected by a rule requiring a two-thirds majority, seems a far more just and democratic way of carrying out constitutional changes than this clumsy scheme, designed primarily to safeguard a constitution which had been composed in secret, without definite authority, and which, under colour of democracy, was drawn up primarily to safeguard the rights of private property. In a Socialist Commonwealth private property—in the sense of the ownership of the means of production—will not exist, so that it is a somewhat naïve idea that we can derive much benefit from the origins of the American Commonwealth. What *can* be deduced, however, with great benefit, is the plain fact that the American people were too busy to take part in the framing of the Constitution under which they were to live. The frontier, with its ever-receding vista of free land, drew the ordinary American with far greater force than the shadowy prospect of discussing a proposed constitution on which he had been disqualified from voting. The struggle for existence, as always, took precedence over the relative luxury of political discussion. To-day, when boundaries have become static once more, it is not so easy to withdraw from politics. Men cannot escape from the framework of government, and they therefore come to demand as a right the power to effect a relatively easy change. The

[1] Appendix I.

American example, with the notable exception of the New England Constitutions, affords them but scant prospect of discovering any practical method. Let us now proceed to consider whether the three Republics that have ruled in France during the last century and a half have offered any more helpful examples for the peaceful change of constitutional shortcomings.

Chapter Three

THE FRAMING OF THE CONSTITUTION IN FRANCE

I

The government of eighteenth-century France was a completely arbitrary monarchy. The Crown had broken the political power of the great nobles, but whereas in England they had been practically eliminated by civil war in the fifteenth century and royal executions under the Tudors, in France, they were still preserved as social parasites necessary to a royal Court. The complete exemption from taxation which was the privilege of the French aristocracy and clergy,[1] very seriously delayed the development of the French bourgeoisie, which flowered only a full half-century later than its English counterpart. While in England this class was constantly expanding, and was permitted to buy its way into the aristocracy, insurmountable social barriers were raised against it in France.[2] Nevertheless, the natural interplay of economic forces might well have enabled it to overcome arbitrary government by decree and to break through the swaddling clothes of heavy provincial protection, which stifled internal trade by a multiplicity of local tariff walls, had not the French bourgeoisie been fatally weakened by the Revocation of the Edict of Nantes by Louis XIV.

This Charter of the French Huguenots was cancelled to satisfy the religious bigotry of a doting King and his grasping mistress. The Revocation had dragooned the people into Catholicism, and was accompanied by terrible cruelties and indignities, which not only sowed the seeds of revolt, but left a legacy of undying hatred

[1] Although the clergy from time to time made substantial "voluntary" gifts to the Crown in lieu of taxation properly so called, both the amount to be raised and the method to be followed were settled by the clerical party in its own representative Chamber. The unprivileged Third Estate, and more particularly the peasantry, is computed to have paid 60 per cent of its income in taxation.

[2] We should distinguish here between the two sorts of nobility, that of the sword and that of the robe. The latter, resulting from high legal office, was a career more or less open to talent, and was therefore somewhat despised by the "true" nobility of the sword, exclusively hereditary.

of the Church. More than any other single act it rendered certain the explosion that occurred almost a century later. The emigration of Protestants assumed alarming proportions. The most industrious, self-reliant and independent members of the French middle class, together with the germs of a later proletariat, were driven into exile, and carried with them to Prussia, to England, and even to the New World, that incessant, ant-like proclivity for industrious toil which is the hallmark of the petty bourgeoisie the world over. Thus the effects of the Revocation of the Edict were ruinous to France; certain districts were nearly depopulated, the centres of commerce and industry, such as Normandy, were reduced to extreme poverty, and there were industries which suffered irrevocably from the drain of emigration.

There remained the intellectuals. Political life was non-existent under the *ancien régime*, but the mental turmoil of the century following 1688 could not be stilled by a royal decree or the threat of arbitrary imprisonment through a *lettre de cachet*. Men might not act politically, but for the most part they were allowed to think: to the ever-growing luxury and purposeless display of Versailles was added a very necessary spice of intellectual *divertissement* from what threatened to become intolerable boredom.

Literary patronage had always been a fashionable habit in the eighteenth century, and at a time when the forms of social and religious government seemed immutable the men of letters alone were permitted to question the existing static order. But these writers usually possessed the defects of their qualities: they were armchair philosophers, abstract analysts, and theoretical builders of paper constitutions: men who might pay lip-service to a republic three thousand miles away, but who were at heart incapable of conceiving of anything more radical than a constitutional monarchy on the English model, resting in turn upon the tolerant slave-owning mentality of a rich, landed oligarchy. To what extent the influence of abstract thinkers on social crises becomes operative in history is a debatable question.

A short review of some of the leading intellectual figures of eighteenth-century France will show how feeble and unreal were their speculations. They might thunder against royalty in the abstract, but they received and enjoyed their aristocratic pensions as a matter of course. Foremost among them we must rank Voltaire, the philistine of "transcendant cleverness," the enemy of entrenched authority, the man who combined fearless polemical writing with an amazingly incongruous lack of personal courage. He persistently hurled his uncompromising attacks against the Church and against every aspect of Christianity, and regarded Roman Catholicism as the most mischievous of all religions. He thought it would be possible to get rid of the priests, monks and friars without risk of serious disturbance by undermining the popular faith. He epitomizes the age, not only in his attacks upon existing abuses, but in his parasitic existence as a courtier in two successive kingdoms. "Like many others of the middle class who have gained wealth and consideration, Voltaire was conservative from fear of the future, not from reverence for the past."[1] Not for him the discomforts of a true revolutionary. He was fond of luxurious leisure and became a supporter of the nobility. He died quietly in his bed at a ripe old age, "the sage of Ferney," bequeathing as a final testament the absolute antithesis of revolution: the doctrine of cultivating one's own garden in peace.

Drawing upon the achievement of the city-republics of ancient or medieval times, Voltaire held the view that a popular government, based on elected representatives was possible in a small country with a homogeneous people. Yet in his *Idées Républicaines* he defines the true function of civil government as "the execution by one or more of the General Will in accordance with the laws voted by all." He declares that a republican constitution is the best because it is likely to be instrumental in ensuring equal rights for personal liberty, property, and the protection of the laws. But Voltaire's attitude towards the problems of his times was largely negative, and consequently his voluminous writings had a comparatively insignificant influence upon the practical issues that concerned the people of France.

Even Rousseau, the neurotic theorist of popular sovereignty, considered the idea of a French Republic to be absurd because the republican form of government was adapted only to a small State. So large a territory as France, he thought, must of necessity require a monarchy to control it, a monarchy less arbitrary, perhaps, than the benevolent despotism envisaged by Voltaire, but still a system of personal government. "How great," he writes, "would be the danger of disturbing the vast masses which

[1] *The Cambridge Modern History*, vol. viii.

compose the French Monarchy! Who could arrest the impulse once given or guard against the possible consequences? Even if the advantages of the new arrangement were indisputable, what men of sense would venture suddenly to abolish old customs, to change old maxims, and to alter that shape which an existence of thirteen hundred years has gradually given to the State?"

It is the same with the other great figures of the time. Diderot, d'Alembert, Holbach, Helvétius, the men of the Encyclopaedia, might all declaim against the rule of kings, but apparently none of them envisaged the possibility of any other form of government for their native country. Montesquieu, as we shall see later, merely wished to reproduce at home his conception of the English model. He believed that the regeneration of France lay in saving her from despotism, which inevitably led to anarchy, and that a return to the old monarchy as it existed under Henri IV or Louis XIII would give France the best polity. But he "would temper monarchy by aristocratic institutions," because undivided sovereignty was the source of despotism. D'Argenson might praise the abstract idea of a Republic, but it was only that he might graft upon the Crown those portions of a democratic system which he thought best suited to France. Even the mathematician, Condorcet, who was to play so large a part in producing the Constitution of 1793, did not, before the Revolution, regard a republican form of government as either possible or desirable in France.

The reason is not far to seek. The ideology of the French Revolution is a purely bourgeois ideology, largely restricted to the upper middle class. The French bourgeoisie had become increasingly powerful, owing to the expansion of commercial enterprise since 1714. It was this class which sought to become a privileged oligarchy in place of the privileged feudal aristocracy. The spearhead of a possible proletariat had been broken off by the revocation of the Edict of Nantes; and therefore these writers were all appealing to a narrow, stunted, politically starved section of the population, extending from the clique of high-born intriguers who surrounded the Throne to the petty provincial nobility and the wholly disfranchised intelligentsia of doctors, lawyers and inferior clergy. In so far as these writers make any concrete proposals they advocate a policy of gradualism, a policy which found its epitome in the short-lived Constitution of 1791, prefaced by the sonorous and heroic Declaration of the Rights of Man. It was only the proletarian struggle of Paris, after Hébert and the *Enragés* had captured the government of the capital, that drove the Revolution forward, despite the right-wing Social Democracy of the Girondins. Secure in the implied support of the Paris "sections," Robespierre was able to push forward to the social revolution which the poor desired as a necessary corollary to the mere transference of political power from the Crown to the well-to-do. Mistaken tactics by Robespierre, as we shall presently see, not only cost him his head but was fatal to the whole principle of the social revolution. The bourgeoisie returned to the attack, and under the despotism of Napoleon they riveted afresh upon the nation this iron yoke, a yoke that to-day bears with redoubled weight upon the ever more powerful and discontented working-class of France.

Fatally weakened at the core, the over-centralized machine of government rolled on, largely by its own momentum. The monarchical centralization facilitated a concerted despotic movement, but the defects of autocracy had become apparent even in the reign of Le Roi Soleil: initiative was discouraged before the overbearing self-assurance of the semi-deified figure of Louis XIV, and the acts of the succeeding Kings of France might have been consciously designed to reveal the fatal weakness of a system deliberately constructed to revolve exclusively about the person of an hereditary autocrat.

The reign of the infant Louis XV began with a Regency notorious, even in that century, for its dissolute character, and the logical consequence of such a training for kingship resulted in a display of purposeless and extravagant immorality which makes the long reign of this monarch one of the most dreary in history. By an ironical chance, the young Louis XVI bore a character of sober honesty that under different circumstances might have averted the disaster which was to sweep him away. Lord Acton aptly describes his reign as "the era of repentant monarchy," but he figured only as a feeble straw, drifting upon the flood-tide of universal corruption. His weak character made him incapable of sustained resistance to a court of determined and self-seeking voluptuaries. A stronger and more ruthless man might perhaps have controlled the new forces unleashed in 1789. The innate conservatism of mankind would have responded in France to a resolute leadership, as was revealed later by the stubborn revolt in La Vendée. But Louis XVI was totally untrained in statecraft. A devotee of hunting, a mighty eater and a passable locksmith, it was not for him, in the words of the poet, "to ride the whirlwind and direct the storm." Perplexed, honest, well-meaning and weak, he passes from the scene, with a personal dignity that would be wholly admirable if it were not so utterly ineffective.

II

The political immaturity of the French at this period needs to be repeatedly emphasized. They had no experience whatever of self-government, even in the most insignificant of local affairs. The *Parlements* of France, which had their seat in most of the chief provincial cities, must be carefully distinguished from the apparently similar English Parliament. They were local, the English equivalent was national; they represented purely the judicial function of government, while the latter was primarily an executive and legislative body. The typical French *Parlement*, such as that of Paris, the most powerful of these Courts, was composed of lawyers who sought, somewhat unsuccessfully, to pose as the final arbiters upon the legality of the actions of the executive —that is, of the Crown. An unsuccessful pose, since the King could, and frequently did, force the *Parlements* to register edicts to which they had previously taken exception, by the process of holding what was termed a Bed of Justice, wherein the bare order to register was sufficient to enforce obedience. The English Parliament itself, on the other hand, indirectly furnishes the Executive, since all Cabinet Ministers must be members of one of the two Houses. To-day, since the passage of the 1911 Parliament Act, absolute Sovereignty in Britain resides practically in the House of Commons. By this measure the Commons re-asserted the principle of forcing the Crown to threaten the creation of a sufficient number of peers to overcome opposition in the House of Lords, while at the same time it severely restricted the independent powers of that body.

Nor were the French particularly well served when they looked abroad at foreign institutions. The eighteenth century has been termed the Age of the Enlightened Despot, and free institutions were at a low ebb. Harrington would have been shocked at the conditions of affairs in his beloved Venice, and in the Netherlands, while the much-vaunted democracy of Britain turns out, on critical examination, to have consisted of a landed oligarchy, entirely composing one House, and largely controlling the other by open and unashamed corruption, rendered possible by a restricted franchise and a steadily diminishing electorate. The great shift in population, due to the Industrial Revolution, rendered a redistributing Bill essential, as year by year the number of rotten boroughs increased and their sale became more open. Montesquieu, in his famous study of British government at this period, totally misunderstood the position, and evolved his celebrated doctrine of the separation of powers, which was to have so great an influence on revolutionary Constitution-makers, declaring this principle to be the lynch-pin of the British system.

According to this theory, the executive, legislative and judicial functions of government were all jealously separated, and could not overlap. The error is not surprising, if we consider the period at which the author wrote. Under George II the office of Prime Minister was uneasily evolving as an unnoticed by-product of the long Ministry of Walpole, but no contemporary realized what manner of new departure was so gradually emerging, and the very title was hotly resented, as hinting at an improvised imitation of French autocracy, directed towards the undermining of the legislative independence of the House of Commons.[1] The King was still the apparent, as well as the titular, executive; Parliaments still dissolved automatically upon the death of the sovereign under whose authority they had been summoned, and the recrudescence of personal monarchy under the young George III—although he did not lead his armies in the field as his grandfather, George II, had done at Dettingen—did but seem to confirm old theories. Finally, the evolution of judge-made law during this century, due especially to the masterful independence of Lord Mansfield, led to the creating of such a body of case law, particularly in commercial matters, and the Chancery protection of Married Women's Property, as wholly to excuse an intelligent foreigner for arriving at the erroneous, if pardonable, opinion that the three powers were in fact totally separate and independent.

In North America, certainly, men did find an example, but it

[1] It was not until the twentieth century that the title of Prime Minister in Britain received formal recognition. Mention of the title then occurs in an Order in Council deciding the relative precedence of various dignitaries at official functions.

was one that appeared too late to be of any great value to the French. The American Constitution was produced only in 1787, and was barely ratified before the French Revolution had begun. The individual States had certainly, for the greater part, produced their first independent Constitutions by 1776, but we have seen that the American record for this period was hardly reassuring to an inquiring democrat who was searching for a suitable form of government for his own country. Largely through the philo-American influence of Tom Paine and Lafayette, two veterans of the struggle for Independence, coupled with the active assistance of the philosopher Condorcet, the so-called "Projet Girondin"—to which we shall have occasion to refer later—flowered into the Constitution of 1793, but the direct influence of America, considering the recent fact of Independence, was not so marked as might have been expected. The chief effect of the revolt of the thirteen colonies was to precipitate national bankruptcy in France, through the heavy increase in expenditure involved by the war with England. It thus definitely speeded up the summoning of the Estates General in 1789, and so led the way to the Revolution. But once representative institutions had in fact been granted, the American example served to provide material for orators rather than for statesmen. It was hard to work out a concrete parallel between countries historically and physically so different as were France and the United States, and the fact that the Paris Commune swung so successfully to the extreme left for nearly twenty months—that is, from August, 1792, till the execution of Hébert in March, 1794—differentiates French history very sharply from that of North America. The tempo of events in France was far more rapid than in America, and while the leisurely Fathers of the American Constitution successfully excluded the revolutionary *canaille*, the "Sons of Liberty" and the "Mechanicks in Union," while they secretly riveted the fetters of private property upon the American people, the French, historically centred about one great city, were swiftly carried away by the revolutionary zeal of those who felt, with Rousseau, that they had nothing to lose but their chains, and were therefore determined to cross the Rubicon, to face the world reaction of the princes fearlessly and without excuse; in a word, as Danton heroically put it, "to hurl at their feet as a gage, the head of a king."

III

It cannot be too strongly insisted that the summoning of the States General in 1789 was due solely to financial embarrassment. France was then bankrupt, but her bankruptcy was a symptom rather than the malady itself. The perpetual spate of pamphlets, satires and critiques upon the *ancien régime* must surely have caused the vacillating mind of Louis XVI to recoil from the indirect approval of such criticism inherent in the summoning of an assembly that had not met for over a century and a half. Circumstances, however, were too much for him: it was the misfortune of this sovereign that his weak will was always subject to the pressure of the last resolute intriguer who could obtain an audience. The tentative reforms of Turgot, his first and greatest finance minister, provoked an immediate outcry from the mob of titled sinecure holders, who rightly saw that their parasitic position was now in danger, and the King was soon induced to dismiss the most brilliant of his servants.

Necker, who succeeded him, was altogether of inferior calibre. He seems to have determined that he at least would not be guilty of his predecessor's fault of endeavouring, however tentatively, to get to the root of the problem, and he therefore proceeded to balance the national budget, primarily by means of a system of ever-increasing and unfunded loans. At this period France was still in form a feudal society, and there was, therefore, no machinery for calculating and administering the national income on "business" principles; that is, in effect, along the lines of bourgeois, middle-class economy. The State's income was farmed out to a ring of wealthy bankers, and it was impossible to provide any check upon the optimistic statements of the royal finance minister.

But we must give him the credit for attempting to mitigate the distress resulting from the scarcity of food in the capital. About a year before the Revolution he suspended the exportation of corn, encouraged its importation by bounties, and spent over 70 million livres in the purchase of foreign wheat. In order to control profiteering and fraudulent practices he issued a decree empowering magistrates and police to inspect private granaries, but all these efforts were rendered useless by corruption among the officers of the State. Cautious though he had been, Necker fell a victim to backstairs intrigue, and was dismissed, to bide his time. Almost certainly he took with him the knowledge that he had definitely brought the State far nearer to an inevitable moratorium.

If a professional banker, such as Necker, could not manage the national accounts, it was certain that his aristocratic successors would make a mess of the business. The Comte de Calonne, after a period of office, resigned in despair, roundly declaring that it was "impossible to govern." Necker's unsound finance was recoiling on the heads of his successors, and the easy years of postponed deficits were a thing of the past. Three-fifths of the country was free from taxation, the Crown, the nobility and the clergy each enjoying approximately equal shares in this immunity, so that the first attempt to grapple with the deficit—by means of an Assembly of Notables—was doomed to failure. The Assembly proved notable merely for a natural refusal to waive its traditional immunities, and a deadlock resulted. The summoning of this Assembly, however, is important, as tending to show the very real reluctance with which the idea of calling the old States General was viewed. Although the Three Estates would presumably sit apart, so that a majority of the houses was apparently assured for reaction, yet the Crown and its satellites were obviously extremely reluctant to admit even so small a fraction of the popular will. In this they proved right enough, as was subsequently proved by the "Cahiers" or "Quires" of grievances of the deputies, while the militant nature of the famous pamphlet by the Abbé Sieyès, "What is the Third Estate?", caused more anxiety among the privileged. At this period, however, Necker forced the King's hand. Popular opinion had long urged his recall, as his previous dismissal had but served to enhance his reputation among those who could not know on what unsound principles he had managed the finances. The courtiers, admitting their inability to handle the financial affairs of the country, seconded the popular vote, and Necker returned to office a popular hero. An astute self-seeker, he suddenly produced an entirely new, and far more accurate, statement of the national accounts, declaring that hitherto he had been misled, through no fault of his own. Out of his own considerable private fortune he lent the State an imposing sum, which might, it seemed, at least postpone the inevitable bankruptcy for a few months. The natural wealth of France, he argued, was obvious for all to see. Only let the King summon the representatives of his people to his aid, and all would yet be well.

It was with such a pistol held to his head that Louis XVI at last consented to the summoning of the Estates General. The popularity of the Crown at once knew no bounds, especially when it was decreed that the Third Estate should have as many representatives as the other two Houses combined. Rightly foreseeing that such conduct would make him a popular hero, Necker no doubt hoped to recover, in a wave of popular approval, all, and far more than all, than he had hazarded. His general calculations were correct: he was, indeed, for a period, the most worshipped man in all France, but the forces he had unleashed proved too strong for this man of putty to control, and he was soon swept away into permanent exile and oblivion.

IV

The inexperience of the French was indeed patent. The accident that the Estate of the Clergy happend to contain a majority of curés and abbés, or small, poverty-stricken priests who were all unanimously for reform, led to the victory of the Third Estate in its struggle to effect a junction with the other two Houses and sit as a single Assembly. The appearance of the Marquis de Lafayette, whose American experience had brought him before the public eye, as presumably expert in the affairs of a practical democracy, helped to win over the nobles, not least upon the ground that so popular a figure would doubtless serve as a brake upon the more exuberant demands of the extremists. Such a term, however, as applied to the personnel of the National Assembly requires some qualification; for the assembly as a whole was thoroughly imbued with conservatism, notwithstanding the presence of many men who were to become leading figures of the Left in the future. In the entire assembly there were only two or three legal members with adequate knowledge of the feudal laws, and there was hardly a single member who aimed further than the abolition of feudal dues and inequalities, for which compensation was generally urged. Indeed, the notorious paper currency of the Revolution, the assignats, originated in December, 1789, as a species of Treasury bond secured upon the Church property that was to be taken over by the State. Later issues, it is true, were to degenerate into a true paper currency, but the basic idea of the first assignats is typical of the bourgeois determination at all costs to reassure the holders of property in France.

Hence we find that the typical handiwork of the National Assembly is the Constitution of 1791, which was merely an attempt to follow as closely as possible the comparatively oligarchical model of contemporary English institutions. This draft—for it can hardly be said to have had more than a very brief life—proposed to substitute a constitutional monarchy, on the English pattern, for the existing absolutism, but apart from this very important feature it was reactionary and static throughout. The franchise, following the English precedent, was extremely restricted, and there was no question of submitting the draft constitution to popular ratification. One may say that as yet the people, as a whole, had not successfully asserted their right to a political life, although the right to have their affairs debated by their representatives was grudgingly allowed. With the appearance of the far more liberal National Convention, elected in August, 1792, on a more restricted franchise than the original Estates General, this cautious compromise was at once swept utterly away on the unchallenged ground that it had never been ratified. This shows the development of political feeling very clearly: the Assembly did not consider that ratification was within the competence of the people. The Convention automatically assumed that the last word must lie with the electorate.

It also explains why the Revolution was at first greeted with almost universal applause in England. Not only Liberals like Charles James Fox acclaimed it, but at first even the British Ambassador could enthusiastically report, with perfect accuracy, that autocracy had been overthrown in favour of Constitutional Monarchy. Only the pessimistic eye of Edmund Burke marked, in the revolutionary upsurging of Paris that swept away the Bastille, the cloud no smaller than a man's hand, which ere long was to sweep away the oligarchic alternative that appeared to have so quickly superseded the system of autocratic absolutism.

The National Convention at once set to work to produce the far more advanced Constitution of 1793, in which Jeffersonian Democracy was crossed with the theories of the French Encyclopaedists. The author of the Declaration of Independence was Jefferson, who appeared in the rôle of a true democrat. The doctrine of Jeffersonian democracy was concerned with the right of self-determination and the theory of popular initiative; but the constitution of the United States, drawn up and adopted while Jefferson was in France, bore hardly any mark of his political philosophy. It was only on his return to America that he realized how he had been tricked, and he at once proceeded to organize the opposition to the Federal Party of all those who had been worsted in the economic struggle that preceded the founding of the Federal Constitution: the small farmers, the debtors, and the unfranchised workmen who had been temporarily defeated by the powerful representatives of Capitalism.

By the unsuccessful flight to Varennes in June 1791, Louis XVI had virtually abdicated, and far more radical opinions were in the air. Although considerably purged and altered under the influence of Robespierre, the draft of this Constitution was in fact ratified by the people, although under coercive methods that made a free vote impossible. In August 1793 the apparently overwhelming figure of 1,801,918 to 11,160 votes was announced.

The American principle of primary assemblies still survived in the final document. One-tenth of these primaries could compel the legislature to order all the primaries to elect delegates to a national convention for the consideration of specific alterations or revisions of the Constitution. Here, then, the important principle of the popular initiative is established. The philosophical contribution of the Encyclopaedists, on the other hand, is to be found in Condorcet's alternative plan for a popular *initiative by stages. Fifty individuals might propose revision in* their own primary assembly. They had then to convince a majority, first of their arrondissement, and next of their department. Should they succeed in both of these attempts, the legislature was then forced to consult the nation.

This precise and mathematical Constitution, although duly ratified, hardly saw the light of day, as it was virtually suspended by a decree which in effect set up a dictatorship for the duration of the interventionist wars, which had broken out in 1792, largely as a result of underground intrigues to which the King, now virtually a prisoner, was a party.

We must now return to the political development of France, or the reader may be in some danger of falling into much the same error as these early makers of paper Constitutions: that is, of drawing up sound projects without any reference to current events, which encompass and automatically condition them, despite their authors' apparent independence of such mundane activity.

V

The French Revolution primarily enfranchised the middle-class, the *laissez-faire* bourgeoisie, who demanded a proportionate taxation of the hitherto immune upper class in order to facilitate their own development. To this end the National Assembly liquidated the hopeless anachronism of the old feudal France. Feudal dues were wiped out and the four pillars of the *ancien régime* destroyed. The historic provinces of France were broken up into the modern departments; the Church was disestablished by the Civil Constitution of the Clergy; the old reactionary, closed corporations were dissolved; and the mediæval concept of the Family was shattered by the institution of civil marriage and a progressively easier divorce law. Finally, the royal army, suspect as the preserve of reaction, and indeed in part composed of foreign mercenaries, was replaced by the National Guard, the armed mass of the newly-enfranchised bourgeoisie.

Nevertheless, despite these widespread reforms, designed to facilitate the assumption of power by the bourgeoisie, the keystone of the bourgeois system was the sanctity of private property. Even the Jacobins never departed from this fundamental concept. They proposed to apply the surplus of the rich to the mitigation of popular suffering, but they did not in the least envisage a confiscation of their capital. Rather they were in line with the views of those modern English Socialists who wish to effect a redistribution of wealth by an ever more steeply-graded scale of taxation to be imposed upon the rich. Indeed, the French bourgeoisie were eagerly awaiting the speedy emergence of the nascent capitalist order as the crown of their triumphant struggle against feudalism. They even abolished the peasants' communal rights for the benefit of the bourgeois speculators.

The Legislative Assembly of 1791 was elected, it must be remembered, upon a very restricted franchise. Men were divided into "active" and "passive" citizens, and the former alone possessed the right to stand for election, while in each case there was a necessary qualification: the citizen must be a taxpayer, and only the more prosperous were included in the "active" category. The artisans, journeymen and small shopkeepers of Paris were thus totally unrepresented in that Assembly, but they were able to capture the local government of Paris, the Commune, on August 10, 1792. These men, the followers of Hébert, known as the "enragés," the "furious," were the real Left Wing of the Revolution. Never represented in the Assembly itself, they exercised a perpetual influence upon it by their membership of the leading political clubs, by their continual presence in the public galleries of the Assembly, and by their control of the municipal government of the capital. These were the men who furnished the germ of truth in the traditional and wholly misleading picture of the French Revolution as a proletarian uprising. They brought about the storming of the Bastille on July 14, 1789, providing by this means a concrete symbol of the fall of the *ancien régime*. It was their womenfolk who, in October 1789 marched to Versailles and forced the King to take up his domicile in Paris instead of twenty miles away. But influential though they were, the *enragés* were at last defeated by Robespierre, the Cromwell of the Revolution, who looked with horror upon their interpretation of Egalité, an interpretation which would automatically have demolished his sacred concept of the inviolability of private property.

It is unnecessary to sketch in detail the history of the Legislative Assembly. The Right Wing Girondins, who had done much to prepare the ground for the ideology of revolt, were unable to see beyond their own upper middle class. They were passionate defenders of bourgeois property, and had little sympathy with the masses. Moreover, they suffered a fatal blow in the treachery of the Republican General Dumouriez, who, though regarded to some extent as a Girondin nominee, deserted to the invading armies of reaction. Even the Jacobins, generally held to be the Left Wing of the Assembly, were also unfortunately class-bound, although they included the much greater mass of the petty bourgeoisie and the peasantry, by whose means they were able to effect the primary results of the great Revolution: that is to say, the final and complete destruction of the obsolete feudal system, from whose ruins arose a petty bourgeoisie and a peasantry at last in actual possession of the land. The famous Civil Code, unjustly associated with Napoleon, in reality owes far more to the early Jacobins than to the First Consul, with its basic principle of perpetual subdivision of the agricultural holding among the descendants of the original small-holder.

It should now be comprehensible why Robespierre fell on the 9th of Thermidor, 1794. The orthodox theory of reaction against bloodshed is simply untenable: for if this were correct the Russian Revolution would long ago have been followed by a bourgeois, "white" reaction, instead of remaining Socialist and consolidating its position. Robespierre fell, not because the people were tired of bloodshed as such, but because he was incapable of developing along sound revolutionary lines. He duly eliminated the lukewarm Girondists, but he then made the fatal mistake of alienating the masses by his suppression of Hébert and the revolutionary Paris Commune. When revolt broke out among his own class followers Robespierre had no one to whom he could appeal with success, for the very driving force of the Revolution had been deliberately stilled for ever by Robespierre himself when he fell upon the *enragés*. The class which had imprisoned the King in the Tuileries; had conducted the Red Purge of the Paris prisons, known as the September Massacres; had pressed for the execution of Louis XVI; had urged the necessity for social laws, such as the celebrated Law of the Maximum, directed against profiteering, and a general policy of taxation designed, in modern American parlance, to "soak the rich": this powerful force now lay headless and bleeding, destroyed by his very own act, while he sought desperately for support against his enemies.

Reaction, therefore, followed the fall of the Incorruptible. The Directory, and Executive Committee of Five, controlled by Barras, became the germ of the Napoleonic dictatorship that was to follow, although the instrument by which it was set up was designed to curb the absolute powers of the Executive, which had come to be vested in the Committee of Public Safety and the Committee of General Security. By the Constitution of the year III, the plural Executive of Five Directors was to be controlled by two Houses, that of the Ancients and that of the Five Hundred, who were to preserve strict financial control, while the Directors retired annually in rotation.

By the notorious Law of the Two-Thirds, the Directory and the Constitution of the Year III stood condemned. Under this measure the remnants of the Legislative Assembly stipulated that two-thirds of the two new Houses of Government should be elected from their own members. Government was at once discredited, when even the framers of the new Constitution appeared to have so little faith in their own handiwork, and the only significant incident during the reign of the Directory was the revolutionary flash, in 1796, of "Gracchus" Babeuf, the leader who fully realized that the Constitution framed by the bourgeoisie defeated the very purpose of democracy.

As he told his judges at his trial: "My companions and I have groaned over the unhappy results of the Revolution . . . it has merely replaced the old gang of scoundrels by a new one." Babeuf was the first to see that the class struggle was inherent in politics: it is true that he had three bloody examples before his eyes, in the events of 1789 and 1793, and the reaction of Thermidor, following the fall of Robespierre; but honour is due to him for drawing the inference which, though it may seem obvious enough to-day, eluded the great mass of his contemporaries. There appears to be something so sacred in the concept of private property that men will not see that this age-old incubus is the source of all our troubles and not a shield against them. "All revolutions centre round the relation of political authority to the distribution of economic power; for, as Madison long ago insisted, 'the only durable source of faction is property.' " So writes Harold Laski.[1] The inference is that the ending of "faction," or class oppression, must therefore involve, as a matter of course, the end of property as a private possession.

Babeuf, then, saw that the capture of a political machine designed to facilitate the purposes of the exploiting class was only a beginning. The intervening period of the "dictatorship of the proletariat," to use the classical phrase of Marx, was apparent to him as a necessity, pending the construction of a new form of democratic government designed to fulfil the wants of the working class.[2]

The plans of Babeuf were cut short by Governmental inter-

[1] The opening words of "Socialism in the French Revolution," forming ch. viii of *Social and Political Ideas of the Revolutionary Era*, ed. F. J. C. Hearnshaw.

[2] Buonarotti, one of the Babeuvist conspirators, and the official historian of the movement, wrote, thirty years later: "It was evident that the inherent necessity of things, even the very success of our enterprise, required an interval between the fall of aristocratic power and the final establishment of a popular democracy."

ference, and he himself was executed. It seems that the ranks of his movement had, for some time, been penetrated by police spies, and the Directory had struck at leisure. Nevertheless, at the height of the resulting confusion, seven hundred men marched to the suburb of Grenelle, and sought to incite the troops there to come to the aid of their comrades. They were dispersed only by a deliberately planned military attack. Further, one of the famous Paris Communards of 1871, that body of workers who for over two months set up a "Soviet" Government in the capital, in defiance of German invaders and French reaction, was a grandson of that Clemence who had sat with Babeuf on his central committee. Thus does the continuity of history reveal itself. The Paris Commune was the ancestor of the Soviet Russia of to-day, and thus we have a revolutionary chain of causation, passing back unbroken from modern times to the emergence of the first modern conditions, a century and a half ago.

VI

What, then, can usefully be learned from the French Revolution? Its function was primarily to destroy an outworn economic system, that of Feudalism, and to substitute for it, not immediately a large-scale Capitalism, which in fact was fully developed in France only under the Dictatorship of the Second Empire, but rather the necessary conditions from which a large-scale Capitalism might later develop; that is to say, the protection of the rights of private property as a sacred fundamental of Society. Land was no longer the great criterion, but wealth in any form; and with the development of French Banking under the July Monarchy of the Orleanist King, Louis Philippe, this "wealth" became, more precisely, ownership of the means of production, and so modern capitalism was made possible. By a system of indirect election and property qualifications, the Constitution of the Year III based the electoral right on wealth, and delivered the Government of the Republic into the hands of the propertied classes. Briefly, it established a régime of the bourgeoisie, adapting it to the Republic; but its ideology was greatly at variance with the "Declaration of the Rights of Man" of 1789.[1]

Thus, for all constructive purposes, the early French Consti-

[1] Appendix III.

tutions are not much more valuable than those of eighteenth-century America, but these too show us how to avoid errors which might otherwise be committed. The French, like the Americans, revealed a lively fear of the consequences of a popular vote, so the franchise was severely restricted. An indirect system of election was established, and on account of the property suffrage only men in easy circumstances could be enfranchised. In brief, the electoral features were extremely conservative. This is not surprising, if we remember that all the Constitutions had this in common, that they were products of the early stage of Capitalism, when political power was still in the hands of comparatively few, whose interest it was to conserve that power as far as possible. The *petite* bourgeoisie of France finally revolted in 1848, against financial exploitation by the ring of bankers and big industrialists who used Louis Philippe as their convenient figurehead. Enlisting the power of the proletariat, now tardily beginning to increase in France, the bourgeoisie rebelled against the yoke of monarchy, but speedily turned against their new allies once the victory had been achieved. Torn and divided amongst themselves, the French fell a victim to Prince Napoleon, who entirely ignored the popular will, and, trading upon the glamour of his name, transformed himself by a *coup d'état* from President to Emperor almost overnight. The Constitution of Louis Napoleon, which bears the date of 1852, was never submitted to the poople. A series of military engagements engrossed the attention of the French people under the Second Empire, and it was not until the very end of this period, in 1870, that a series of liberalizing amendments to the Constitution of 1852 were adopted in the forlorn hope of staving off an internal explosion.

With the fall of Napoleon III and the disastrous Franco-Prussian War of 1870 the last flicker of popular government in France appeared in the short-lived Paris Commune of 1871. The French bourgeoisie, which managed to destroy it, under the leadership of Thiers, was terrified of the possible effect of even so brief an experiment. The Commune of 1871 actually introduced cheap government by the destruction of the standing army and the civil service bureaucracy of "fonctionnaires." For these two chief props of bourgeois capitalism it substituted the simple function of workmen and managers, who performed their duties at workers' wages. The unrestricted power of vocation, which could remove any person previously elected by universal suffrage, was a sure safeguard against the danger that a new bureaucracy might develop along the old bourgeois lines, albeit recruited from the working class. When we compare this system with the existing French Constitution of 1875 it will readily be seen why the Third Republic, friendless and loved of none though it may appear, was in reality, despite the presence of various monarchist groups, the most perfect device of its kind for riveting the yoke of the French bourgeoisie upon the nation.

The Third Republic is the reverse of democratic. Both the armed forces of the State and all Frenchwomen are denied the right to vote. Deputies for the Chamber must be at least twenty-five years of age, while candidates for the Senate must have attained the age of forty. Even the President, the prisoner of the Elysée, as he has been bitterly termed, is not elected by the people, but by the two Chambers in joint session. At every step we see traces of the determination of the terrified bourgeoisie to prevent a further outbreak of democracy. This is especially apparent in the deliberate under-representation of Paris in the National Assembly. Over five million persons live in Greater Paris to-day—that is to say nearly one-eighth of the population of modern France—yet Paris herself is allowed but ten Senators out of the national total of 314, and 59 Deputies out of a total of 615. Again, in general, the French Mayor, the only elected official in France who is vested with executive power, is responsible for the control of the police of his municipality, but in Paris, Lyons and Marseilles the municipal police pass under the control of the Government, as is also the case in the great naval arsenal of Toulon, controlled by the Prefect of the Var Department.

The reason is not far to seek. The bourgeoisie is in deadly fear lest the revolutionary tradition of these cities should lead to the control of the police passing, by a perfectly proper reflection of public opinion, into the hands of those who might be opposed to the maintenance of the *status quo*, and to the preservation of bourgeois capitalism.

In the early days of the first Revolution, traces of the old feudalism were responsible for the old view that man is by no means equal to his fellows. The men who framed the Declaration of the Rights of Man had in mind, primarily, their own class, and not by any means the sum of all French citizens. Helvétius,

Condorcet and other Encyclopaedists believed in the rights of private property, but realized the necessity for minimizing the sharp contrasts between rich and poor within the social order. Yet the entire constitutional edifice was founded on particular rights or special privileges. Such a view is confirmed by the division of the electorate into the categories of "active" and "passive" citizens. That is, those who lacked the property qualifications for suffrage became passive, and those who possessed them, active. This is not to belittle the magnificent wording of the Rights of Man, but only to point out that these noble words, as a concrete expression of the philosophical ideas of the time, have so far been unworthily confined in their application to but a section of the community, instead of being extended to mankind at large. To-day we have granted the political right to equality, but have largely nullified it by the disproportionate influence of wealth in the modern State.

We are therefore forced to conclude that the forms and distribution of property determine the nature of the State. The social configuration arising from different degrees and kinds of property-possessions and occupations distorts the fundamental basis of democracy unless the Rights of Man are protected by the socialization of the means of production and distribution. "The freest government, if it could exist, would not be long acceptable, if the tendency of the laws were to create a rapid accumulation of property in few hands and to render the great mass of the population dependent and penniless. In such a case, the popular power must break in upon the rights of property, or else the influence of property must limit and control the exercise of popular power. Universal suffrage, for example, could not long exist in a community where there was great inequality of property." Thus wrote Daniel Webster in America, at the time of the great Secession controversy. So long as property in the hands of small groups and estates remains as a measure of power, there can be no hope of the survival of democratic ideals. That is why the doctrines of liberty and equality proclaimed by the French Revolution did not affect the constitution or the structure of the government. The French bourgeoisie attacked the evils rooted in feudalism, but ignored the majority of the nation. Eager to possess political power, so as to enjoy the fruits of expanding commerce and industry, they secured a large share in the Government, but failed to observe the close and inevitable parallelism between the trends of economic and political movements.

Yet the French Revolution served its purpose: it gave birth to a new France. It postulated the thesis that in order to preserve the inherent dignity and worth of man, he must learn to demand the bestowal of sovereign power upon the people; he must strive to establish social relationships which will not degrade human worth, and which will deliberately challenge the hierarchical organizations of Society. Even though it resulted in a conquest of power by the French bourgeoisie, its results, from 1789 to the Commune, brought about fundamental changes in the national psychology. For one thing, it showed that revolution was in reality a part of the evolutionary process by which human progress was accomplished, and that it carried within its ideologies such elements of development as are revealed to-day in the Union of Socialist Soviet Republics, where socialism in action is demonstrating what *can be* the basis of an enduring form of democracy.

Chapter Four

CONSTITUTIONAL CHANGES WITHIN THE BRITISH EMPIRE

Contrasting the English and French Revolutions, Sir Henry Campbell-Bannerman made the following observations: "When we make a Revolution, we do not destroy our house. With care we preserve the façade, and, behind that façade, reconstruct a new house. You, Frenchmen, act differently: you pull down the old building and reconstruct the same house with another façade and a different name." Although the first phase of the French Revolution was an attempt at a modification of the constitutional structure within the existing political framework, it soon developed into a radical stage. We have seen, in the last chapter, that there was no possibility of setting up a Constituent Assembly by constitutional means, in view of the character of the *ancien régime*, with its outworn combination of feudalism and autocracy.

Since the history of the British Dominions provides examples of constitutional changes without revolution leading to their present status of sovereign States, we shall, in this chapter, survey these circumstances with a view to examining whether the analogy of Constituent Assemblies in the Dominions is applicable to the case of India demanding national independence.

I

A. Canada

The first of the British Colonies to receive self-government was Canada. The early history of European penetration and exploitation of Canada is bound up with the pioneering work of French explorers such as Cartier and Champlain. In the seventeenth century the French established themselves in Quebec, which remains French in language and sentiment to this day. Late in that century, the British came into conflict with the French. The first era of the history of British Canada ended in 1713 with the Treaty of Utrecht—the general settlement which brought to an end the War of the Spanish Succession. By this the Hudson's Bay Company, founded in 1670, received back from the French its fortified posts and its vague, undefined rights over the great North-West—an area nearly as large as Europe. France also ceded Nova Scotia, and acknowledged the British claim to Newfoundland. The final conflict between Britain and France for the possession of Canada came nearly half a century later, when Quebec surrendered to Wolfe, and French Canada passed into British hands by the Treaty of Paris in 1763.

When the British lost the American Colonies a few years later, there was a considerable migration from these former possessions of "United Empire Loyalists" to Nova Scotia, New Brunswick, Cape Breton and Prince Edward Islands. In addition to this, emigration from Great Britain, and the systematic exploitation of the country's economic resources by the great trading companies, accelerated the general development of the Colony, and raised the problem of its constitutional position.

The first legislative enactment of importance was the Constitutional Act of 1791, whereby Upper Canada was divided from Quebec; a Governor-General was appointed for all Canada, and a Lieutenant-Governor for each province, assisted by a nominated executive Council. Each province was also to have a bi-cameral legislature—the nominated Legislative Council and an elected Assembly; the latter had powers of taxation, but did not control the Executive, which was not responsible to it.

The constitutional problem was solved for a time, but after some years it became apparent that the Act of 1791 could not permanently determine Canada's constitutional position. The independence of the Executive in respect of the elected Assembly led to complaints and disputes, especially in Lower Canada, where the French Canadians deplored the predominant influence of English Protestants in the Executive and Legislative Councils. In Upper Canada the endowment of livings for the clergy of the Episcopal Church was resented by the Scottish Presbyterians and other Nonconformists. There was trouble, too, over the control of customs revenues, over finance, and the provision of the Civil List; and thus the same issue which in England had arisen between King and Parliament in the constitutional conflicts of the seventeenth century, and which to-day cuts at the root of India's so-called autonomy, demanded a solution.

In 1833 the leaders of Lower Canada asked for a Convention which should effect a constitutional settlement, and subsequently sent a petition to the King, urging that "delegates freely and indiscriminately chosen by all classes and out of all classes of the community, so as to be in harmony with the interests of the province," should "recommend the proper modifications" in the machinery of government. They insisted that "a general Assembly of this kind would prove to be a faithful interpreter of all interests of the Colony taken collectively."[1]

But the response to this petition was unsatisfactory. The Secretary of State for the Colonies declared that "the object of the Address is to pray His Majesty to sanction a National Convention of the people of Canada for the purpose of superseding the legislative authorities. . . . His Majesty can never be advised to assent, as deeming it inconsistent with the very existence of monarchical institutions." The resolutions demanding a convention of the people passed by the Lower Canada Assembly in 1834 were likewise rejected by the British Cabinet. The Assembly then had recourse to the threat of revolution.

In 1837 this discontent resulted in a rebellion. After it had been suppressed the Earl of Durham was sent out as Governor-in-Chief and High Commissioner to investigate the position. His *Report on the Affairs of British North America* recommended the union of the two Canadas; and although he rejected the idea of federalism, mainly because of the necessity of anglicizing French Canada—thereby underrating the unusual fertility of its population—he proposed a Legislative Union.

One feature of this memorable document is of special interest to India. Lord Durham had the courage to admit that the policy of the British Government was largely responsible for the racial antagonism and religious conflicts in Canada. "I expected to find," he writes, "a conflict between a government and a people, but I found two nations warring in the bosom of a single State. I found a struggle not of principles, but of races. . . . Unhappily the system of government pursued in Lower Canada has been based on the policy of perpetuating that very separation of the races, and encouraging these very notions of conflicting nationalities which ought to have been the first and chief care of Government to check and extinguish. From the period of the conquest to the present time, the conduct of the Government had aggravated the evil, and the origin of the present extreme disorder may be

[1] See Kennedy, *Statutes, Treaties and Documents of the Canadian Constitution.*

found in the institutions by which the character of the Colony was determined. . . . The Imperial Government . . . has shaped its policy so as to aggravate the disorder. In some instances it has actually conceded the mischievous pretensions of nationality in order to evade popular claim. . . . The alternate concessions to the contending races have only irritated both and impaired the authority of Government." He then goes on to propose remedies for these abuses, and suggests that deep-rooted causes of racial antagonisms could be removed by "the efficacy of reform in the constitutional system."

The main proposal of the *Durham Report* was therefore responsible domestic government. "It is worth noting," writes Professor Egerton, "that even Durham's conception of responsible government did not include the management by the colonial authorities of questions of trade, the Crown lands, or military defence."[1]

Lord Durham's definition of responsible government is, nevertheless, of interest. He writes that the establishment of such a form of government demands "no change in the principles of government . . . (but) it needs but to follow out consistently the principles of the British Constitution. . . . The Crown must submit to the necessary consequence of representative institutions; and if it has to carry on the government in unison with a representative body, it must consent to carry it on by means of those in whom that representative body has confidence. . . . The Governor, as the representative of the Crown, should be instructed that he must carry on his Government by heads of departments in whom the United Legislature shall have confidence. . . ." This ideal of representative government, which in its clear-sightedness reveals the conditions necessary for responsible self-government, whether in nineteenth-century Canada or present-day India, was not applied for some ten years, and it was not mentioned in the *Union Act* of 1840 which gave effect to Lord Durham's recommendation for the union of the two Canadas—the Upper and Lower Provinces. This Act further provided for a United Legislature consisting of a nominated Council of not less than twenty members; also an Assembly whose members were to possess certain property qualifications and to be elected in equal numbers from the two Provinces.

Obviously, this settlement was far from being the Act of a

[1] Egerton, *Federations and Unions in the British Empire.*

sovereign people asserting its rights through its elected representatives, and it was, in particular, coldly received by the French Canadians, who considered the Act of Union to be a challenge to their separate nationality. One step further towards full parliamentary autonomy was attained, however, in 1847, when responsible government was actually introduced. Instructions were sent to Lord Elgin, the son-in-law of Lord Durham, and at that time Governor-General, "to act generally on the advice of the Executive Council, and to receive as members of that body those who might be pointed out to him as entitled to be so by their possessing the confidence of the Assembly."

The Act of Union and the introduction of responsible government did not mean that the Canadian Constitution was finally determined. For one thing, there was no homogeneity in outlook between Ontario and Quebec; and without agreement on fundamentals, democracy cannot successfully function. Differences in population and consequent change in the balance of political representation between the two Provinces made each fearful that what it valued most would be sacrificed if the other were predominant. There was, therefore, little harmonious working of the parliamentary machine. Other questions, such as imperial preference, and boundary disputes with the United States, became urgent at this time, and demanded a solution.

Meanwhile, a number of notable Canadian statesmen were becoming convinced that a permanent solution of the Canadian Constitutional problem could be attained only through confederation. In 1858 a Federal Union of British North America had been advocated by the Canadian Government; and although the suggestion received little encouragement in England, there was a growing feeling in Canada that it would eventually be necessary to find some other means of making laws for Canada than in a single parliament representing the population. Differing motives had brought this idea into active consideration. As Professor Egerton writes: "If, then, we confine our gaze to Canadian party controversy there is ample ground for the assertion that the adoption of federation was a mere counsel of despair, occasioned by the bankruptcy of party government. No doubt economic motives were also at work. Fears at the coming termination of the Reciprocity Treaty of 1854 with the United States marked the danger of isolation. The restrictions on inter-colonial trade were more and more felt irksome, and the powerful interest of the Grand Trunk Railway Company worked, though silently, in the same direction. Beyond and above all this there was besides, in the background, and for a time hardly consciously, a nobler motive at work. The idea of a greater Canada had for years been in the minds of thinking men. . . . It is certain that the recognition of the need of a greater Canada to secure an outlet for future population, and fear and suspicion of Canada's mighty neighbour to the south, were main contributing causes to the speedy success of the federation movement."[1]

It was felt that federation would resolve the difficult problem of the union of Upper and Lower Canada, and would also make for a closer bond of sympathy with the Maritime Provinces and the two Canadas than had hitherto been possible. It was the only way, too, of comprising the vast territories of the North-West and British Columbia within a single union.

The matter had been submitted to Bulwer Lytton, the British Colonial Secretary at this time (1858), and his attitude towards the project had not been encouraging. The suggestion was discussed at an inter-colonial conference at Quebec in 1862. Of greater importance, however, was the Charlottetown Convention two years later, which was attended by eight Canadian Ministers. This conference was adjourned to Quebec, where it met on October 10, 1864. In the course of that month some seventy-two resolutions were passed, which represented in the main the substance of the British North America Act. Canada, Nova Scotia, New Brunswick, Prince Edward Island and Newfoundland were all represented at this Conference. The resolutions were then laid before the Canadian Parliament and approved, and in 1866 Canadian delegates came to England and met Lord Carnarvon, the Colonial Secretary, and in co-operation with him the British North America Act was drafted. Unlike Lord Lytton, the new Colonial Secretary was sympathetic towards the idea. Nor was there any serious opposition to the Act by the Imperial Parliament.

Thus on July 1, 1867, the self-governing Dominion of Canada came into existence. Although the Constitution was not framed by the representatives of the people especially elected for the purpose, Canadian public men were content to recognize the

[1] Egerton, *Federations and Unions in the British Empire.*

sovereignty of the British Parliament. The executive power was vested in the British Sovereign, represented in Canada by the Governor-General. It was expected (although not definitely stated in the Act of Parliament) that the Governor-General would act on the advice of a Parliamentary Cabinet. Legislation was to be enacted through a Senate and a House of Commons, and there was to be a Privy Council of Canada. Like that of its great southern neighbour, the nominated Canadian Senate represents the federal principle, as does the elected House of Commons. The Constitution as laid down by this Act is supreme; in contrast to the terms of the Australian Constitution, it can be amended only by the Imperial Parliament, though in practice it is always at Canada's request that any such alterations are made. The British North America Act determined also the relations between the Dominion and the several provinces.

In each of the nine provinces now constituting the Dominion, there is a Lieutenant-Governor appointed by the Governor-General, and a single-chamber Legislature to which the Executive is responsible. In 1867 there were only four provinces in the Dominion, but the British North America Act provided for the admission of other territories, and Manitoba joined the federation in 1870, British Columbia in 1871, Prince Edward Island two years later, and finally Alberta and Saskatchewan, although this was not until the beginning of the twentieth century, in 1905. The administration of the remaining Canadian Territories, the North-West Territory and the Yukon, is in the hands of Commissioners.

The framers of the Canadian Constitution took all precautions against leaving political power weak at the centre, and hoped that provincial autonomy would make possible the co-existence of the diverse racial elements. In reality, it did not succeed in allaying the fear of the French, a minority group, who are "consciously on the defensive against absorption in the maelstrom of Anglo-Saxon life." It has also given rise to complex economic and constitutional problems in federal and provincial relations, and has certainly failed to maintain cohesion within the country. As Professor Berriedale Keith writes: "It appears to have been the laudable, if idle hope of the framers of confederation that they would be able to produce a measure which would so definitely assign to the federation on the one hand and to the provinces on the other their respective sphere of authority that no question of conflicts of law could ever arise. If so, their hope was utterly defeated, for the number of complexities which have arisen regarding the interpretation of the Constitution is deplorable. . . ."[1]

Both the hegemony of the centre and the development of provincial particularism have contributed to a steady deterioration of Canada's constitutional unity. A recent writer sums up the situation as follows:

> ". . . there is a conflict between the economic and the legal realities in Canada. The large corporations cannot be effectively controlled in the public interest by nine provincial legislatures, while their efficiency is hampered by the multitude of varying and vexatious laws and taxes to which they are subject. The Dominion, on the other hand, is incompetent to meet concentrated economic power with an equal political authority, or to provide remedies for economic problems which are essentially national in scope. This failure of the Dominion to act produces, by a curiously inverse process, a greater degree of provincialism and sectional feeling, for the economic policies formulated by the financiers and industrialists in the past have borne heavily upon the extremities of the Dominion and upon the agricultural exporters, who complain they are sacrificed to the money power and who blame Ottawa for tolerating the exportation.
>
> "Thus to the separatist and divisive influences of geography, race and religion must now be added the disintegrating force of provincial sovereignty. Canada has made slow progress in the task of nation-building, and in recent years has lost constitutional ground. . . . Only recently, because of the greater need for governmental action, has the seriousness of the constitutional situation been appreciated, but already the sectional feeling is so strong that the political problem of securing amendments to the British North America Act appears almost insurmountable. Bold leadership and statesmanlike appeal for co-operation will be needed if sectionalism is to be overcome, and of these there is at the moment little indication."[2]

[1] Keith, *Dominions as Sovereign States.* [2] Scott, *Canada To-day*, 2nd ed., 1939.

We are not, however, concerned here with the working of the Constitution of 1867. What is important for us to note is that the Act is now viewed more as a statute than as a constitution for a growing nation, and that the claims of Dominion Sovereignty did not arise in drawing up the British North America Act.

II

B. Australia

If federation was recognized to be the only constitutional means of permitting the co-existence of two different and mutually unsympathetic race groups in Canada, in Australia it was the consciousness of danger from outside which in the end made federation possible and necessary. In the last thirty years or so of the nineteenth century, European expansion in the Pacific was proceeding apace. In 1863 the French established a penal station in New Caledonia; and isolated instances of convicts escaping to Australia excited alarm. In 1884 Germany annexed part of New Guinea, and two years later established a protectorate over Samoa. In the third place, the United States, whose interest in the Sandwich Islands had been apparent for some time, annexed that group in 1898.

It was this new situation in the Pacific, arising from the world expansion of the Great Powers at the end of the nineteenth century, which gave a new impetus to the movement for federation among the Australian Colonies.

From the early days of the European colonization of Australia at the end of the eighteenth century the problem of inter-colonial jealousy had been acute, and time served to increase rather than lessen this disunity. Different tariff policies, disagreement as to the reciprocal use of one another's railway systems, and a general provincial pettiness which was not prepared to make any large sacrifices for the common good, led some observers to believe that they might one day be involved in civil war. The dangers inherent in this situation were aggravated when the co-ordinating authority of the Imperial Government was removed by a grant of responsible government to the several colonies.

The constitutional development of New South Wales can be briefly cited as an example of the colonies' progress towards responsible government. Although at first the Government of this former convict settlement was purely military, in 1823 a nominated Legislative Council of five to seven members was set up, and two years later an Executive Council was created. In 1828 a further stage was reached, when the membership of the Legislative Council was increased to fifteen, and the powers of the Governor and Chief Justice were restricted.

The next development of importance in the constitutional history of New South Wales was the passing of an Act of Parliament in 1842, by which the Legislative Council was to consist of thirty-six members, one-third of whom were to be Crown nominees, and two-thirds elected on a franchise with moderate property qualifications. The nominated members were appointed for the duration of the Parliament, which was five years. At intervals in the following decade this form of constitution was extended to the other colonies—Tasmania, Western Australia, South Australia, Victoria, and (in 1859) Queensland. Further, the Governor of New South Wales was given the position of Governor-General, and had in theory certain supervisory rights over the other colonies, but in practice he had no real constitutional power, and could exert little influence outside New South Wales. In 1861 the office of Governor-General was abolished.

Responsible statesmen in Australia realized that some effective means of inter-colonial co-operation could alone afford a permanent solution which would end the disunity among the growing communities. In 1846 Deas Thompson, the Colonial Secretary of New South Wales, suggested that some authority should be set up to deal with problems affecting Australia as a whole, an idea which met with the approval of Lord Grey, the British Minister for the Colonies. Inter-colonial rivalry, however, prevented Grey from carrying out this idea. An Act of Parliament passed in 1850, authorizing responsible government in Tasmania and South Australia, included the suggestion of a customs union and a federal authority, but this project had to be abandoned, largely owing to the unwillingness of the colonists themselves.

In 1853 Select Committees of the Councils of New South Wales and Victoria approved the idea of federation, but the Imperial Government refused to take action, as the suggestion had emanated from two Colonies only. Undeterred by this failure, the supporters of federation took action in other directions. For instance, a "General Association of the Australian Colonies" was organized in London, and it was this Association which issued in 1857 a memorandum urging federation, and proposed that the Imperial Government should pass an Act enabling two or more colonies to summon a Convention, or Constituent Assembly, which would prepare a scheme of federation. This suggestion again met with a refusal, mainly on account of unwillingness among the colonies themselves. As an Australian historian writes: "Australian federation could not be built up simply by the vision of a few statesmen such as Wentworth, Thompson and Duffy. Its real basis must be a general understanding that all the colonies had interests in common, and that it was sometimes necessary that Australia should act as one."[1]

The tariff question provided the strongest internal argument in favour of federation. Attempts to form a customs union were unsuccessful. However, in spite of this failure, there were annual colonial conferences, and matters of common interest were discussed. As a result of these conferences of Ministers, and of improvements in the means of communication, a national loyalty was gradually emerging.

But it was the trend of external affairs that made Australians of all the colonies realize that the development of cohesion within the country was necessary for their safety. When, in the third quarter of the nineteenth century, the Pacific had become the scene of rivalry among the Western Powers, Australians for the first time felt that their security from external aggression was precarious, on account of their small population and their isolated geographical position.

One of the foremost advocates of Australian federation was Henry Parkes. At conferences in 1880 and 1881 he brought forward a scheme for a customs agreement and a Federal Council; but Victoria was jealous of New South Wales, and no definite result was forthcoming. In 1883, however, conditions were more favourable, and the German threat to New Guinea in that year gave an impetus to greater inter-colonial unity. At a conference of prominent Australian statesmen a scheme was adopted for setting up a Federal Council. The British Parliament passed an Act to bring it into force in 1885, but the Federal Council was only partially successful: its powers were too small, and it was

[1] Wood, *Constitutional Development of Australia.*

condemned in advance by the refusal of New South Wales to participate in it.

In 1889 the publication of a report on the defence of the Australian Colonies by General Sir Bevan Edwards directed attention once more to the need for increased co-operation among the Colonies. At an informal meeting in February 1890, Henry Parkes proposed the union of the Australian Colonies under one legislative and executive government, and urged that any federal constitution which might be set up should both respect and safeguard the privileges of the several States, and yet also be a Government with full powers to undertake responsibilities such as the defence of the country and other matters in which the interests of all the colonies were involved. Although the attitude of the representatives from South Australia and Western Australia was not too friendly, it was agreed to ask the several legislatures of the Colonies to nominate delegates to a National Australasian Convention which should be able to discuss and make recommendations for a federal constitution.

The Convention, consisting of forty-three delegates, met at Sydney on March 2, 1891, under the leadership of Sir Henry Parkes. The idea of federation was now taken seriously, the details of the proposed federal constitution were set out, and a Bill was drafted. But the issue of Australian federation was far from settled. As Professor Egerton writes: "Although the Bill of 1891 had been the outcome of some five weeks' hard work on the part of the delegates, there was no readiness on the part of any of the Colonial Legislatures to accept its conclusions as more than the starting point of a future measure."[1] Several causes were responsible for this setback. In New South Wales, the Labour Party doubted the value of federation, and Free Traders disliked a possible supremacy of the advocates of protection in Victoria. Although Victoria, South Australia and Tasmania took action in 1893, New South Wales indefinitely postponed consideration of the Bill.

Yet the idea of federation was not allowed to lapse. Public propaganda was conducted by the Australian Natives' Association and the Australian Federation League, with its several branches throughout the country. At a conference of the Association in 1893 at Corowa a resolution was passed suggesting that

[1] Egerton, *Federations and Unions in the British Empire.*

each Colony should pass an Act providing for the election of representatives to attend a statutory convention which should be empowered to adopt a Bill for the establishment of a Federal Constitution for Australia; this could afterwards be referred to each Colony for approval by means of a referendum.

This Convention met in March 1897, at Adelaide, and it was attended by delegates from all the Australian States except Queensland. A Bill was drafted embodying the suggestions made at this conference. After the several Parliaments had considered the proposed Bill and it had been referred back to the Convention, the Bill was put to the test of popular support. In Victoria, Tasmania and South Australia it was approved; but in New South Wales the prescribed number of 80,000 votes was not forthcoming.

After agreement had been reached on points of difficulty, New South Wales passed an enabling Bill by which a majority vote only was necessary, and this was forthcoming in June 1899. Queensland, also, now gave her approval to the federation scheme. The approval of Western Australia was the last to be obtained. It was granted later when the Bill was passing through the Imperial Parliament, in return for the right of imposing inter-colonial customs dues for a term of five years.

The Bill was taken to England by a deputation of Australian Ministers, and their views were found to be in substantial agreement with those of the Imperial Government, except that a provision to abolish the right of appeal to the Privy Council in matters affecting the rights of the Commonwealth and the States between themselves was at first opposed, although later a compromise was reached. The Commonwealth of Australia Constitution Act was passed by the Imperial Parliament in July 1900. Under the Act large powers were granted to the Commonwealth, but the residue of powers is vested in the States. Unlike the Lieutenant-Governors of the Canadian provinces, the State Governors are appointed by the Crown, and the Legislatures have power to amend their own Constitution, subject to a Crown veto.

Here again the National Convention or Constituent Assembly was not concerned with the question of Dominion sovereignty. It drew up a constitution, and the acceptance of the constitution having been determined by referendum, it was submitted to the

Queen, the Assembly praying that the constitution thus adopted should be passed into law by the Imperial Parliament.

III

C. South Africa

In contrast to Australia, the constitutional development of the South African colonies was attended by insurmountable difficulties. While in Australia the forces working for the federation of the whole continent received many setbacks due to conflicting economic or political interests, in South Africa the interests of the four partners to the Union had been so much at variance that less than ten years before the Union was finally brought about they had been at war among themselves.

The clash of racial and economic interests and views on social policy, particularly in relation to native affairs, had caused the Great Trek in the middle of the nineteenth century—the secession of many of the Boer farmers and their families from the Cape Province and their migration over the Drakensberg Range into the Transvaal, which together with the Orange River Colony became independent republics, largely Boer in outlook and sympathy.

A federation of the four South African colonies was suggested by Sir George Grey in a speech to the Cape Parliament in 1859. To his suggestion for a "federal union amongst all these territories in which great individual freedom of action should be left to each province, whilst they would all be united under British rule," the Imperial Government turned a deaf ear; and it was not until half a century later that union became a reality.

The need for some kind of union is ably summed up by Professor Egerton: "The revenues derived from duties levied at Cape Town and the other Cape Colony ports were taken by Cape Colony for its sole exclusive use; while the inland States paid the additional cost on their goods, occasioned by these duties. Again, only by a federal union could the South African Colonies become so strong and so united in policy and action as to make impossible the danger of a native rising. . . . Under the policy of separation South Africa had become a land of small States, wherein petty and parochial issues filled men's minds; but federation would open out a wider horizon, along which would appear wider questions and more general interests."[1]

When the question of federation was again raised in 1871, South African opinion regarded the over-hasty enthusiasm of the Imperial Government with some suspicion. Besides, the attitude of the Transvaal towards the British connexion was none too favourable. At any rate, the South African Colonies held the view that if federation was necessary for their own stability, it should come at the spontaneous request of the people themselves. A Bill providing for federation was, however, passed by the Imperial Government in 1877, but was never carried into force.

The prospect of federation receded even farther into the background with the ill-advised annexation of the Transvaal and the recovery of its independence. The powerful Boer republic, enriched by the newly discovered gold of the Rand, became intensely hostile to England. The clash of opposing interests led up to the notorious Jameson Raid, and eventually, at the close of the century, to the Boer War.

After a war lasting three years, which at first threatened to exhaust Britain's resources, the Imperial Power found itself in possession of the small but gallantly defended Boer republics. The Orange River Colony and the Transvaal were annexed to the Crown, and in 1906 responsible government was introduced in the Transvaal and in the Orange River Colony a year later, in the hope that this would "in due time lead to the union of the interests of the whole of His Majesty's dominions in South Africa."

Such a union became a reality more quickly than might have been thought possible. There was a fairly general realization that common problems affecting the interests of the sub-continent as a whole could best be solved by some political authority which could speak on behalf of a united South Africa. The most pressing problem was, for instance, the formulation of a native policy. Great differences existed between the native policies of Cape Colony and Natal, on the one hand, and the Orange River Colony and the Transvaal on the other; in Cape Colony the native had the franchise, whereas in the two latter colonies there was the strongest opposition to any such extension of the suffrage. Labour, too, gave rise to problems which could best be handled

[1] Egerton, *Federations and Unions in the British Empire.*

by a central authority. The policies of the different Colonies, mainly in respect of imported Asiatic labour (chiefly Indian), caused great embarrassment and administrative inconvenience. Lord Selborne, in a valuable memorandum,[1] stressed the artificiality of continued disunion.

In addition to the native and labour questions, the problem of the tariff and of railway rates also afforded abundant evidence of the need of a central controlling authority for the four colonies. If the colonies were to be financially stable it was evident that a customs union such as that formed in 1889, and again after the South African War, was necessary; but this economic co-ordination could be completely successful only in the event of political union; and if this political union had not finally materialized it is fairly certain that the Customs Union would not have survived. Competition between the railways of the four Colonies could also be obviated only by union.

Summing up the position in 1908, Professor Egerton writes: "Public opinion in South Africa was ripe for a change. An active campaign had been carried on for some two years in favour of union in which the Memorandum issued by Lord Selborne played a leading part. Several of the brilliant young men introduced by Lord Milner into South Africa threw themselves heart and soul into the movement. Closer union societies were set on foot. In this state of things the four Colonial Parliaments were willing to send representatives to the memorable Convention which met at Durban in October 1908."[2]

This conference resulted directly from the failure of a conference at Pretoria to deal satisfactorily with the customs and railway problems. Unlike the body which first framed the draft of the Australian Constitution, it met in secret. After adjourning to Cape Town, the conference finally completed its work in February, 1909. Much consideration was given to the form of the constitution—whether it should be unitary or federal. The draft of the proposed constitution of a Union was then referred to the four parliaments for consideration and approval. Support for the plan from the Transvaal was unreserved. In Cape Colony and the Orange River Colony, however, difficulties were experienced in respect of the validity of votes cast in urban and country

[1] *Review of the Present Mutual Relations of the British South African Colonies* (1907).
[2] Egerton, *Federations and Unions in the British Empire.*

constituencies, and also concerning the native franchise. Natal, on the other hand, a Colony strongly British in sentiment, resented inclusion in a union in which the Dutch element would probably predominate. Opposition, however, was less strong than had at first been expected, and Natal approved the new constitution by a referendum of the people—the means adopted in this Colony, as compared with parliamentary sanction in the others. The South Africa Act, 1909, was passed by the Imperial Parliament, and formally established the new Constitution.

This Constitution was unitary rather than federal, as in the case of those introduced in Canada and Australia. The principal objective was to find a solution of the economic problems, such as the railway and tariff systems; but the main reason for the adoption of a unitary constitution was the relationship between the white and coloured races. As Kennedy and Schlosberg observe: "It inspired the first Free State address on union to Sir George Grey in 1858; it was the central theme of Lord Selborne's Review in 1907. If a sudden disturbance broke out in one Colony that Colony might not be strong enough to meet the crisis; but, under a single national control of the military and constabulary establishments, the forces of a united country might be moved easily and swiftly to every part of a vast territory."[1]

At any rate, the change effected by the South Africa Act of 1909 was not fundamental; nor did it invest the Government with a vestige of sovereignty. "The Constitution of the Union is a replica on a large scale of the pre-existing constitutions of the four colonies. . . . The real change effected was the substitution of one responsible government system in place of four responsible government systems, and the consequent centralization of powers in that one government, at the same time granting the control of more or less minor or local matters to the four local and entirely subordinate provincial legislatures."[2]

IV

D. Dominion Sovereignty

Although the constitutional changes in each of the three instances cited above were effected by the existing legislatures,

[1] Kennedy and Schlosberg, *Law and Custom of the South African Constitution*.

[2] Ibid.

through the method of summoning a constituent Assembly, they did not involve the question of the sovereignty of the Imperial Parliament. The impelling motive behind these changes was economic and strategic rather than nationalist, for the forces of nationalism were not at the time sufficiently powerful to inspire any claim to Dominion sovereignty. Consequently the analogy of the constituent Assemblies which drew up the Dominion constitutions is wholly irrelevant to the consideration of India's demand for independence. We may now ask: "How have the Dominions, then, acquired the status of Sovereign States?" Without entering into details of the intricate character of Dominion sovereignty, which lie outside the scope of this book, we shall record here a few instances in which the Dominions have asserted their rights as Sovereign States. It was the trend of such developments that led finally to the passing of the Statute of Westminster in 1931.

The introduction of responsible self-government in the Dominions involved, in the main, the control of internal affairs, although, as Professor Wheare observes, "the limitations upon colonial and Dominion legislative competence which arose from disallowance, from reservation, from the supremacy of the United Kingdom Parliament as expressed in the Colonial Laws Validity Act, and from the lack of extra-territorial power were considerable. But it must be emphasized that within the sphere confided to the colony, subject to these restrictions, the colonial legislature was supreme and sovereign."[1] There was no thought at this time that the Dominion should be master of its external relations. Indeed, before the War of 1914–18 no Dominion seriously raised the question of independent participation in the conduct of foreign affairs.

Distinct rumblings of discontent on the part of the Dominions were audible on occasions. For instance, the decision at the Hague Conference of 1907 to establish an International Prize Court to which appeals could be sent from national courts, gave rise to animated discussion at the Imperial Conference of 1911. The Imperial Government then promised to adopt the procedure of consulting Dominion views in matters relating to the agenda for future Hague conferences. But the first formal action on the part of the Dominions in international negotiations took place in 1912 at the Radiotelegraphic Convention, to which Dominion dele-

[1] Wheare, *The Statute of Westminster and Dominion Status.*

gates were appointed by the King on the advice of their own Governments. The Dominions sent their representatives to that Convention as plenipotentiaries.

Such tendencies received an inevitable impetus during the Great War. The inclusion of the Dominion Prime Ministers in the Imperial War Cabinet in 1917 was the first step towards active participation in foreign affairs by the Dominions Governments. Under the exigencies of the War the Imperial Government recognized the need of joint consultation between them, and it was evident that they would never revert to the pre-war conditions of having no voice in determining both defence and foreign policy. Indeed, in a resolution of the Imperial War Conference in 1917, it was stated that the readjustment of constitutional relations within the Empire should be postponed until after the War. "They deem it their duty, however, to place on record their view that any such readjustments, while thoroughly preserving all existing powers of self-government and complete control of domestic affairs, should be based upon a full recognition of the Dominions as autonomous nations of an Imperial Commonwealth, and of India as an important portion of the same, (and) should recognize the right of the Dominions and India to an adequate voice in foreign policy and in foreign relations, and should provide effective arrangements for continuous consultation in all important matters of common Imperial concern. . . ."[1]

At the close of the War, mainly through the persistent efforts of Sir Robert Borden, the Canadian Prime Minister, the Dominions were given separate representation at the Peace Conference as individual nations, and not as dependent States of the British Empire. It was the first recognition in the international field of the new stature of the Dominions. Sir Robert Borden also succeeded in getting the Imperial Government to agree that "the treaty must be ratified for the Empire only after it had been approved by the Dominion Parliaments.

Perhaps the most fruitful achievement of Sir Robert Borden, however, was the admission of the Dominions to membership of the League of Nations as Sovereign States, and, as such, the recognition of their distinct character from the Empire was emphasized by according them a permanent seat on the League Council. Their position was further strengthened by the grant of

[1] Cmd. 8566, 1917.

the rank of distinct States under the Statute of the Permanent Court of International Justice in 1920.

But the growth of national self-consciousness in the Dominions made them, as Professor Dawson says, "somewhat restive in a position where they had little control of any kind over their relations with other countries."[1] Matters concerning a Dominion had to be negotiated through the Imperial Government, as the Dominions had no diplomatic representatives of their own. Therefore they sought to secure the freedom and power of diplomatic representation. The appointment of a Canadian Minister at Washington gave rise to some opposition on the ground that such a precedent would tend to weaken Imperial unity, but the privilege could not be refused to Canada. The letter of appointment, however, stated that the Canadian representative would work in the closest touch with the British Ambassador at Washington. The Halibut Fisheries Treaty of 1923 was negotiated by Canada with the United States and signed by the Canadian representative alone, without a British signature, because the subject of the Treaty concerned Canada and Canadians only. This assertion of Canada's right to act independently as a Sovereign State met with the approval of the Imperial Conference of the same year.

Credit is also due to Canada for asserting her right to take independent action in foreign affairs. When the Treaty of Lausanne (1923) had been concluded and signed by Britain, Canada signified her reluctance to ratify it, as she had not been invited to send representatives to the Conference, had consequently taken no part in its deliberations, and had not signed the Treaty, although she had in common with all the Empire been at war with Turkey. Finally Great Britain ratified the Treaty in the name of the Empire, although Canada and the Irish Free State denied responsibility.

About a year before this event, during the Chanak crisis, when Britain had to face the revolutionary Turks, Mr. Lloyd George (then Prime Minister) made a melodramatic appeal to the Dominions for aid, only to receive a cold douche from Canada and South Africa. As Professor Hancock observes, "In the first place, Canada would not accept joint responsibility where there was no real joint control. In the second place, Canada would not

[1] Dawson, *The Development of Dominion Status.*

accept joint control as a desirable end. The Liberal Government of Canada admitted no other responsibility save that to the controlling Canadian Parliament: its purpose was to extend the old doctrine of responsible government further into the field of foreign affairs, and to disentangle Canadian policy from the imperial policy pursued by the British Foreign Office."[1]

Notwithstanding Mr. Lloyd George's announcement[2] in 1921 in the House of Commons that the foreign policy of Great Britain would be henceforth the joint policy of the British Empire, both the Chanak crisis and the Treaty of Lausanne not only revealed a divergence of ideas, but also raised a serious constitutional issue regarding the position of the Dominions *vis-à-vis* the Imperial Government. It seemed clear that the Imperial Government had no intention of consulting the Dominions under normal circumstances in matters of foreign policy, and it did not escape the vigilance of the Dominion Governments that, while they were asked to send troops to fight in Asia Minor, they were not allowed representation at the conference convened to settle the terms of the peace. But it was not merely the question of consultation with the Dominions, or the absence of appropriate machinery for doing so, that agitated the Dominion Governments. The proposal of the Labour Government (1924) to summon an informal Imperial Conference to discuss improved means of consultation between the Dominions and Britain met with a rather lukewarm response. What was wanted Mr. Mackenzie King explained in the Canadian Parliament: "I believe that the future of this Dominion will be the happiest and best, most prosperous and in every way most to the good, if its development is . . . towards a fuller recognition of national status within the community of free nations which comprise the British Empire. . . ."[3]

By 1924, the diplomatic representation of the Dominions in foreign capitals was considerably extended. We have seen that the principle had been conceded four years earlier, when Canada

[1] Hancock, *Survey of British Commonwealth Affairs*, vol. i.

[2] "The sole control of Britain over foreign policy is now vested in the Empire as a whole. . . . The advantage to us is that joint control means joint responsibility and when the burden of Empire has become so vast it is well that we should have the shoulders of these young giants under the burden to help us along. It introduces a broader and a calmer view into foreign policy. It restrains rash ministers and it will stimulate timorous ones." (*Hansard*, House of Commons, December 14, 1921.)

[3] Canadian Parliamentary Debates, June 9, 1924.

appointed a Minister to Washington. The Government of the Irish Free State followed this up, and sent its own representative to the United States, to take charge of all affairs relating to the Irish Free State.

In 1925 the Imperial Government created a separate Secretaryship of State for Dominion Affairs. It implied recognition and confirmation of the position of a Dominion within the Empire, and in a way, it heralded the statement of the Imperial Conference a year later, to which we shall presently refer.

While criticism of Imperial relations with the Dominions was more articulate in Canada, and while she had been more insistent in demanding a full recognition of national status than the other Dominions, South Africa was not slow in asserting her growing nationalism. At the Imperial Conference in 1917, General Smuts observed: "Although in practice there is great freedom, yet in actual theory the status of the Dominions is of a subject character. Whatever we may say, and whatever we may think, we are subject provinces of Great Britain. That is the actual theory of the Constitution, and in many ways . . . that theory still permeates practice to some extent." Already in South African elections (in 1920 and 1921) the secession of South Africa from the Empire had become a live issue.

The truth is, the increasing section of the Afrikaans-speaking people in South Africa does not share the traditional enthusiasm of the English-speaking South African for the Imperial connection. The resurgent spirit of this community, supported by a cultural revival, regards the Imperial bond as an impediment to full expression of national sovereignty. To the Afrikaans nationalist, to quote a recent writer, "the Empire stands, not for democratic liberty and the full and free development of personality, but for conquest and exploitation. . . . He remembers the Boer War as an adventure of foreign capital which destroyed that political isolation his pioneering forebears had preferred, at considerable cost, to progress dependent on the restrictions of ordered government. . . . He remembers as a symbol of the situation of his people that the mining industry, which defeated him and conditioned all his subsequent existence, still sends some 60 per cent of its profits out of the country to overseas investors."[1]

At the Imperial Conferences, the representatives of the Union

[1] M. Ballinger, "South Africa and the Empire," *Political Quarterly*, vol. ix, 1938.

of South Africa lost no opportunity of asserting their own national entity as a self-governing Dominion. It was through their active support of Sir Robert Borden's proposal that the 1923 Conference had to agree to the Dominions' right to conclude their own treaties without any British interference. During the Chanak incident General Smuts, the South African Prime Minister, replied that he could not commit the Union to participate until Parliament had met.

In contrast to the attitude of Canada and South Africa, Australia had been satisfied with her constitutional relations with the Imperial Parliament, contending that it was unnecessary, or even dangerous, to attempt statutory definition of what had been achieved through usage and convention. "In effect," declared Mr. W. M. Hughes, the Prime Minister of Australia at the Imperial Conference (1921), "we have all the rights of self-government enjoyed by independent nations. . . . I know of no power that the Prime Minister of Britain has, that General Smuts has not."

We must, however, take into account the facts that determine the texture of Australian nationalism. Its main interests are the preservation of Australian territory from invasion, the security of Australian sea trade routes, and the maintenance of a reasonable measure of freedom of world trade in raw materials. So long as these interests were well served by Australia's close connexion with Britain, she was not prone to attach much importance to her constitutional position.

But the trend of events necessitated a clear definition of intra-imperial relations. In the realm of Imperial foreign policy, the Treaty of Locarno (1925) constituted a new departure. Britain assumed liability under that Treaty independently of the Dominions, who had no primary interest in Britain's European commitments. Although they were informed of the progress of the negotiations by Britain, they were not consulted, and they took no part in the consultations. It was explicitly provided that the Treaty should not apply to the Dominions and India unless they actually chose to accept liability. Thus, in the words of Professor Dawson: "Unity of foreign policy had disintegrated before the constant attack of divergent interests throughout the Empire. The position of Great Britain as a European Power had finally driven her into conflict with the Dominions, whose chief desire was to withdraw from active participation in world affairs and to abstain from any act which would involve them in European wars. . . . Great Britain took sole responsibility for the Locarno Treaty. . . . It was a bold step, but it brought into Empire relations a refreshing touch of realism in place of the Imperial sentimentality of the past."[1]

Reference should also be made to a crisis in the constitutional relationship between Canada and Britain, in which it became clear that the question of Dominion Status needed a precise definition, and could no longer be left to the exigencies of circumstances. The dispute arose in consequence of the action of Lord Byng, the Governor-General, who had refused to dissolve Parliament at the request of the Premier, Mr. Mackenzie King. Mr. King considered the action of the Governor-General a breach of constitutional convention, fought an election on the issue, and resumed office. Professor Keith asserts: "Lord Byng . . . has challenged effectively the doctrine of equality in status of the Dominions and the United Kingdom, and has relegated Canada decisively to the colonial status which we believed she had outgrown."[2] Furthermore, the decision of the Judicial Committee of the Privy Council in 1926, that the legislation of the Canadian Parliament purporting to abolish the appeal in criminal cases to the Judicial Committee was invalid, was another indication of the anomalous position of the Dominions in regard to their constitutional rights. Thus, the status of the Governor-General, the operation of the Colonial Laws Validity Act (1865), the absence of legislative power in extra-territorial matters, and the power of the Privy Council were some of the positive hindrances to Dominion Sovereignty. Canada, South Africa and the Irish Free State were now determined to readjust their constitutional position *vis-à-vis* the Imperial Parliament.

V

At last the Imperial Conference in 1926 undertook to clarify this vexed problem of intra-imperial relations, and referred it to a committee under the chairmanship of Lord Balfour. In its Report,[3] the Committee defined the status of the Dominions in

[1] Dawson, op. cit.

[2] Keith, *Speeches and Documents on the British Dominions.*

[3] Cmd. 2768.

the following terms: "They are autonomous Communities within the British Empire equal in status, in no way subordinate one to another in any aspect of their domestic or external affairs, though united by a common allegiance to the Crown, and freely associated as members of the British Commonwealth of Nations." The King's title, the Governors-General's status, the operation of Dominion legislation, the lack of legislative powers of the Dominions to enact laws having extra-territorial validity, the legislative supremacy of the Imperial Parliament as enforced by the operation of the Colonial Laws Validity Act, merchant shipping legislation, appeals to the Judicial Committee of the Privy Council, procedure in relations with foreign countries in respect of treaties, representation at international conferences, the conduct of foreign policy—all these questions which involved legal inequality of status were discussed at the Conference. While the Conference recognized that "existing administrative, legislative and judicial forms" were not in harmony either with the spirit of Dominion nationalism or with the definition of Dominion status quoted above, no attempt was made to express that status in legal terms. Consequently the Report of the Conference gave rise to varied interpretations, and its implications were not fully realized. To some "it summarized and re-stated the customs which had recently been established, and gave them unquestioned acceptance and authority"[1]; to others it marked a significant stage in the process of decentralization which strengthened rather than severed the unity of the Empire. On the other hand, General Hertzog maintained that the right to secede had been accepted and declared after the Conference: "No one need bother in future about South Africa breaking away from the Empire. As a result of the work of the Imperial Conference, the old Empire no longer exists."[2]

Perhaps the general opinion on the Report among responsible British statesmen is adequately expressed by Professor Hancock, who says: "The Balfour Report is impressive not merely for its philosophic imagination but for the sharpness of its insight into actual circumstances. It was, first and foremost, finely accurate description. With admirable economy of words it cut through the thickets of legalism and skirted the marshes of vague moralizing, and revealed the British Commonwealth as it was in the year

[1] Dawson, op. cit.

[2] *The Times*, December 15, 1926.

1926. . . . Its insight was historical. It described not merely the form but the motion of a community. The principle of motion which it professed to discern was the same principle which Mr. Asquith had acclaimed in the Imperial Conference of 1911: 'Liberty operating within Unity' . . . The Balfour Report recognized that Liberty and Unity were not reconciled through the free association of equals. 'Equality of status' it declared, 'so far as Great Britain and the Dominions are concerned, is then the root principle governing our inter-imperial relations.' It exorcized something which might have been called, in a jargon fashionable at the time, the inequality-complex."[1]

The problem of carrying into effect the recommendations of the Report of the Imperial Conference (1926) was undertaken by a Committee on Dominion Legislation and Merchant Shipping Legislation. It was appointed in 1929 and presented its report in 1930. In general the report recommended the legislative independence of the Dominions. The Colonial Laws Validity Act should not apply to a law made by a Dominion Parliament. No law made by a Dominion should be invalid because it was contrary to the statute Law of Great Britain; no law enacted by the Imperial Parliament at Westminster should be valid in any of the Dominions except at the request and with the consent of the Dominion. Concerning Merchant Shipping the Committee made similar proposals.

The Imperial Conference of 1930 approved these decisions and recommended that the Imperial Parliament should pass an Act (the Statute of Westminster) embodying those resolutions of the Conference, in statutory form, which definitely stated certain legal inequalities in Dominion status. The Conference resolved that the appointment of a Governor-General should be made by the King on the advice of the Dominion Government concerned. The practical use of the power of disallowance was made virtually impossible. Reservation also was allowed only by the Governor and not by the Imperial Parliament. But no proposals were made with regard to appeals to the Judicial Committee. It was agreed that the draft of the proposed Statute should be placed before the Dominion legislatures, and with their approval the Imperial Parliament should proceed with its enactment. On November 10, 1931, the Speech from the Throne announced: "In conformity

[1] Hancock, op. cit.

with the undertaking given to the representatives of my Dominions in 1930, a measure will be laid before you to give statutory effect to certain of the declarations and resolutions of the Imperial Conferences of 1926 and 1930. This measure is designed to make clear the powers of Dominion Parliaments and to promote the spirit of free co-operation amongst members of the British Commonwealth of Nations."

The Statute of Westminster[1] Bill was accordingly passed by the Imperial Parliament, and it received the Royal Assent on December 11, 1931. Since then the Dominions have interpreted and applied the Statute for asserting their legal independence, although the operation of terms of strict law combined with conventional rules—the combination aimed at in framing the Statute—has not been wholly successful in defining the independent character of Dominion Status. The Statute forms, as Wheare put it, "a part and not the whole of the body of rules, legal and non-legal, which define Dominion Status. Its enactment was necessary if the fundamental non-legal rule in the definition of Dominion Status—equality between Great Britain and the Dominions—was to be made effective."[2]

Opinions differ, however, as to the efficacy of the Statute in defining without ambiguity the constitutional rights of the Dominions *vis-à-vis* the Crown and the Imperial Parliament. "The Statute was passed," writes Dawson, "partly for the sake of political convenience, but chiefly to satisfy those sensitive Dominions and fussy persons who were not content with constitutional practice as enunciated in 1926 but who demanded legal as well as practical equality. It necessarily failed in its main purpose. The awkward fact remained, and must remain, that if the Imperial Parliament could grant complete legal powers to the Dominions it could at any time withdraw them by the same method; and to argue that the British Parliament would never repeal the Statute of Westminster is simply to admit that Dominion powers depend now, as they depended before, upon constitutional usage. Apparently the only way in which complete powers in the absolute sense could be obtained would be for the Dominions to declare their independence and then re-enter the Commonwealth as independent States."[3]

On the other hand, it is held that the Statute confers upon

[1] Appendix IV. [2] Wheare, op. cit. [3] Dawson, op. cit.

Dominion Parliaments wide extension of powers which promote the Dominions to virtual independence. Such limitations as are imposed on the operation of the Statute arise from voluntary agreements by Canada, Australia and New Zealand. The Canadian Provinces, for example, were unwilling to surrender the safeguard of the existing processes of constitutional amendment contained in the British North America Act. At their request and with their assent, clauses were inserted into the Statute of Westminster which placed the Constitutions of Canada, Australia and New Zealand beyond the range of the powers which the preamble of the Statute conferred upon Dominion Parliaments.

While the Statute of Westminster brought about a great measure of Dominion autonomy, its implications in regard to matters such as foreign relations and defence became an essential part of the efforts of the Dominions to acquire their rights as Sovereign States. In 1934, the Union of South Africa passed two Acts (The Status of the Union Act and the Royal Executive Functions and Seals Act) defining its constitutional status, the purpose of which was to locate the sovereignty of the Union in its own Parliament. It removed all limitations upon the delegation of the King's executive power. Thus, "there is no longer any obligation on the Governor-General to reserve for the Royal assent certain kinds of constitutional amendments. . . . In certain circumstances also, Acts of the Union Government which required to be formally expressed under the Union Great Seal no longer require the sign manual, so that personal application to the King is unnecessary."[1] Under its provisions, as Hancock says, "it would be entirely in order that while the King's Ministers in Great Britain were advising him to declare war his Ministers in South Africa should be advising his representative there to declare South Africa's neutrality."[2] As a matter of fact, the issue was raised by General Hertzog, then the Premier of the Union, on the outbreak of the present war. Although his motion for the right of the Union to remain neutral was defeated, it must be recognized that the participation in a war declared by the Imperial Government was decided by the South African Parliament. The purely formal character of the connexion of the Union of South Africa with the British Crown has been emphasized ever

[1] Jennings, *Political Quarterly*, 1938.
[2] Hancock, op. cit.

since the growth of nationalist influence within the Union Parliament; but it was stated in clear terms in the Letters Patent and Instructions to the Governor-General (March 11, 1936). "In strict law there seems no obstacle," writes Professor A. B. Keith, "to the Governor-General issuing a proclamation of neutrality in the event of the Crown declaring war on the advice of British Ministers. There seems further no obstacle to the Governor-General assenting to an Act which would sever the connexion between the Union and the Crown."

The reality of the position of the Dominions as Sovereign States was demonstrated by the Irish Free State on several occasions. The connexion with the British Crown is retained, as we shall see in the next chapter, under a subsidiary Act, but not in the Constitution itself. And the Crown is regarded only as an "instrument" for action in external affairs, subject always to the advice of the Eire Ministers. On the abdication of King Edward VIII the Dáil passed an Act of their own confirming the new succession a day later than the United Kingdom Act. Again, "Mr. de Valera's decision to recognize the Italian conquest of Abyssinia *de jure* in December 1937 before recognition by the British Government was doubtless influenced by the opportunity thus afforded of accentuating the sovereign independence of Ireland and the purely subordinate position of the Crown, the King being compelled to appear in the rôle of a King with Two Faces, recognizing, for Ireland, the King of Italy as Emperor of Ethiopia, and, for the rest of his Dominions, the exiled Emperor as sovereign *de jure*."[1]

In regard to matters relating to foreign affairs, Canada has been equally concerned with the safeguarding of her sovereignty. As early as 1921 she was opposed to the renewal of the Anglo-Japanese Alliance, which might become a menace to friendly relations between the Empire (and therefore Canada) and the United States. Recently the Canadian Federal Legislature frankly expressed disapproval of Britain's negotiations with Italy (February 20, 1938) and of the recognition of the conquest of Abyssinia *de jure*. Following the annexation of Austria by Germany, and realizing that the interests of Canada would be well served by keeping her safe from European entanglement, Canada encouraged the policy of isolation, and claimed the right of

[1] Keith, *The Dominions as Sovereign States.*

neutrality by declaring that when Britain was at war, Canada was not necessarily at war.

These are, then, some of the instances where the Dominions have demonstrated the reality of their position as Sovereign States. Whether the sovereign independence derived from the Statute of Westminster is real or whether these developments are due to the flexibility of the constitutional relationships between the Imperial Parliament and the Dominions cannot be considered here. What is important for us to remember is that in its early stages the interpretation of Dominion Status has not had the same significance as it has now acquired and that the enacting clauses of the Statute of Westminster, notwithstanding its preamble incorporating the famous Balfour Declaration of 1926, allow of different varieties of Dominion Status. We should, however, note that in all the three instances which we have cited in this chapter the peoples concerned were not regarded as *subjects* of the British Empire. Their constitutions were all drafted by National Conventions, which were formally registered without question by the Imperial Parliament. But the steady growth of Irish nationalism led to a bitter struggle with imperialism, a brief account of which may be of special interest to us.

Chapter Five

THE IRISH STRUGGLE FOR CONSTITUTIONAL FREEDOM

I

The Irish claim to national sovereignty dates from the early part of the seventeenth century. In 1782 unsuccessful efforts were made to grant legislative powers to Ireland, and even the Act of Union passed two years after the rebellion of 1798 was doomed to failure from the beginning because it entirely ignored the demands of the people and adopted a policy of thwarting Ireland's economic development. Grattan's Parliament and the Constitution of 1782 were not the genuine expression of the growing national consciousness of the Irish people.

The feudal character of the landlord system, which had its origin in the confiscation and plantations of earlier centuries, was maintained with the primary object of promoting the interests of a landed aristocracy. And "not a single nation in Europe can boast of having raised an aristocracy that accomplished its work of monopolizing the land with anything like the rapacity and ferociousness of Scotch and English landlords."[1]

Nearly half a century later, the consequences of reducing Ireland to a servile state revealed themselves in the tragedy of a great famine. Thousands of emigrants left Ireland in "coffin ships" for America. The truth that Ireland was being ruled in the interests of England and of those few Irishmen who acted in partnership with England for the exploitation of the people appeared in a relentless light, and the moral was driven home with such unanswerable force by the callous attitude of the governing class that the sovereignty of the Irish nation could no longer be left in the hands of Britain.

The Irish Republican Brotherhood was founded in Dublin in 1858 by James Stephens, "as a secret oath-bound Society" to work for the freedom and welfare of the whole people of Ireland.

[1] Paul Lafargue, *The Evolution of Property*.

Its members, known as "Fenians,"[1] had not much faith in "political concessions from England," and prepared the ground for a sustained struggle with Britain and her Irish supporters. It was due to the Fenians that the two aspects of the Irish problem, namely, Land Reform and Home Rule, featured so prominently in the national struggle. Through inflexible will and tenacity of purpose, Parnell, in collaboration with leaders of the Land League founded in 1879, succeeded in passing the Act of 1881, which gave the tenant a right in the land and reduced his rent. But these measures of economic reforms were totally inadequate in the absence of Home Rule for Ireland. The politically conscious Irish agreed with Parnell's declaration that "none of us will be satisfied till we have destroyed the last link which keeps Ireland bound to England." Thousands of emigrants in the United States of America pledged themselves to return and fight for Irish freedom.

The agitation for Home Rule bore no fruit until the storm-clouds appeared on the European horizon, and the outbreak of the war in 1914 altered the whole face of the Irish question. Early that year a Bill was passed which, in principle, was somewhat akin to the Morley-Minto Reforms enacted in response to the Indian demands in 1910. The Home Rule Bill (the Government of Ireland Act of 1914) did not go further than a series of safe provisions of devolution; it set up an Irish Legislature, but severely restricted its powers both in external and internal affairs. Although the Bill was placed on the Statute Book, an amending Act was rushed through the Parliament suspending the enforcement of the Bill until six months after the termination of the war.

But the outbreak of the war offered a fresh opportunity to the Irish nationalists for pressing their claims. They agreed to stand by Great Britain in the emergency, in the hope that the status which would enable the Irish nation to choose a form of government compatible with the needs of a free people might now be granted by the Imperial Government. They made it plain that without the settlement of the Irish question, there could be no conscription in Ireland. Indeed, the temper of both Nationalists and Labour ran high, and when Asquith, then Premier, went to Dublin to appeal for recruits, it was the labouring class who announced: "*We serve neither King nor Kaiser—but Ireland.*"

[1] The name is derived from the famous "Fianna" of Irish legend.

However in 1916 an Act was passed introducing conscription in Ireland.

But no step was taken to recognize the Irish demand for political freedom. While an Irish Convention called by Lloyd George failed to come to an agreement on account of the uncompromising hostility of the Ulster Unionist members, he did not hesitate to announce that in Ireland all males between eighteen and fifty-one would at once come under the operation of the Conscription Bill. The Irish Parliamentary Party left the House of Commons as a protest, and Labour declared a day of general strike.

This act of imposing conscription on Ireland against her will for service in the British Army did more than any other single factor to convince all organized political parties (the Catholic Hierarchy, the Nationalists, Sinn Féin, the Irish Volunteers, Labour) that the Imperial Government had no intention of implementing the main principle of the Report of the Irish Convention, signed on April 8, 1918. They now realized the urgency of a nation-wide campaign of resistance, but the only men in a position to take up the challenge were the Irish Volunteers. In this connection, a note of warning from the famous Irish poet A.E. (George Russell) may be of interest. He wrote:

> "I cannot expect many in England to sympathize with Irish feeling, but I may ask them to consider it in relation to the future weal of the Empire. If they persist in forcing military service on Ireland, if they insist on breaking the Irish will, there will not be a parish here where blood will not be shed. There will grow up a hate which will be inextinguishable, lasting from generation to generation. It will be fed by tradition everywhere, and our people live by tradition. 'Here this man fell.' 'There that group made their last stand.' No expression of regret after the deed is done will wipe out those memories. They will be like that stain upon the hand of the Queen in the darkest of all tragic dramas—the stain which was ruddy to the spiritual sense, and no purifying water could cleanse it. It will spread over the Empire. It will invade that great Republic where so many millions of our exiled children have their home. The Irish are capable of the most bitter as of the most gentle

speech, and the darker side of that eloquence shall be turned against you. Millions of the bitterest tongues in the world will be incessantly wagging, breeding sedition in your dominions, and hostility against you in whatever alien State they may live. . . . What moral strength can come to you from a nation broken in its pride, shamed and bleeding? What aid to military power will be those who would now as readily turn their arms upon your officers as the enemy, for to such a pass has the unwisdom of our rulers brought this country? I say to the English people, drop this thing and seek the way of friendship. It is not yet too late."[1]

It was the conscription issue that precipitated at Easter Week (1916) a rebellion which broke out in Dublin, and violent repressive measures were adopted to stamp out insurrection. Some of the leading Sinn Féiners were taken prisoner and promptly executed.

On that occasion Bernard Shaw expressed his resentment at the manner of dealing with the insurrection in the following terms:

"My own view is that the men who were shot in cold blood after their capture or surrender, were prisoners of war, and that it was therefore entirely incorrect to slaughter them. The relation of Ireland to Dublin Castle is in this respect precisely that of the Balkan States to Turkey, of Belgium or the City of Lille to the Kaiser, and of the United States to Great Britain. . . . An Irishman resorting to arms to achieve the independence of his country is only doing what Englishmen will do if it be their misfortune to be invaded and conquered by the Germans in the course of the present war."[2]

Although the insurrection failed to achieve its object, it succeeded in bringing about sufficient cohesion and organic strength within the Irish National Movement. It liberated one of those inevitable psychological reactions which make the peoples under oppression courageous and united for a determined struggle. Indeed, it was this Easter insurrection in 1916 that eventually led to the creation of the Irish Free State.

[1] A.E. (George Russell) in the *Manchester Guardian*, May 11, 1918.
[2] Quoted in *On Another Man's Wound*, by Ernie O'Malley, 1936.

The Sinn Féin issued a Proclamation which read:

> "We declare the right of Ireland to the ownership of Ireland, and to the unfettered control of Irish destinies, to be sovereign and indefeasible. The long usurpation of that right by a foreign people and Government has not extinguished the right, nor can it ever be extinguished except by the destruction of the Irish people. In every generation, the Irish people have asserted their right to national freedom and sovereignty. . . . Standing on that fundamental right, we hereby proclaim the Irish Republic as a Sovereign Independent State. The Republic guarantees religious and civil liberty, equal rights and equal opportunities to all its citizens. . . ."

Undaunted by repression and opposition, various Irish movements became affiliated to Sinn Féin, which elected Eamon de Valera as President. In 1917 the National Convention, summoned by the British Government and composed of representative Irishmen in Ireland, met in order "to submit to the British Government a constitution for the future government of Ireland within the Empire." But it failed to arrive at a compromise, although the Chairman of the Convention claimed, to quote his own words, that "a larger measure of agreement has been reached upon the principle and details of Irish self-government than has ever yet been attained." The Ulster Unionists strongly opposed the Nationalists' demand for fiscal independence, and Sinn Féin boycotted the Convention because it repudiated the Irish claim to national sovereignty. After the failure of the Convention the Irish Nationalist party lost all claim to speak for the Irish people, and Sinn Féin gained a victory in the election of 1918, which was fought on the issue of independence. The aims of Sinn Féin were stated in clear terms: that is, to establish an Irish Republic and to "make use of every and any means available to render impotent the power of England to hold Ireland in subjection." The elected members assembled in Dublin on January 21, 1919, and it was this assembly which assumed the character of the first Dáil Eirean (the Assembly of Ireland) and reaffirmed the proclamation of 1916. The precise objective of the Irish struggle is stated there in clear terms[1] and the Irish leaders realized that

[1] Appendix V.

every step deliberately taken towards the goal would accelerate the *rate* of the national movement.

Simultaneously with this Declaration, the Dáil Eirean adopted a "message to the free nations of the world" in which the national aspirations for self-determination were expressed in terms which represented the whole of Ireland as anticipating the design of the Imperial Government to force its partition. The first Dáil, assembled in defiance of the British Proclamation that forbade all public meetings without a permit from the military or police, appointed a provisional ministry, and developed through its activities an internal administration functioning in opposition to that of the British Government. The organization of the Dáil Government was thus directed mainly to two programmes, one of internal affairs and the other of an intensive propaganda in foreign countries. The Dáil proclaimed the *Saorstat Eirean*—i.e. the Free State of Ireland, and at a Sinn Féin Convention De Valera was elected as President.

Meanwhile Lloyd George proposed an Amending Act for the Home Rule Bill, stipulating that all Ireland was to be self-governing, but Ulster, consisting of the six counties in which Protestants had a majority, would be separated from the Dublin Assembly, representing twenty-six counties with a majority of Catholic population. Thus the Government of Ireland Act, 1920, divided Ireland, and greatly accentuated the conflict of religion by a permanent political cleavage.

Each Irish Parliament was to consist of two Houses—an Assembly and a Senate; but the financial control was to remain mainly in the hands of the Imperial Government as before! Each Parliament was to be given "minor taxing powers," together with the administration of its own jurisdiction, and the Bill provided for an annual Imperial contribution of £18 millions, £10 millions from Southern Ireland and £8 millions from Northern Ireland.

II

Sinn Féin refused to work the Act, but at the general election for the Dublin Assembly, provided in the Act, the Party won 124 seats out of the total of 128. While the four solitary non-party members met and immediately adjourned, the other 124 constituted themselves the second Dáil Eirean. They took an oath of allegiance to the Irish Republic, which proceeded to function as an independent Sovereign State. But Northern Ireland took immediate advantage of the Act, and the new Parliament in Ulster was opened on June 22, 1921, by the King.

Great Britain's answer to the Irish demand for independent sovereignty was the infamous orgy of violence known as the advent of "the Black and Tans."[1] "The history of every country, England included," writes the Right Hon. Sir James O'Connor, "has its dark and shameful chapters. But I doubt if that of any civilized community in modern times can show anything which for cowardice, wickedness, stupidity and meanness can equal the handling by the British Government of the situation created for them by a couple of thousand Irish peasants and shopboys."[2] Sir Hamar Greenwood's boast that he would establish "law and order" in Ireland by a policy of violent repression proved to be empty bluster.

After a dreary and horrible record of reprisals and counter-reprisals, a truce was declared and the British Government outlined proposals for a settlement[3] on the basis of Dominion Status. They suggested that the terms of settlement between Great Britain and Ireland should be embodied in the form of a Treaty.

But the invitation to Ireland for the purpose of negotiations raised the question of the status of Ireland as a Sovereign State. Although it was stated "that Ireland shall assume forthwith the status of a Dominion," Mr. de Valera declared that he would agree to send the representatives of the Dáil only as "envoys plenipotentiaries from the elected government of the Republic of Ireland." To this the British Government could not consent, but issued a fresh invitation "to a Conference in London on October 11th, where we can meet your delegates as spokesmen of the people whom you represent, with a view to ascertaining how the association of Ireland with the community of nations known as the British Empire may best be reconciled with Irish national aspirations."[4]

The respective positions of the parties appeared to be under-

[1] The British-recruited allies of the Royal Irish Constabulary were so hastily sent to Ireland that they first appeared in khaki trousers and the black jackets of the police—whence the name.

[2] Sir James O'Connor, *History of Ireland*, 1925.

[3] Cmd. 1502.

[4] Cmd. 1539.

stood and Mr. de Valera accepted the invitation. However, on December 6, 1921, the draft treaty submitted by the British Government was rejected by the Irish delegation, but an altered draft produced on the same night was agreed upon. By the "Articles of Agreement for a Treaty between Great Britain and Ireland," Ireland was recognized "as a free partner in the Commonwealth of Nations forming the British Empire." The agreement was to be submitted to the Parliaments of the two countries and eventually ratified by necessary legislation. The ratification in Ireland was, however, to come not from Dáil Eirean, which was the Legislature of the militant Irish Republic, but from "the members of Parliament of Southern Ireland convened in a special session for this purpose and for the further purpose of constituting a Provisional Government."

While the Treaty with representatives of the Irish people was approved by both Houses of Parliament, it raised a controversy in Ireland. The British Government expressed surprise at the indifference with which Ireland greeted a transaction which was going to alter radically the political status of the country. Mr. de Valera opposed it on the ground that the Treaty did not adequately recognize the national sovereignty of Ireland, and that it perpetuated the injustice of the partition. He put forward an alternative draft, but it was rejected, and only by a narrow margin the Dáil Eirean decided to accept the Treaty. Thereupon Mr. de Valera resigned and Mr. Arthur Griffith was chosen as the President of the Dáil. In strict conformity with the Treaty, a Provisional Government was formed and a Committee was appointed to draft the new Constitution for the Irish Free State.

But the opposition to the Treaty grew alarmingly into a civil war. The Irish Republic was set up by the Irish people at the elections which took place during the Anglo-Irish Conference, and therefore acceptance of the Treaty which did not recognize the Republic was regarded as a betrayal of the struggle for national independence. Certain concessions, such as control of taxation, including customs and excise, did not seriously endanger the essential economic and strategic interests of Britain; and, above all, the six counties of North Ireland were excluded from the provisions of the Treaty. The Irish struggle was for a united as well as independent Ireland, and therefore the acceptance of the Treaty amounted to a repudiation of National Sovereignty.

Even the Dominion Status, which seemed to have impressed the Irish delegation, would be negatived by intricate legal formalities and administrative subtleties. Mr. de Valera and the Irish Republican Party were so convinced that the British policy in Ireland would fail in practice that they remained in opposition and awaited developments.

The truth behind the main currents of Irish nationalism is explained by a writer in the preparatory paper submitted to the second Conference on British Commonwealth Relations held at Sydney in 1938. He says:

> "After the French Revolution nationalism took two forms which ever since have competed one with the other, the desire to establish an Irish state virtually independent of England, but entirely on the English model and owing allegiance to the Crown, and the more revolutionary policy of establishing an Irish republic modelled on that of France. . . . Indecision as between these two aims has been the great mark of Irish politics from that day to this.
>
> "At first Dominion Status was accepted with some enthusiasm by the great majority, but it was accepted not as something positive, but as the temporary *de jure* expression of actual freedom. The inevitable policy of Irish statesmen has been, so far as possible, to bring theory into harmony with the Irish view of the facts."[1]

Those who were in favour of accepting the Treaty regarded it as offering the substance of sovereignty inherent in the status of a Dominion. It was to confer upon Ireland fiscal independence and to free her from all British taxation. They were persuaded to believe that the legal formalism of a Dominion Constitution would not in any sense jeopardize the preservation of Irish independence and integrity. Besides, rejection of the Treaty would amount to a declaration of war.

There was also a strong and persistent dislike of the Treaty in Britain, principally from that section of the Conservative party whose means and methods of organizing resistance are familiar to political India. The Die-hards, as they are called, inspired every possible agitation to jeopardize the recognition of Irish nationhood, and instigated Northern Ireland, the citadel of re-

[1] H. V. Hodson, *The British Commonwealth and the Future*, 1939.

actionary forces, to oppose any advance towards Irish unity or Irish autonomy. When this section of the British governing class had done its utmost to take advantage of the difficulties of the Provisional Government, Mr. Neville Chamberlain, then a private member, observed:

> "One of our great difficulties undoubtedly, in dealing with Ireland in the past, has been the fact that we have so often changed our policy, and thereby given grounds for suspicion that we are not to be trusted to keep to our undertaking. That consideration alone would make me hesitate a long time before throwing on the scrap heap a policy which has been sanctioned so recently."[1]

Eventually it was this point of view which prevailed upon the Coalition Government, and the Anglo-Irish crisis was allowed to remain in incubation.

But not for long. The financial adjustments between Britain and Ireland, the future relationship of Northern Ireland with the Irish Free State, and the delimitation of the boundary of Northern Ireland—all these adjustments required to be made in the letter and spirit of the Treaty. Yet in each of these cases the British Government, in its negotiations, produced the impression of bad faith and evoked suspicion and resentment. It soon became evident that the Treaty did not grant Ireland what was implied by Dominion Status.

On the other hand, the assertion of Irish national sovereignty marked every step of the Irish Free State Government—a government constituted sovereign by the consent of the Irish people. It registered the Treaty with the League of Nations and used its own Seal on its documents in 1924. The British Government entered a formal protest against the procedure on the ground that common allegiance to the Crown debars the Irish Free State from being classed as an independent Sovereign State, and consequently the terms of Article 18 of the Covenant could not be applied in the Irish case. The Irish, however, refused to accept this interpretation, and held that the obligations of the Article were applicable to every member of the League. Again, in 1929 the Irish Free State accepted the optional clause of the Statute of the Permanent Court of International Justice providing

[1] *Hansard*, February 16, 1922.

for the compulsory arbitration of legal disputes "on the sole condition of reciprocity."

However, the "Irish-Irish War" blazed forth in an ominous way in June 1922 and made the task of the Provisional Government increasingly difficult. They were forced to take ruthless measures against their own compatriots and comrades, but the open hostilities were not allowed to continue long after the Constitution was brought into operation on December 6, 1922.

III

Let us now turn to the work of the Constituent Assembly. The Constituent Committee, charged with the responsibility of framing a Draft Constitution, submitted its report within a month, on the basis of which the Provisional Government prepared the final draft. The Committee went thoroughly into all relevant issues relating to the basis of a Constitution in conformity with the spirit of the Treaty. They compiled a volume of select Constitutions of the world, and collated such provisions from them as seemed applicable to Ireland. Although it was declared that the British Cabinet were consulted on the contents of the draft "as of courtesy and not as of right," Lloyd George "applied his blue pencil to the draft and left a Constitution wholly different in effect from that which the Irish Committee had devised." It finally emerged from the Committee bearing the interpretation of the Treaty by the British Cabinet rather than by the Irish Provisional Government.

Meanwhile the election was held on the burning issue of the acceptance or rejection of the Treaty. The Provisional Government released the draft Constitution for publication on the morning of the polling day. By arrangement between the leaders of Sinn Féin and the opposition led by Mr. de Valera, candidates were put forward on an agreed panel. As a result, 94 of the panel candidates (58 Pro-Treaty and 36 Republican) were elected and 34 other members. The national mandate seemed to be in favour of the Treaty, and the Third Dáil declared itself to be a Constituent Assembly, but it did not meet until September. It should be noted that the Constituent Assembly, though it functioned as the third Dáil Eirean, was regarded as a constituent and not as a legislative body. As Mansergh observes: "This rigid separation of the Constituent and Legislative Power emphasized the more important issue, namely that, unlike the Dominion Constitutions, that of the Free State emanated from a National Constituent Assembly."[1]

The final draft was submitted to the Assembly in the form of a Constitution Bill. It was debated article by article, and went through considerable revision and amendment. The Bill was entitled "an Act to enact a Constitution for the Irish Free State and for implementing the Treaty between Great Britain and Ireland signed at London on the 6th Day of December 1921."

Thus, the Constitution of the Irish Free State, enacted by Dáil Eirean on October 25, 1922, was brought into operation by Royal Proclamation on December 6th after the Imperial Parliament had passed a Confirmatory Act. The significance of the procedure adopted by both the Constituent Assembly and the Parliament lay in the fact that the Irish Republican régime was legally converted into the status of a Dominion Government. Although the interpretation of the stages through which the Constitution came finally into being gave rise to controversy as to the location of Sovereignty, the Provisional Government had no doubt as to their own competence and authority in enacting the Constitution. They believed that their legislative independence was fully recognized by the terms of the Treaty, and by the methods subsequently adopted for the enactment and ratification of the Constitution. They declared in the Preamble to the Act that "Dáil Eirean sitting as a Constituent Assembly in this *Provisional Parliament, acknowledging that all lawful authority* comes from God to the People and in the confidence that the National life and unity of Ireland shall thus be restored, hereby proclaims the establishment of the Irish Free State and in the exercise of undoubted right decrees . . ." the new Constitution. But we shall presently see how the British governing class provoked a conflict over the constitutional relationship between the Irish Free State and Great Britain by raising objection to Ireland's realization of what was implied by the Dominion Status.

The Constitution set up a Parliament (the Oireachthas) consisting of two Houses, the Senate and the Dáil. The Senate was to consist of sixty members, of whom one-half were to be

[1] N. Mansergh, *The Irish Free State* (1934).

nominated in the first instance; but thereafter all senators would be elected from a panel to be furnished by both the Houses. The Dáil was to be an elective body, on the basis of proportional representation and universal adult suffrage. The franchise of the Dáil was to be enjoyed by all citizens over twenty-one years of age without distinction of sex, but the franchise of the Senate was to be restricted to persons who had reached the age of thirty years.

We are not concerned here with the details of the structure of the Constitution, which had been modelled on the basis of democratic self-government; but we should note that the framer of the Constitution realized the utmost importance of party discipline in the Dáil, and "embodied every known device for the subjection of political parties," because in the initial stages of constitutional development "the greatest requirement of the Irish Free State was independence of political thought and opinion." The trend of circumstances, however, led almost inevitably to the emergence of party dominance in the Dáil.

Perhaps one of the most interesting features of the Constitution is the fact that the State has been vested with extensive powers to take initiative in such measures as are calculated to satisfy the fundamental rights of the Irish people. It declares: "All citizens of the Irish Free State have the right to free elementary education": it asserts that the natural resources of the country "shall not be alienated and their exploitation by private individuals must be in the public interest and under State supervision."

Realizing that the Constitution would necessitate a great deal of adjustment in course of its operation, the Constituent Assembly provided that amendments to the Constitution might be made by ordinary legislative procedure during the first eight years after its enactment. The ideal of submitting each constitutional amendment to a referendum was kept in view, but in practice this method proved to be too complicated and cumbersome. Accordingly the term of amendment by the ordinary channels of legislation has been extended to a further period of eight years.

But the *Fianna Fáil* party under the leadership of Mr. de Valera took no part in the newly constituted Dáil. De Valera insisted that if and when "an unfree people gave allegiance not to the legal government but to a rival body, that rival body becomes the *de jure* government." His party claimed persistently that the ratification of the Treaty by the Dáil was both illegal and *ultra vires* because the Second Dáil had sworn fidelity to the Irish Republic. The oath of allegiance to the Crown, provided in the Constitution, was unacceptable, and the fiscal policy agreed upon was inimical to the interest of Ireland. Thus the spirit of hostility initiated by the Fianna Fáil party continued to form Irish public opinion in favour of amending the Constitution in strict accordance with the principle of national sovereignty. In the process of completing the Treaty settlement, the governing class of Britain gave ample confirmatory evidence to convince the Irish Nationalists that the era of British domination in Ireland had not passed, and that the struggle for her sovereignty would call for a compact and homogeneous national unity.

We have already referred to the British protest against the registration of the Treaty with the League of Nations. When the question of financial settlement with the Irish Free State came up for discussion, it became apparent that Great Britain, unwilling to recognize the sovereignty asserted by the Oireachthas, proposed to wage "economic warfare" against the Irish Free State. A drastic tariff was imposed upon imports of Irish produce in the hope of aggravating her internal economic crisis. Similarly, the Boundary Agreement executed on December 3, 1925, resulted in a bitter controversy. All these circumstances gave Mr. de Valera and his party ample opportunities for insisting day in and day out on the national position in relation to the Treaty, and they had no difficulty in gaining the sympathies of a considerable portion of the country. Thus the inevitable reaction of Irish opinion to the weakness of the Cosgrave Government brought Mr. de Valera into power at the beginning of 1932. He and his party had already formed the parliamentary opposition since 1927, when the question of the oath of allegiance was made a condition of nomination. Strengthened by the vast mass of Republican opinion, Mr. de Valera was now in a position to assert the constitutional independence of the Irish Free State. "While fully adhering to his Republican and anti-Treaty convictions he assumed control of the Government and administration established under the Treaty and, as a matter of practical statesmanship, conducted both on the basis that the Treaty was *de facto* operative. He announced that the decision whether the Treaty was to be maintained or repudiated must be the decision of the

Irish people at a general election taken on that specific issue—and that in due course and at an appropriate juncture that decision would be taken."[1]

IV

Although the Irish Free State became virtually a sovereign State in its internal politics, its relations with the British Empire had to be adjusted in consonance with the goal of independence. In the year after the passing of the Statute of Westminster (1931) the Irish Free State raised the question of abolishing the oath, which reopened the validity of the Anglo-Irish Treaty of 1921. It also pressed for fiscal independence and for the abolition of the office of Governor-General. In pursuance of the terms of the Statute, the Irish Free State passed a series of amendments to the Constitution, and thus prepared the way for fundamental revision of the Constitution in 1937.

De Valera lost no time in informing the Imperial Government that the oath of allegiance was not mandatory in the Treaty, and that he proposed to remove it from the Constitution at the earliest opportunity. In 1932 he raised the question of the land annuities which the British Treasury had received from the Irish Free State since the Treaty, and withheld payment. The Imperial Government sought to realize the amount by imposing a tariff upon Irish imports, and the Irish Government exercised its fiscal independence by laying special duties upon various imports of British goods. The conference which was held in that year for the purpose of establishing amicable relations between Eire and the United Kingdom led to no result. The plea to terminate the Anglo-Irish "Economic War," as it was popularly known, was of no avail. Referring to the need of establishing happier relations between Eire and the United Kingdom, Mr. de Valera wrote to Mr. J. H. Thomas, then Secretary of State for the Dominions: "These friendly relations cannot be established on pretence, but they can be established on the solid foundation of mutual respect and common interest, and they would long ago have been thus established had the forces that tend to bring us together not been interfered with by the attempts of one country to dominate the other."

[1] Henry Harrison, *Ireland and the British Empire*, 1937.

The new Constitution of Ireland (Eire) was published in May 1937, and came into force in December. It is no longer the Constitution of the Irish Free State, but of the historic Ireland—Eire.[1] It was submitted to the electorate in 1937 and ratified by plebiscite (on December 29, 1937). It greatly modified the Constitution of 1922, and incorporated as many as seventeen items of constitutional changes made by the Dáil from 1922 to 1937, notwithstanding the terms of the Anglo-Irish Agreement of 1921. It declared the right of the Irish people to choose its own form of government, to determine its relations with other nations, and to develop its national life in all its aspects without the intervention of Great Britain. The Irish tongue became the official language, and the Governor-General was superseded by the President (Uachtaran) of Eire, elected by the direct vote of the people of the twenty-six counties. In short, the Constitution asserted Ireland's position as "a sovereign independent democratic State," and included the whole of Ireland as its territory. "On December 29th," writes the *Fianna Fail Bulletin*, "we enter a new phase of national history. The old Constitution, drafted in Westminster, amended and excoriated by successive Fianna Fáil amendments until it is an empty symbol of imperial domination, will become a scrap of paper." Nevertheless, one fundamental question remained unsolved; namely, the partition of Ireland. This perpetuates a situation in which political solidarity has become impossible; it accentuates the conflict of religious beliefs, and renders Ireland's relations with the British Commonwealth perverse and difficult. The Irish leaders declare that "the crime of conquest can be repaired by evacuation, but the crime of having divided the conquered house against itself is not so easily repaired."[2]

The Irish Parliament consists of a President and two Houses. The representatives of the Lower House (the Dáil) are elected by manhood suffrage, but those of the Upper Legislature (Senate) are chosen from five vocational panels: namely, agriculture and fisheries, education, labour, industry and commerce, public administration and social service. The elected President holds office for seven years. The Dáil, through the President, appoints a Prime Minister (Taoiseach) who, in turn, appoints his Ministry

[1] *Eire* is the name for Ireland in the Irish language.

[2] George O'Brien, *The Four Green Fields*, 1936.

from both the Houses. The Deputy Prime Minister and Minister of Finance must, however, be selected from members of the Dáil.

The Constitution establishes the principle of the Referendum, and satisfies, once for all, the claims of the Irish people to sovereign independence. It contains no mention of the Crown, but under a subsidiary Act the Crown is empowered, subject to the advice of Irish Ministers, to act in matters relating to external affairs.

It is interesting to note that the Constitution of Eire is not recognized by the Imperial Government; nor have they formally denounced it. They consider it best, as an Irish writer puts it, "to turn a Nelson eye on Ireland." Professor A. B. Keith observes that "while in the case of the Dominions it has been frankly *conceded* that the *Constitutions rest without exception on the* basis of Imperial Acts, the Irish view has always been that the Constitution was valid apart from the Imperial Acts, on the ground that all power in Ireland came from the people of Ireland and not from any British grant, a doctrine not naturally accepted in the United Kingdom, and in 1935 formally repudiated by the Privy Council."[1] However it was subsequently announced by the Imperial Government that "they are prepared to treat the new Constitution as not effecting a fundamental alteration in the position of the Irish Free State as a member of the British Commonwealth of Nations." Although no Irishman takes the oath of allegiance, internationally Ireland is still regarded as a member of the British Empire. The fact is a proof of strength rather than of weakness in the Empire's connection with Ireland.[2]

The position of Ireland within the Commonwealth is envisaged as follows by a writer in a preliminary paper read before the second Conference on British Commonwealth Relations held at Sydney in 1938. He observes:

> "English political and social institutions have no meaning for the Irishman and call forth no loyalty from him. It is therefore a matter of common honesty and wise realism for

[1] A. B. Keith, *Dominions as Sovereign States.*

[2] The attitude of the British Conservatives towards the new Constitution was expressed by the *Morning Post*, which spoke of "de Valera's antics," and warned the Irish that "the more Ireland separates herself from the British connexion, the more insignificant she becomes in the world's estimate." (*The Morning Post*, July 17, 1937.)

Irish nationalists to insist on a radically different status for their country from that of the self-governing Dominions. If loyalty to the Crown is a real force, binding together the other self-governing parts of the Empire, it is presumably because those Dominions recognize a common origin from a common Motherland, of which they may be justly proud. The Crown is to them a rallying point, a symbol of their community life, as it is still in England. In Ireland there can be no question of any such symbolic rôle. What is possible, and all that is possible, is the use of the Crown in external affairs, as a sign of our association with the British Commonwealth. But the association must be from outside, analogous rather to the relationship of Egypt and the Sudan than that of India, to mention two other communities where native loyalties have prevented in the past, and still prevent, the development of loyalty to the English Crown. To an Irishman, it seems strange that the Commonwealth should have any objection to such an obvious solution of the problem. It would, indeed, appear to open the door to a rearrangement of the complicated relationships binding the solid kernel of the British Commonwealth to an outer fringe of States, which show varying degrees of strategic and economic dependence on the Empire."[1]

Notwithstanding somewhat anomalous constitutional relations between Eire and Britain, the Anglo-Irish Agreements of 1938 have brought the two countries much closer together. "It is possible," writes O'Sullivan, "that the growing threat from Nazi Germany was a factor in inducing the British Government to go as far as it could in the way of establishing a friendly Ireland on the western flank of Great Britain."[2] At any rate, with three Agreements of outstanding importance, Great Britain closed an unhappy chapter in her association with a constituent part of the Empire. In the first place, under the terms of the Treaty, the British Government was entitled to keep armed forces in three fortified harbours—Cork, Berehaven and Lough Swilly—and to obtain further facilities in times of strained relations with a foreign Power. The new Agreement provided that the transfer of these three ports should take place not later than December 31,

[1] H. V. Hodson, *The British Commonwealth and the Future*, 1939.

[2] Donal O'Sullivan, *The Irish Free State and its Senate.*

1938. The responsibility for these defences rests now with the Government of Eire.

Secondly, with regard to land annuities, the claim was finally settled on the payment of a lump sum of £10,000,000 sterling. These annuities are the annual rent which the Irish farmer pays the Land Commission. The amount thus collected was being paid to the British Exchequer under British rule, but the Irish Republican Party insisted that Ireland never owed the land annuities to Great Britain, and they argued that "if there should be any question of an outstanding account between the two countries Britain would be the debtor instead of the creditor." However, with due regard to the interests of Ireland's industrial policy, Mr. de Valera met the British case with a compromise.[1] The penal duties imposed by both Governments which had been in force since 1932 were removed, but the freedom of the Irish Government to give their nascent industries adequate protection remains unimpaired. Thus, the economic war which continued over a period of six years was brought to an end. It was estimated that the penal duties had cost the Irish people the colossal sum of forty-eight millions sterling.

The third Agreement was a trade agreement which was in the nature of a mutually advantageous commercial treaty. Under its terms, Irish goods were to be admitted free of customs duties into the British market, with certain provisions concerning the quantitative regulation of imports of agricultural products. The Irish Government, on their part, guaranteed the right of free entry for certain classes of British goods and undertook to remove or modify the duties on certain other classes to be determined by the Irish Prices Commission.

These three Agreements reflect the constitutional position of Eire in relation to Great Britain. Eire became a Sovereign State and entered into a free alliance with Great Britain. She did not merely desire self-government, but directed her efforts toward the acquisition of that political freedom which would confer sovereign status. By virtue of this status Eire was able to keep out of the war (1939) and to refuse to open her ports to the

[1] Sir John Marriott in a letter to *The Times*, pointed out that the financial agreement with Eire imposed a heavy burden on that patient camel—the British Taxpayer," because it would mean, so he argued, the addition of about £100,000,000 to the National Debt, being the amount of capital "advanced to Irish landlords for the purchase, by the tenants, of their estates." (*The Times*, May 5, 1938.)

British Navy. If she permitted any part of her territory to be used by one belligerent against another, Eire would probably become a cockpit of the present war. The supreme test of a nation's freedom is its right to neutrality in war.

We now come to Northern Ireland. The *de facto* position with regard to these counties is recognized by Article 3 of the Eire Constitution, which reads: "Pending the reintegration of the national territory, and without prejudice to the right of the Parliament and Government established by this Constitution to exercise jurisdiction over the whole of that territory, the laws enacted by that Parliament shall have the like area and extent of application as the laws of Saorsta't Eircann and the like extra-territorial effect." But the British Government do not recognize any provision in the Constitution which "involves any right to territory or jurisdiction over territory forming part of the United Kingdom of Great Britain and Northern Ireland, or affects in any way the position of Northern Ireland as an integral part of the United Kingdom of Great Britain and Northern Ireland."

But the partition issue remains in the forefront of Irish politics. The Irish people hold Britain responsible for that iniquity of partition which, they believe, could not continue if there were no outside interference. It appears that without a solution of this question of the restoration of what Mr. de Valera declares as "Ireland's natural unity" there can be no comprehensive adjustment of Anglo-Irish relations.

Chapter Six

THE CONSTITUENT ASSEMBLIES IN POST-WAR EUROPE

I

It may now be instructive to draw upon the recent experiences of certain European countries whose constitutional struggles took place against a revolutionary background. The critics of India's demand remind us that "the Constituent Assemblies, elected on a wide franchise, which have sought to combine the securing of unity among diverse elements with the writing of the new Constitution itself, have not always had a happy result."[1]

But their failure was not due to any inherent weakness in the concepts underlying the Constituent Assembly. It failed in some instances to accomplish its task, because the forces of democracy had not been adequately mobilized for capturing the vital organs of the Government it sought to replace. Again, when it was not possible to set up political forms of a permanent character, the Constituent Assembly adjourned after declaring the basic principles of a democratic constitution, and left it to be adjusted to suit changing circumstances. The reconstruction of a political system cannot take place overnight, and there must be a period of transition when the economic bases of democracy have to be created and consolidated. The success of a Constituent Assembly depends upon the preparation and leadership of the peoples as well as upon the clear perception of the goal.

It should, however, be apparent that a Constituent Assembly is not just a body of selected personages brought together for the purpose of drafting or amending a Constitution. In a debate in the House of Lords on the Viceregal pronouncement that "His Majesty's Government will be very willing to enter into consultation with representatives of various communities, parties and interests in India and with Indian Princes with a view to securing their aid and co-operation in framing all such modifications of the 1935 Act as may seem desirable," Lord Samuel suggested

[1] Sir Maurice Gwyer's address to the Benares University Convocation.

that such a proposal was not very far removed from the Constituent Assembly which the Congress desired. This implies a total misconception of the Indian national demand and ignores the main issue involved in our struggle for freedom.

Nor is it the function of a Constituent Assembly to act as a *deus ex machina* in solving all the problems that confront the protagonists in such a political struggle. While the Imperial Government refuses to recognize India's sovereign rights to determine her own destiny, Indian bourgeois politicians argue that the institution of a Constituent Assembly would be unable to solve the Indian constitutional problem, which they cynically declare as "a riddle wrapped in mystery inside an enigma." They fail to admit the fact that to-day our will to win freedom is sufficiently strong to regenerate India in spite of a foreign Government and of the reactionary forces assembled by them in order to frustrate India's struggle. The demand for a Constituent Assembly is indeed a concrete expression of that national will.

We shall now turn to the success and failures of Constituent Assemblies in certain countries of post-war Europe.

II

The Union of Socialist Soviet Republics, consisting of over one hundred and seventy-nine nationalities and ethnic groups, embraces eleven national and twenty-two autonomous Republics. It is a multi-national State, the formation and stability of which have shown beyond doubt how divergent interests may be successfully reconciled on the basis of democratic socialism. The lesson is of special interest to India.

In the fourth year of the Great War the Tsar of Russia abdicated, and it looked as though power would be seized by the great landlords and the plutocrats. They had long acquired considerable influence in the economic as well as in the political sphere. Indeed, the expanding Russian bourgeoisie had become the mainstay of Tsardom. But neither the autocratic Court nor the influential bourgeoisie reckoned that the discontent among the masses of the workers and soldiers was increasing to serious dimensions, and that they would now make a bid for freedom and power.

The abdication of the Tsar was followed by a Provisional Government formed by the Executive Committee of the Duma. Bearing in mind the influence of the Council of working-men and soldiers, which had then come into being, the Provisional Government adopted a conciliatory attitude towards the demand for a democratic Constitution by issuing a Proclamation that an immediate step would be taken for "the preparation and convocation of a Constituent Assembly, based on universal suffrage" They promised that this Assembly would establish a stable régime by drastic elimination of those obnoxious forces of Tsardom which had so long oppressed the masses, and that Russia's political structure would now conform to the real interests of the country.

The proclamation of the Provisional Government did not, however, reassure the revolutionary spirit. The Executive Committee of the Duma failed to grasp the deeper significance of the Revolution; for "this *coup d'état*," as Guchkov put it, "is not the result of a clever conspiracy of a few masked conspirators, for whom the secret police were searching in the dark. It is a ripe fruit pulling its own weight; it is an historic event. In the fact that it was not the artificial result of mere conspiracy, that it was the result of natural forces, that it is an historic necessity: in this lies the guarantee of its durability."

Indeed, the ferment that had been at work among the masses for over half a century was activated by the vicissitudes of the revolution, and could no longer be kept under control by the palliative measures adopted by the liberal and professional classes, who, having formed themselves into the Constitutional-Democratic Party, occupied a prominent place in the Provisional Government. The Constituent Assembly, the elections to which were held prior to the October Revolution, was dissolved because of its refusal to recognize the decrees passed by the Congress of Soviets.

We must understand that the first stage in the creation of the framework of the new Constitution was the reconstruction of urban and village councils or committees, called Soviets. The structure of these organizations bears a striking resemblance to Indian *Panchayet*, or perhaps one should say, to democratic working-class organizations all the world over. But in the case of Russia the Soviets were so developed as to become the main functional organs of the State. The unique character and function of these councils or Soviets were described by Lenin as follows:

> "The Soviets are the new State apparatus. . . . This apparatus represents a connection with the masses, with the majority of the people that is so intimate, so indissoluble, so readily verifiable and renewable, that nothing like it was even approached in the previous State. This apparatus, because it is elective, and because its personnel is subject to recall in accordance with the will of the people without any bureaucratic formalities, is far more democratic than were the former ones. It represents a firm connexion with the most diverse occupations, thus facilitating all sorts of radical reforms without resort to bureaucracy. . . . It makes it possible to combine the advantages of parliamentarism with the advantages of immediate and direct democracy, that is, to unite, in persons of elected representatives of the people, both legislative and executive functions. Compared with bourgeois parliamentarism this is a step forward in the development of democracy which has an historical world significance."

The Constituent Assembly, elected in November 1917 by the votes of about forty-five millions, proclaimed Russia to be a Socialist Federative Soviet Republic and then adjourned, leaving the task of framing the Constitution in the hands of the Central Executive Committee. The Assembly promulgated the basic principles of the Republic in the Declaration of Rights which laid down as a law the right of the peoples of Russia, irrespective of their nationalities, to "unhampered development and complete equality." The Declaration also indicated the steps to be taken to realize the ideal of a society organized on socialist lines, and to adjust the relations between the divergent peoples by providing equal facilities in respect of participation in public affairs.

The Constitution of the Soviet Republic was adopted at the Fifth All-Russian Congress of Soviets on July 10, 1918. The Congress consisted of representatives of town Soviets on the basis of one delegate for every twenty-five thousand electors and of provincial congresses of Soviets on the basis of one delegate for every one hundred and twenty-five thousand inhabitants. The Central Executive Committee was elected by the Congress, composed of two chambers, the Union Council and the Council of Nationalities. The system of franchise was widely diffused, but it was one of indirect election. At a later stage the system was replaced by direct election and the secret ballot.

So much for the initial stage of development in the Soviet Constitution. When circumstances led to the federation of a number of autonomous States within Russia, the Union of the Soviet Socialist Republics was formed in 1922, and the first Constitution of the Union was adopted in 1924.

The years between 1924 and the beginning of 1935 may be described as "fluid periods" in the history of Soviet Russia. After various strategic retreats in the economic sphere (such as the New Economic Policy in 1921) great efforts had to be made in carrying out the national planning; small individual peasant farms with primitive forms of agriculture had to be brought under an all-embracing collective system; and, above all, the relations between the peoples of a multi-national State had to be adjusted. By 1935 these developments had advanced sufficiently to justify amendments to the Constitution of 1924, for the purpose of consolidating a new social and economic order.

The new Constitution, drafted by the Constitution Commission appointed in 1935 by the Seventh Congress of Soviets, was submitted for public discussion throughout the U.S.S.R. and finally presented to the Congress in 1936.[1] It provides for universal adult suffrage with the secret ballot, direct election, and equality for women and for all races within the Union; it recognizes the *right of voluntary organization, freedom of conscience, of worship*, of speech, of press and of assembly; and it firmly adheres to the Declaration of Rights promulgated soon after the establishment of the Soviet Republic. In short, it introduces the democratic elements missing in the earlier Constitution, and enshrines the fundamental gains of the Russian Revolution in legislative form. By breaking the chains of capitalism the Constitution harmonizes economic and political interests, and this invests the Constitution with a character which renders it "one of the most interesting political experiments that the world has ever seen." The rights of divergent nationalities and ethnic groups—numbering over one hundred and seventy-nine—are protected by the Constitution, which declares that "the equality

[1] Appendix VI.

of citizens of the U.S.S.R., irrespective of their nationality or race, in all fields of economic, State, cultural, social and political life, is an irrevocable law."

"Any direct or indirect restriction of these rights, or conversely the establishment of direct or indirect privileges for citizens on account of the race or nationality to which they belong, as well as any propagation of racial or national exceptionalism or hatred and contempt, is punishable by law." Women are accorded equal rights with men in all fields of economic, political, social and cultural life.

The unique feature of the representative system evolved by Soviet Russia is of special interest to us. Here, as the Webbs remark; "Man is represented in three separate capacities, as a citizen as a producer and as a consumer. In each case the franchise is the widest in the world, though with peculiar and steadily dwindling disqualifications, whilst the extent to which the entire population actually participates in elections is without parallel."[1] With the rapid liquidation of illiteracy, the universal electorate is being provided with a wide opportunity to participate effectively in public affairs. The Constitution declares the formal rights of citizens, and at the same time provides the possibilities of conditions necessary for exercising these rights. Therefore it is not so much the actual structure of the Soviet Constitution that engages our attention, but the essential principles of a democratic social order, coupled with the rapid technological progress, that strike our imagination. We note also that the Constitution represents a federation not of territorial units, but rather of peoples. Here a great variety of peoples, races, languages and cultures is brought together under a common government which recognizes no principle of racial superiority, but insists upon the common adherence to the principles of democratic socialism.

For our purpose, the procedure adopted in framing the Soviet Constitution is of special interest. It was the Constituent Assembly which laid down the Fundamental Law, and the present Constitution was drafted by a Constitution Commission appointed by the Congress. The draft was then thrown open to nation-wide discussion, lasting over five months, and finally submitted to the Eighth Congress of Soviets. Whatever may be the criticisms of that Constitution, its democratic character embodies the victory

[1] *Soviet Communism* by Sidney and Beatrice Webb, 1936.

of Socialism. While we are inclined to agree with Laski[1] that the conditions of the Russian Revolution in 1917 are not likely to be reproduced elsewhere, it may be admitted that, like the French Revolution, the developments in Soviet Russia have brought about an era of revolutionary dynamics. The emergence of a Socialist State comprising multiple nationalities with their variegated patterns of culture, founded upon a system that promises a definite break with the bourgeois capitalist economic structure, cannot but interest the bulk of mankind.

III

We now turn to the Grand National Assembly of *Turkey*.

The history of the Turkish Nationalist Revolution, which at last succeeded in emancipating the Turkish people from the petrified political traditions of the Ottoman Empire and the dead weight of a religious hierarchy, affords a profound lesson for India. The achievement of the Republic, its increasing stability and progress within the short space of eighteen years, makes an inspiring record. Credit for this astonishing transformation of Turkey into an advanced State must go to Mustafa Kemal, an outstanding personality, in whom we find a happy blend of realism and bold intellectual radicalism. It is this combination that invested his policy with the hall-mark of genius, and enabled him to gather round him divergent elements within the Nationalist Revolution, unified by the single purpose of the liberation of their country. He did not create the Nationalist movement, but gave it a new orientation, and finally led it to victory.

"Unlike many other famous generals," observes *The Times*, "he did not allow victory to obscure his judgment. He had succeeded to a troubled heritage. Turkey had been bled white by eight years of almost continuous warfare. Communications, trade and agriculture were in ruinous disorder; the Kurdish provinces were out of hand; the survivors of the Committee of Union and Progress, which had involved Turkey in the Great War, were jealous of their former critic, who had saved the country from irremediable disaster; while Pan-Islamic intriguers,

[1] H. J. Laski, *The State in Theory and Practice*.

excited by his triumph, hoped that he would again make Turkey the spearhead of militant Islam."[1]

The revolt against the Ottoman Empire dated as far back as the third decade of the nineteenth century. The contact of Young Turkey with the ideas behind the French Revolution, and the Nationalist movements throughout the Western world, together with the positive influence of the non-Mohammedan subjects in Turkey, awakened among the rising generation a spirit of challenge to the social and political structures which bore the stamp of a bankrupt inheritance from the past. Being so close to the currents and cross-currents of Western civilization, Turkey developed within the State "a dualism which has no historical parallel." To meet the demands of its non-Mohammedan subjects, the monarchy reluctantly had to embark upon certain reforms in the field of social service; the cultural influence of Western civilization permeated the educated Turkish communities, and military necessity compelled the Government to reorganize an army on Western models. Yet Turkish society as a whole remained imprisoned in an antiquated mould. The character of this dualism is described by a recent writer as follows:

> ". . . Public administrations fulfilled their functions in accordance with Western laws; professors taught the civil schools on Western lines; religious institutions changed not an iota of their rules, and gave their schools a teaching that was twelve centuries old. The Sultan was both temporal Sovereign and religious head (Khalif). As Sovereign, he had a civil representative, the Grand-Vizier; as Khalif, a religious representative, the Sheikh-ul-Islam. If a declaration of war were contemplated, the secular leaders were required to satisfy themselves by obtaining a "fetva"[2] from the Sheikh-ul-Islam that the war in view conformed to religious dogmas."[3]

But the continued interplay of contradictory forces within a nation is bound to accelerate the process of social transformation. If it gives rise to sharply differentiated class-conscious groups, it

[1] *The Times*, November 11, 1938.

[2] Religious rulings on a given problem with a juridical conclusion.

[3] *The New Turkey*, by Falih Rifki Atay. *The Times* (Turkish Number, 1938).

also tends to bring into full operation "the law of social equilibrium," which, under certain circumstances, cannot dispense with the necessity of alliance with the forces of revolution. This is what happened in the evolution of New Turkey.

After the Armistice the attitude of the Allies in their negotiations with the Turkish Government made it apparent that they meant "to leave Turkey no shadow of independence." They attempted to deprive Turkey of a large part of Anatolia, and the Peace Conference authorized a military occupation of Smyrna by the Greek Army. The Turkish Government had neither the power nor the will to offer any resistance. Meanwhile, under the protection of Allied warships, the Greeks actually landed (May 15, 1919) at Smyrna—the key to Anatolia. The decision of the Allied Powers to humiliate Turkey with the help of a sworn enemy of the Turks was actuated by the motive of disrupting the forces of nationalism in the Near East. The Greek Army appeared to the exhausted Powers "a convenient instrument" which might well be utilized to satisfy the ambition of the Greek Premier, M. Venizelos, who was then carrying on a most unscrupulous propaganda against Turkey. He faked statistics to show that the Turks were in the minority in those territories which should belong to Greece; and, in order to impress the Peace Conference, he forged documents purporting to prove that the Turks were preparing for a wholesale massacre of Christians.

But the ultimate plan of the Allied Powers was frustrated by that inevitable reaction which transformed a rather vague intellectual opposition to an alien Power into a dynamic movement. A sort of guerilla warfare between the Turkish irregulars and the troops of the Allies continued to embarass the Government, and Mustafa Kemal was appointed to the post of Inspector-General of the army in Anatolia. This gave him an opportunity to defend his country by reorganizing the army and to carve out his way to the leadership of New Turkey.

The Congress of the Nationalists which met at Erzerum (July 1919) laid down, without a single dissentient voice, the following principles:

1. All territory within the national frontiers forms one indivisible whole.
2. The nation will unite to resist any foreign occupation or intervention.

3. If the Central Government is incapable of defending the independence of the country, a Provisional Government shall be formed by election at a national Congress.
4. Sovereignty belongs to the people.
5. No privileges infringing this Sovereignty can be granted to the Christian races.
6. No Mandate or Protectorate shall be accepted.
7. A National Assembly shall be called and placed in power at once.

At a Congress of Nationalists held under his direction, it was decided to form a League for the Defence of Rights of Anatolia and Roumelia (September 7, 1919); and from this organization there eventually emerged the People's Party (Half Firkasi) which functioned as the pivot of the Turkish revolution. The principles on which the Party based its programme are as follows:

> "National will and Sovereignty spring from the people. It is one of the essential principles of the Party that in return for the exercise of this sovereignty and will, the individual owes reciprocal duties in his relation with the State. The Party is convinced that the form of government which best represents national sovereignty and best permits it to manifest itself in practice is the republican. It is one of the fundamental principles (of the Party) to regard the people of the Turkish Republic not as a mass composed of distinct classes, but as a community which portions out social and individual work. . . . The work of every person is an obligation imposed on him out of consideration for the life and well-being of all others. The Party aims at substituting social order and solidarity in the place of class warfare, at establishing a harmony between interests which will eliminate all possibility of conflict. Interests are measured by merit and work."

The leadership of Kemal and the methods he employed in organizing the life of the community gave rise to discontent among the privileged classes, who feared that Turkey was following in the footsteps of Soviet Russia. The capitalists were alarmed by the risk of substituting "the supreme function of the State for the limited function of the individual," which might lead to the control of all the means of production by the State. Men imbued with the liberalism of the Western democracies felt that the country was menaced by the advent of a dictatorship.

But Kemal realized that the liberation of Turkey would never be possible if divergent political creeds were allowed to add confusion to the imperfect political education of its citizens. The communities whose political life was undeveloped required a definite objective, and certain straightforward principles to guide them in understanding the line of action adopted by their leaders. While taking measures to suppress active opposition to the policy of the new régime, Kemal lost no opportunity of impressing upon the minds of the masses that unity was essential if Turkey was to gain national sovereignty, and that there could be no rival theories or rival parties in matters concerning the life and death of the Turkish nation. Therefore, the first essential step towards the formation of a Republican Government was to subordinate minor differences between political groups to the fundamental aim of securing the independence of their country. In his appeal to the people Mustafa Kemal said:

> "The nation has already suffered much from clashes between political parties. In other lands parties are formed to safeguard class interests. The bitter after-taste which we are experiencing is the direct result of the formation of parties here which emanated from the preconceived idea that we too were divided into classes. In speaking of the People's Party, we must understand a Party embracing the whole nation."

Kemal's passionate appeal to end all feuds among the various political groups is characteristic of his leadership. For the success of his audacious programme of Reform, he needed a Government which would, at least in its initial stage, represent a single political party. But intrigues against his personal supremacy over the Assembly and the People's Party were fostered by the court circles in Constantinople. A section of young Turkish politicians, intellectuals and conservative adherents to the Ottoman régime, formed a new party which rose in opposition to Mustafa Kemal and his policy. Since the Constitution and the programme of the People's Party[1] were based on principles of democracy, Kemal encouraged the growth of opposition parties until they led to

[1] The word "Republic" was added to the designation of the Party in 1924.

serious conflicts threatening to disrupt the homogeneous character of the Nationalist movement. The moment patriotism becomes subordinated to party politics, there are no depths to which the leaders of sectional interests will not descend. He realized that the Allied Powers were counting upon the Turkish reactionary forces to join them in frustrating the Nationalist movement which was pledged to give Turkey the status of a modern State. It was therefore necessary to suppress the growth of opposition parties and not to allow any compromise to the basic principles of Turkish nationalism. He also knew that the conversion of the masses to those principles would alone guarantee their realization.

In a sense, the People's Party was the precursor of the Grand National Assembly (the Kamutay) which proclaimed the establishment of the Republic and became the *de facto* Government in Angora.

The Sultan's Government was still in Constantinople, and the Grand Vizier, Damad Ferid Pasha, was attempting by intrigues to curb the influence of the Nationalist Party. But in the general elections that followed the fall of the Damad Cabinet in October 1919 the Nationalists gained an overwhelming majority, and demanded an organized resistance against the plans of the Allies to partition Turkey. The Allied Powers, especially Britain and France, were of course hostile to the Nationalist movement, and persuaded the Sultan to take drastic steps against an Assembly dangerously dominated by a Nationalist majority. They were none too pleased with the pact between the Nationalists in Constantinople and the "Kemalists" in Angora, which affirmed as a fundamental condition of Turkey's existence that she should enjoy complete independence and liberty, and that the Nationalist movement was opposed to any restrictions inimical to the attainment of that goal. The Pact, legally adopted by the Assembly in Constantinople, appeared to the Allies as a constitutional declaration against them and their agreed plan to partition Turkey. Consequently they took possession of Constantinople (March 16, 1920), arrested a number of leading Nationalists (including several members of the Cabinet), and deported them to Malta. The protest of the Assembly was of no avail, and it adjourned *sine die.* The administration was left under the control of Allied officers, who even inspired the Caliph to issue a *fetwa* proclaiming the Nationalists to be rebels deserving of excommunication.

Kemal was not slow to take full advantage of the situation. He summoned the Turkish Parliament to meet at Angora, but "as the British authorities had prevented the departure of the deputies, he issued writs for a new election." The new Assembly then met at Angora on April 29, 1920, and was christened the Grand National Assembly. By virtue of its representative character, the Assembly declared itself to be the sole representative of the nation. This meant a virtual repudiation of the Sultanate and his Government in Constantinople. The Assembly lost no time in drawing up a constitution based upon Republican principles, and set in motion the work of administration with full confidence in the support of the people. But the formal declaration of the Republic was not made till October 29, 1923. During the interim period, while Turkey was governed by the "Government of the Grand National Assembly," the Congress and the People's Party were preparing the ground for initiating radical reforms in both social and economic spheres. Regionalism, feudal influences in economic life, the conservative attitude of the privileged classes, the stranglehold of religious ideology, with all its ingenious laws (Sheri), upon the masses, and the tragic circumstances inseparable from illiteracy—all these obstacles to the birth of a new Turkey required to be overcome, not by the slow and cumbrous process of compromising with opposition, but by a determined will inspired by revolutionary spirit and action. The Nationalists passed from village to village, impressing upon the masses the fact that the abject conditions of their life and labour were bound up with the traditions of the Ottoman Empire, and that drastic steps would have to be taken to secure their emancipation from the tyranny of a theocratic régime.

We now turn to the Constitution of the Grand National Assembly. It declared without ambiguity that "Sovereignty belongs to the Nation"—the phrase which has since become the motto of the Turkish Parliament—and that the Assembly would exercise the right of sovereignty in the name of the nation through the elected representatives of the people. The Assembly was to be a single Chamber of Deputies, to be elected every two years. The electoral system was based on universal adult suffrage. Every Turkish citizen over eighteen had the right to vote, but only candidates over thirty years of age were eligible for membership of the Assembly. Women were given equal rights. The introduction of a common roll obviated the risk of racial or class conflicts and, indeed, prepared a sound basis for investing the Grand National Assembly with a representative character.

The immediate task before the Grand National Assembly, composed of three hundred and forty-two deputies, was to establish a Provisional Government and to draw up a formal scheme for a new Turkish Constitution. A Council of Executive was accordingly formed, with deputies selected on the basis of having administrative experience and special knowledge of the national problems. The President of the Assembly also presided over the Council. But Kemal and his associates had no easy task in hammering out a National Constitution when the moribund Sultanate was still looming large in the horizon. As a matter of fact,[1] the first Assembly was divided on the question of retaining the House of Osman and the Caliphate; but Kemal took care not to weaken the solidarity of the Nationalist Party by stressing any objective other than that of Turkey's political independence. Should the Assembly give sufficient indication of its organic vitality, which had to be reckoned with, and succeed in establishing its prestige and power among the masses, then opponents of the Party programmes would understand the deeper meaning of the struggle. With that understanding the task of raising the authority of the Assembly "above every other Power" would be comparatively easy.

A formal Constitution, or rather "the Fundamental Law," was drawn up on January 20, 1921, and the Provisional Government set about in earnest to consolidate its authority within the country. In other words, the function of the Constituent Assembly did not cease with the proposal of a new constitution for Turkey, but it proceeded to formulate a programme and carry it out. The leaders of New Turkey had not only to educate the National Assembly up to the methods of applying republican ideals in the Administration, but also to strengthen the position of the Party by undertaking such measures as would inspire the confidence of the masses. The inertia inextricably ingrained in their

[1] Recently a Turkish writer observed: "The first National Assembly was wholly reactionary and clerical. One member declared that no Turk could attend an Assembly which dared enact laws when the Koran existed. A Ministry of Public Instruction formed by this same Assembly opened four hundred new religious schools and prohibited drawing-lessons in the secular ones." (*The Times*, Turkish Number, August 9, 1938.)

character and habits had to be overcome through *organized* efforts; an understanding with Turkey's neighbours (e.g. the Union of Socialist Soviet Republics) had to be established on a sound footing; and, above all, sources of internal conflict had to be eliminated in order to protect the vital interests of the nation.

In November 1922 the Assembly deposed the Sultan and declared that Turkey had at long last rid herself of the basis of the Ottoman Empire. The Administration of Constantinople passed into the hands of the Angora Government. They now invited the foreign Powers to recognize the rights of a new Turkish sovereign State, announcing that such control as they exercised over the country would not be tolerated any longer. The Treaty of Lausanne (July 1923) not only freed Turkey from the capitulations[1] but established a new basis in her relations with foreign Powers. Thus, step by step, the administration of the Government of the Grand National Assembly reached a stage when it became necessary to give the constitutional form its true name. Hence the declaration of the Republic in October 1923, followed by the introduction of its Constitution in April 1924. The Proclamation of the Republic was hailed with joy throughout Turkey.

Nevertheless, one relic of the past régime still remained in the country, which had been so long a citadel of conservatism, and it had to be removed in order to secure the new Constitution from a source of religious fanaticism. Although the influence and prestige of the Caliphate had been considerably undermined, its continued existence would not be desirable within an essentially Moslem State now pledged to democratic principles. Its preservation, even in a modified form, was incompatible with the supreme duty of raising the nation to an independent status. A Bill for the "abrogation of the Ministry of Religion and the Ministry of Pious Foundations" was therefore passed by the Grand National Assembly on March 2, 1924; and as a precautionary measure the decision was followed by the expulsion from Turkey of all the members of the House of Osman. Such was the end of the Caliphate, over which a section[2] of Indian

[1] Judicial, commercial and economic privileges granted to foreigners.

[2] While the demise of the Caliphate caused little stir in Turkey, an appeal for its revival came from Indian Moslem leaders (e.g. H.H. the Aga Khan and the Rt. Hon. Sayyid Ameer Ali). The appeal gave Mustafa Kemal an opportunity of stirring up an agitation. He declared the Aga Khan "a special agent of the British." "England,

public opinion shed bitter tears. The Indian Moslems did not realize that the Nationalist movement since 1920 was not concerned with pan-Islamism, and that the separation of religious organizations from the State was in complete accord with the spirit of the Republican Constitution adopted by Turkey. Kemal's nationalism was not inspired by the illusion of pan-Islamism or pan-Turanianism.

Addressing the Assembly, he declared: "I am neither a believer in a league of all the nations of Islam, nor even in a league of the Turkish peoples. Each of us has the right to hold to his ideals, but the Government must be stable with a fixed policy, grounded on facts, and with one view and one alone—to safeguard the life and the independence of the nation within its natural frontiers. Neither sentiment nor illusion must influence our policy. Away with dreams and shadows! They have cost us dear in the past." Kemal's action in abolishing Islam as the State religion was warmly greeted by the young Turks, for it removed the danger of the use of religion for political ends.

It must not, however, be inferred that by the severance of the State's official connexion with Islam, the Turkish Republic proposed to dispense with religion or to undermine the disciplinary effect of Islam on the people. On the contrary, the Nationalists were conscious of the injury done to the Islamic faith by the rabble of *Mullahs*,[1] *Softas*[2] and even *Ulemas*,[3] and removed them from their privileged position. They abolished the Caliphate and encouraged the progressive laicization of the country; nevertheless, the Grand National Assembly created suitable organizations for the instructions of *Immams*[4] and *Ulemas*. It is true that the original article of the Constitution of 1924, whereby Islam had been constituted the religion of the State, was repealed in 1928 by a unanimous vote; but this was not equivalent to discarding the Islamic faith. Ostrorog, in his penetrating analysis of modern Turkey, writes that this breach

the crafty, subtle enemy, who had failed to destroy Turkey through the Greeks was at her intrigues again, using the Indian Moslems and the Aga Khan to back the Caliph and split the Turks into two camps" Thus Mr. H. C. Armstrong describes the reaction to the Indian Moslem leaders' letter of protest. (*Grey Wolf*, 1937.)

[1] *Mullahs:* Teachers in Islamic Law.

[2] *Softas:* Students of Islamic Law and Religion.

[3] *Ulemas:* Men learned in the Quranic Law.

[4] *Immams:* Men trained as preachers.

with the religious past caused "religion to recede from the halls of human conflict and ascend to the stronghold of Conscience, to dwell there in much greater dignity and security than when its ministers pretended to rule earthly interests as well as moral aspirations."[1]

The Proclamation of the Turkish Republic and the introduction of its new Constitution (April 1924) as it emerged from the Grand National Assembly were regarded by the Western Powers not only with suspicion, but with consternation. But all their efforts to throw Turkey "back into the ruin of its bitter past" were of no avail. To those who prophesied the inevitable collapse of the new régime, Kemal replied that: "A nation which makes all possible sacrifices to ensure its existence and independence does not fail; failure would mean that the nation is dead." Conscious of the fact that the success of the movement for national emancipation depended upon unity among its architects and upon their positive achievements in winning the confidence of the masses, he sought to overcome conservatism among his colleagues in executing such measures as would lay the foundation of a republic. Therefore, the initial task before them was not to draw up an imposing constitutional structure, but to bring about the economic and social circumstances favourable to the proper functioning of a State as a *real* instrument of popular liberty and welfare.

A Supreme Economic Council was entrusted with the execution of a well-planned scheme for the development of agriculture, industries, progressive labour legislation, transport and communications. In 1934 a five-year plan was drawn up for initiating directed economy, especially in the spheres of agriculture and industry. Since the backbone of the State is the Turkish peasantry, large-scale agricultural reforms have now been undertaken, and a number of agricultural industries have been established. Stage by stage the economic structure is being so adjusted as not to allow the Turkish bourgeoisie to attain power over the working-class. The future of the Turkish Republic will depend largely upon its success in controlling economic factors and in maintaining a balance of economic groups within the State. On one occasion Kemal was asked: what was the appropriate designation of his party?—to which he replied that he recognized no classes,

[1] Count Leo Ostrorog, *The Angora Reform*, 1927.

and that the party behind the Republic was the People's Party. It is this definite goal of the Turkish Republic that should ensure its stability.

In order to make the impact of Western civilization upon Turkish social and economic life really stimulating and fruitful, the Republic proceeded to adopt various measures which had proved fundamentally sound both in theory and practice in some of the advanced countries. Kemal's youthful Minister of Justice, for example, was deputed to study law and jurisprudence in Switzerland, so that the Swiss Civil Code might be modified to meet the needs of the Turkish community. They embraced the whole field of family law, the law of inheritance, property, and contracts, and were adopted in 1926. Similarly, the Penal Code was adopted, with necessary adjustments, from Italy, and the Commercial Code from Germany. Other changes supplanting the Turkish systems included the adoption of international time, and the international calendar, the Metric System, and Arabic and Latin figures.

Three years before the introduction (1931) of compulsory primary education, the Government removed a serious handicap to the spread of education by the compulsory adoption of the Latin script. Of all the social reforms initiated by the Turkish Republic, none has paved the way towards adjusting the nation to the needs of contemporary life more surely than the measures taken to fight against illiteracy.[1] "By teaching every member of the Turkish nation to read and write," observed Kemal's successor, Ismet Inonu, "we have undertaken a great task which will give glory to the coming generation. The fight against ignorance is the first item on our programme, and to-day the whole country has been turned into a classroom."

But the great legacy which Mustafa Kemal, the maker of the Turkish Republic, has left behind him is a dynamic faith in the future of his country and his people. Though he was not inclined to indulge in picturesque illusions about Turkish traditions, he had the clear vision to realize that in the Turkish people "there were hidden springs of vitality which only awaited the touch of a leader's wand to burst forth and revivify the State." That is

[1] The number of students attending schools rose from about 359,000 in 1923–24 to over 770,000 in 1935–36. Most of the Primary and Secondary Schools have adopted advanced pedagogic methods.

why he remained undaunted by the opposition of reactionary forces and could impose with confidence upon the people such social and political changes as were necessary to bring Turkey into the comity of independent nations. "I have known all nations," he assured the Turkish people, "I have studied them on the battlefield, under fire, in the face of death, when the character of a people is laid bare. I swear to you, my people, that the spiritual strength of our nation transcends that of all the world. . . . I will lead my people by the hand along the road until their feet are sure and they know the way. Then they may choose for themselves, and rule themselves. Then my work will be done." These noble words are not the words of a dictator, but they are imbued with the ideology of a true democrat. The authoritarian methods employed by him at the early stage of the Turkish Revolution were directed to training his people in courage and discipline—courage to face reactionary threats, and discipline to follow the path of hardship in order to reach the goal of independence. It was only by adopting a determined line of action that Kemal was able to liquidate the excrescences of a theocratic State steeped in mediaeval traditions, and to create circumstances favourable to the emergence of a new Turkey.

If the leaders of new Turkey have shown their ability to make a harmonious whole out of very diverse elements, both of thought and of human material, the credit is also due to the Turkish people themselves; for, "it was," to quote a Turkish authoress who played a prominent rôle in the Young Turk Movement, "the man in the street, the peasant on the soil, who had to do both the acting and the thinking. It was the surging up of elemental forces that brought about the new government of the people."[1]

Thus, all attempts of the Ottoman Empire to suppress the concept of freedom have proved futile. To-day, two verses of Namik Kemal, who lived in the beginning of the last century, have engraved themselves into the Turkish consciousness:

> How magic, art thou, O Freedom!
> Although when we are free, we become thy slaves.

[1] Halidé Edib, *Turkey Faces West*, 1930.

IV

We now take a glimpse into the social-democratic period of *Germany*. After her defeat in the War (1914–18) Germany adopted a Republican form of government which had been acclaimed by many as the ideal democracy in action. In its dread lest the nightmare of the Russian Revolution should be transplanted into Germany, the nation achieved a remarkable unity. All majority parties seemed to endorse the goal of a parliamentary democracy, and to approve of the democratic practice inherent in the idea of a Constituent Assembly. Although the elections to a Constituent Assembly were held in the critical period of German history that began in August 1918, the poll was heavy. The Social Democrats (including Independents and Progressives) polled a total of 76·1 per cent, while all the parties of the Right, the staunch supporters of the old régime, polled only 10·3 per cent. Indeed, the pendulum swung violently from right to left.

The German National Assembly, which met at Weimar, had two main tasks—to conclude the negotiations for the Treaty of Peace and to determine the lines on which the new constitution for democratic Germany was to be framed. We must bear in mind that there had been no revolution in Germany in the proper sense of the term. The Social Democratic Party did not by any means desire a break with the institutional spirit of Germany. What the party aimed at was to effect a radical change in the State, and to inaugurate a Republican form of government. This was established by the German National Assembly at Weimar on August 11, 1919.

The Weimar Assembly may well be regarded as a spiritual descendant of that which met at Frankfurt in 1848. The influence of the French Revolution had then extended to Germany, where it developed into a liberal bourgeois discontent. In pursuance of the demand for the convocation of a Constituent Assembly, the Federal Council ordered the election of German national representatives by universal franchise. The aim of Assembly was to combine the spirit of nationalism with that of democracy. About six hundred elected members assembled in the church at Frankfurt as the German National Assembly, and remained in session for one year.

In the course of its deliberations disputes arose over the character of the head of the future German Federal State. Was he to be a hereditary monarch, who would share the responsibility of government with Federal ministers responsible to the elected Parliament, or should Germany leave the leadership to Prussia? Ultimately the Assembly proposed a House of Commons elected by universal and equal franchise, and an Upper House composed of the ruling princes and one hundred and sixty-one elected members. The King of Prussia was elected as the head of the State, but his reply to the deputation was characteristic of the Prussian tradition. He declared that he "wished to reign by the grace of God, and not by the will of the people," and that "the National Assembly only wanted to put a dog-collar round the neck of the King to bind him indissolubly to the sovereignty of the people." It was, however, his brother who in 1871 became the Emperor William I.

Various circumstances contributed to the failure of the Frankfurt Assembly. It declared that the sovereign power should emanate from the people, but in actual practice it was left in the hands of a centralized bureaucracy. The individual States were jealous of their powers; the middle classes were without political experience and were not organized; and the rising generation of the working classes had no political consciousness of its rights and duties. The failure of the Assembly left the way open "for the gospel of blood and iron."

Yet the dynamics of the social-revolutionary idea existed in the country. Workmen's Unions and Leagues were springing into existence. Marx and Engels warned the Assembly against the growing military-bourgeois reaction and issued a manifesto setting forth a comprehensive programme, the main items of which were as follows:

> "One indivisible German Republic, payment for the people's representatives, arms for every man (the workers' armies are at the same time productive labour organizations), free administration of justice, abolition of all feudal burdens, transformation of princely and other feudal lands into national property, agriculture to be carried out on a grand scale according to scientific principles, mortgages on farms to become national property, rents and ground rents to be

paid to the State, a national bank to replace the private banks, ending the mastery of the great financiers and creating credit for the whole people, all traffic facilities to be nationalized, salaries to be graded only according to the number of persons in the family, not according to rank, complete separation of Church and State, limitation of the right of inheritance, progressive taxation, no more taxes on consumption, erection of national workshops, guarantee of existence for all workers, care for unemployables, universal free education."[1]

But the members of the Assembly could never summon up the courage to break away from the past and the German Workers' Movement, still too undeveloped for political organizations of their own, was not sufficiently awakened to ideas of freedom.

Karl Marx summed up the result of the Frankfurt Assembly of 1848 in the following terms:

> "Thus vanished the German Parliament, and with it the first and last creation of the Revolution. Its convocation had been the first evidence that there actually *had been* a revolution in January; and it existed for so long as this, the first modern German Revolution, was not brought to a close."
>
> "Chosen under the influence of the capitalist class by a dismembered, scattered, rural population, for the most part only awakening from the dumbness of feudalism, this Parliament served to bring in one body upon the political arena all the great popular names of 1820 to 1848 and then utterly to ruin them. . . . The industrial and commercial capitalist classes were more severely defeated in Germany than in any other country. . . . Political liberalism, the rule of the bourgeoisie, be it under a monarchical or republican form of government, is for ever impossible in Germany."[2]

Mutatis mutandis, the above judgment may well stand for the epitaph of the Weimar Republic.

To return to the Constituent Assembly at Weimar: It produced a remarkably comprehensive constitutional document outlining

[1] Veit Valentin, *1848: Chapters of German History*, 1940.
[2] Karl Marx, *Revolution and Counter-Revolution.*

the political form of a democratic Republic in Germany. Clothed in the verbiage and the ideology of democratic liberalism, the Weimar Constitution sought to preserve what its framers regarded as "the peculiar merits of the old régime." But "the conflict between that past and their present," writes Clark, "they never resolved; in the end they not only crippled the Socialist movement which was the best basis on which to build a democratic Germany, but they crippled that democratic Germany from the start. If the first actor in the tragedy of the German Republic was the old régime, the second was the first revolutionary government, and the reason was the same inherent repugnance to positive action and to the possession of a positive policy."[1]

Not only was the old régime imbued with the spirit of Prussian militarism, but the Army itself represented a powerful political institution. It controlled the Civil Government through a model bureaucracy, and therefore the régime had no roots in the people. In October 1918, after the military defeat, the civil power revolted against the domination of Prussian militarism, and sought to subject it to the control of the new constitutional authority set up by the German Chancellor, Prince Max von Baden; but here again the efforts were abortive.

Meanwhile, the collapse of the German Empire and the flight of the Emperor created a situation comparable to a revolution. It was just a twelvemonth since the October Revolution had brought Lenin into power, and already there was a network of Workmen's and Soldiers' Councils (Soviets) in Germany. While the Spartacus League—the extreme revolutionary group which came directly under the influence of Soviet Russia—raised the banner of revolt in the cities and boycotted the elections for the National Constituent Assembly, the Social Democrats and Independent Socialists voted in its favour. They stemmed the tide of revolt by providing a constitution which, they thought, contained a promise of natural development. The adoption of the principle of direct appeal to the nation by referendum and the plebiscite, and the creation of a system of occupational councils, designed to give economic control to the working class, were regarded as effective criteria for social democracy. While such concessions as were made to secure popular sanction proved largely illusory, the compromise to satisfy the powers of the authoritarian elements

[1] R. T. Clark, *The Fall of the German Republic*, 1935.

which still "survived in the General Staff and Officers' Corps, in the Civil Service, in great industrial concerns and in the East Elbian aristocracy," bore the seeds of death within the constitution. It was these powers that finally sabotaged the German Republic.

As early as 1907 Max Weber had told the Germans clearly: "If the party seeks political power, and yet fails to get control of the one effective means of power, military power, in order to overthrow the State, its dominance in the community and in public corporations and associations would only show its political impotence still more distinctly, and the more it sought to rule simply as a political party and not objectively, the quicker it would be discredited."

But the architects of the Weimar Constitution, far from establishing a new political and social order by taking full advantage of the situation caused by the downfall of the Imperial régime, yielded to the policy of "gradualism" and created a bourgeois republic. They lost touch not merely with the realities of the situation confronting the nation, but with the nation itself, which fretted under the leadership of Prussianism. And the fact that political freedom had need of its economic counterpart was not fully realized by the delegates of the Constituent Assembly. The result was deplorable. The constitutional edifice, however elaborate and impressive, built upon compromise in regard to essentials of democratic socialism, could not endure for long.

The Treaty of Versailles was signed on June 28, 1919, and the Weimar Constitution[1] came into operation six weeks later. As regards the structure of the Constitution itself, the Assembly had produced a remarkable constitutional charter with a long array of provisions for the protection of personal liberty. It was a rigid constitution, embodying the minutiae of political theory, but it overlooked the practical problems of application under the circumstances facing the nation. Being unable to find a basis of agreement between the parties, it provided for the working of the multi-party system based on proportional representation and the broad franchise. Not only did the system condemn Germany to "the utter weakness of perpetual coalition government," but it preserved those discordant elements which wrecked the success of democracy from the outset.

[1] Appendix VIII.

There were, however, other circumstances which militated against the working of the Weimar Constitution. The devaluation of currency was rapidly bringing down the mark into the abyss, food supplies became scarce, foreign garrisons remained in occupation on German soil, and finally France, determined to take revenge on Germany, invaded the Ruhr in January 1923 on the ground that the reparation instalments due to her were in arrears. The population of the Ruhr offered passive resistance, and the Government of the Republic was faced with a sense of frustration of all its efforts to stem the tide of reactionary forces within the country. During the period between 1924 and 1930, there had however been a large inflow of foreign loans, and in 1929 exports reached a peak of 13 milliards of marks. The growing interests of international finance led eventually to an international understanding with Germany. The reparation problem was provisionally settled by the Dawes Plan in 1924, which was modified in 1929. Germany signed the Locarno Pact of 1925 renouncing her claim to Alsace-Lorraine, and entered the League in the following year. On the last day of June 1930, the army of occupation left the Rhineland. Meanwhile National Socialism came into being as an antidote to any possible attempts at the "bolshevization" of Central Europe, and the party was financed by big business interests and supported by the immensely powerful Reichswehr, whose co-operation was secured on the understanding that general conscription and rearmament would be introduced. The political ideology of the party is well outlined in the following words:

> "The peasant and urban middle class has been ear-marked as the political field of energy from which to mould the community on the basis of the racial idea. On this system all the forces that imperil the political and social position of the middle classes are designated as an 'anti-Reich'—Social Democracy and Communism as political mass phenomena on the one hand, capitalist large-scale enterprise on the other, and Jewry, since it has a leading place with each of these adversaries."[1]

Of course, once the machinery of the State had been captured by the party in March 1933, the paymasters exacted their toll:

[1] Von Erich Voegelin, *Rasse und Staat*, 1933.

finance capital riveted its hold on national economy, and the Reichswehr demanded, and secured, a considerable reduction in the "private armies" of the National Socialist Party. Dissentient elements were "liquidated" in the purge of June 30, 1934.

Against this formidable attack of the Party, the Social Democrats had no effective defence. Their allegiance to the peasants and workers was feeble, and could not bear the strain of repressive measures adopted by the National Socialist Party. "The peasants and artisans," writes Mayer, "were until very recently still in the same condition as was depicted . . . in Marx and Engels' analysis of class forces in 1848. The Weimar Republic made hardly any progress in educating the political consciousness of these social groups. Even in 1932 it was impossible to convince peasant-farmers in Eastern Germany that Chancellor Heinrich Bruening was not a Social Democrat. The middle class, which lost its savings in the inflation, strengthened the bloc of malcontents who faced the Weimar Republic with indifferent non-co-operation or with hostility. Meanwhile, from 1932 to 1933, unemployment figures rose to six millions."[1]

The burden placed on the Republic was, however, heavy. The conditions of peace imposed by the Treaty of Versailles, a series of diplomatic reverses since 1931, inflation and the world economic crisis—all these discredited the Government in the estimation of the petty bourgeois. The National Socialist Party reaped the full advantage of the chaos and confusion of the period. The representation of the Party in the Reichstag had already leapt from twelve in 1928 to one hundred and seven in 1930. *Its leaders used the lower and middle bourgeois class for* the purpose of reinforcing the movement; for they realized that a virile bourgeois consciousness is an effective defence against communism. The "Red Peril" was therefore made the battle-cry, and all possible means and methods were adopted to stampede the German people into the National Socialist fold. When the Social Democrats discovered that with the rise of National Socialism the freedom of the nation was in peril, they appealed to the working class in a manifesto which concluded thus: "Defend yourselves, defend your independence as citizens against your oppressors, against the upper ten, against the miserable minority of the barons, against the capitalist. Break their economic

[1] J. Mayer, *Political Thought.*

and political power! Fight with us for the expropriation of the landowner and the distribution of the land to the peasant and agricultural labourer! Fight with us for the socialization of the heavy industries, for the construction of a socialist-planned economy!" But these words rang terribly hollow, as Clark says, "after the official party had been possessed of power for years without realizing socialism, and fourteen years before had on political and patriotic grounds deliberately rejected the socialist revolution as unrealizable and undesirable."[1] At all events, it was too late.

By the beginning of 1933 the German Republic had ceased to exist, although the Weimar Constitution had not been formally abolished. In the contest for the ascendancy of "Weimar" over "Potsdam" the latter was victorious.

V

The failure to establish a democratic republic in *Spain* on firm foundations is another instance in which the reactionary forces frustrated all efforts to recognize the sovereignty of the people. It is one of the tragedies of modern history that the Spanish struggle should have ended in a civil war; but here again we see that a lesson is to be derived from the grave consequences of internal weakness and contradictions among the Republicans themselves.

Spain is the poorest country in Western Europe. Its economic structure is feudal, and consequently the agrarian problem has always been acute. The bulk of the peasantry lives in abject poverty, and owing to the wretched conditions of life of the increasing number of landless agricultural labourers rural Spain presents a grim picture. In Andalusia many families of this class live in caves and pits dug out of the hillside. Villagers have been known to feed on boiled grasses and roots.

The character of rural economy may be seen from the distribution of agricultural land. Out of 45 million hectares[2] of cultivable land, the landed aristocracy owns more than 23 million hectares. While 5 million hectares are cultivated by a million peasants, there are over one million two hundred and fifty thousand tillers of the soil who cling to a million hectares of land

[1] R. T. Clark, op. cit.

[2] 1 hectare = 2·47 acres.

without any possibility of obtaining anything more than the barest livelihood. In twenty-seven out of fifty provinces, according to the register of 1931, 76·5 per cent of the people owned 4·7 per cent of the land, while 2 per cent owned 67 per cent of the land. According to a census of one section of the country, taken in 1925, some eight hundred and fifty thousand peasants live on an income of less than one peseta (about sixpence) a day. And in 1933 there were over two million landless agricultural labourers whose average daily wage was three pesetas, without board or lodging, and that of the women was half this amount; but farm-labourers are generally unemployed from four to eight months in the year.

Side-by-side with the economic servitude of the masses, there is the unholy alliance of the Catholic Church with the feudal landlords and their parasitic cliques. Only when we realize the significance of the secular power wielded by the Roman Catholic Church do we understand the anti-clerical character of all Spanish mass movements since the seventeenth century. The Catholic Church is the largest landowner, holding under its control millions of peasants, and through a Catholic Agrarian Confederation the vast network of a usurious system of money-lending was spread over the rural areas. In industrial and urban centres the Church invests its ill-gotten wealth, owns house property, controls banks and manufacturing concerns. El Banco Espiritu Santo (Bank of the Holy Ghost) is one of the five large banks of Spain. It is estimated that the Roman Catholic Church in Spain owns as much as 90 per cent of the accumulated wealth of the Peninsula. If Spain has earned the distinction of being the most religious of the principal European nations, she is also the most illiterate. It is the conspiracy of the Church with feudalism and capitalism that has become a menace to Spain.

The inevitable consequences of this conspiracy of feudal landlords and a secularized and powerful Catholic Church are reflected in the social and political history of the Spanish people. Until 1931 the Church controlled the education of the people through the various religious Orders, and exploited every possible means of arresting the spread of secular education. It is the Church which conspires against religious liberty and condemns every progressive movement for its attainment as being inspired by an anti-religious bias. Education has been neglected and in some provinces the illiterates in rural areas exceed 85 per cent of the population. For decades past distress and discomfort among the rural population have created a serious disequilibrium in economic and social relations, but neither the monarchy nor the liberal politicians achieved anything towards the solution of the problem. Most of the landlords were absentees and cared little about their tenants, and the system of land tenure gave rise to numerous parasitic interests.

Agriculture, which is the basis of the national life, has been allowed to remain in a backward state; the result of disequilibrium in the productive relations of agriculture, on which some 78 per cent of the people depended directly for a living, was reflected in the general economy of the country. A greater part of the cultivable land remained uncultivated; the mode of cultivation never passed beyond a primitive stage; distributory channels were not developed; while the means of transport and communication in rural areas remained in a state of backwardness that precluded the possibility of bringing rural life into contact with that of the urban centres.

It is this unprogressive state of affairs that has led to the saying that "Africa begins at the Pyrenees." The persistence of a feudal economy results in the perpetuation of almost mediaeval methods of agricultural production and distribution. Only 40 per cent of the land is actually cultivated and of this one-fourth lies fallow annually. About one-third of the land is cultivated by the share system, which supports a number of sub-tenants and middlemen. Feudal dues, called *foros*, *subforos*, *censos*, are exacted from the primary producers, irrespective of crop output. In the wine-growing districts the feudal share is often as high as 66 per cent of the total crop. Spain, with its arid soil, is not a very fertile country, and "the secret of the flourishing state of industry," to quote Karl Marx, "in Spain and Sicily under Arab rule was to be found in irrigation works." But rational reconstruction of agriculture involves a corresponding change in the general social and economic structure of the country. Since this remains under the control of landlords, the Church, and other interests, the precarious agriculture of Spain cannot ensure even a bare subsistence to the great bulk of the population.

Let us now turn to the tragic failure of the Spanish Republic proclaimed on April 14, 1931. The dictatorial régime of General

Primo de Rivera[1] collapsed towards the close of 1929, and the monarch assumed the full responsibility of government. But the conflicting forces within the country, the demands of the oppressed masses, and the incompetence of the Liberal politicians, brought about circumstances with which the Government were unable to cope, and consequently, within a year, the monarchy vanished from Spanish soil, making way once again[2] for the proclamation of a Republic.

Here we must refer to an important feature of the Spanish Revolution which led to the proclamation of the Republic and its subsequent development: namely, the growth and nature of the Spanish labour movement. In addition to an industrial proletariat of over two millions, there are many miners and large numbers of landless agricultural labourers in Spain. These various groups came under the influence of the Liberal movements of the nineteenth century. One section became adherents of Marx and the other of Bakunin; the former joined the Socialist movement and the latter the Iberian Anarchist Federation. It is interesting to note that the initiative for the spread of radical education among the Spanish people came from the Anarchists, whose influence also permeated a new generation of progressive writers that arose after the last flickering light of Spanish imperialism disappeared as a result of the Spanish-American War of 1898.

In recent years, notwithstanding the tardy development of industry and commerce, the problem arising out of the growth of industrial wage-earners assumed serious proportions in Spain. Being one of the larger countries of Europe which had remained neutral in the Great War, Spain found an opportunity of building up her industries with the alliance of foreign capitalists. A negative trade balance of about 248 million pesetas in 1913 was transformed into a favourable one of over 577 million pesetas by 1917. During the period of the War prosperity industry grew by leaps and bounds, the production of minerals rose to a pheno-

[1] In 1923 King Alfonso XIII handed over the government to the military dictatorship of this general. He was a pompous and impulsive administrator, who in a short time brought the country to the verge of bankruptcy. Under his régime, however, the long-drawn Moroccan war came to an end, thanks to his tactful alliance with the French. He died a few weeks after his withdrawal from the Government.

[2] The first Republic in Spain was proclaimed in 1873, when Amadeo of Savoy abdicated, but it was ended within a year by a military *coup*.

menal level, and a vast capital was invested in the electrical industry. The steady influx of foreign capital, however, paved the way for foreign intervention in internal affairs, and aggravated the conflicts among the social classes.

But when the War ended the era of prosperity suffered a setback. With the first sign of economic depression in 1927 the hostility of the labouring class towards the State became manifest, as is shown by the increase of the membership of the Confederacion Nacional de Trabajo (C.N.T.) from 25,000 in 1914 to 1,500,000 in 1931, the year of the declaration of the Republic. It should also be pointed out that the recurrence of strikes followed rather closely the decline of the issue of new capital. This is illustrated by the following table:

Year	*Issue of Capital*	*Number of Strikes*
1927	1,709 million pesetas	107
1928	2,824 ,, ,,	87
1929	213 ,, ,,	96
1930	802 ,, ,,	402
1931	534 ,, ,,	734
1932	42 ,, ,,	681
1933	51 ,, ,,	1,039[1]

In view of the economic depression, Primo de Rivera imposed tariffs on industrial goods, converted some foreign-owned monopolies into State-owned monopolies, and introduced certain forms of subsidies. A Regulating Committee of Industrial Production was set up in 1927, but all these efforts proved abortive during the world economic crisis of 1929, and labour unrest became universal throughout the Iberian peninsula. We may indeed say that Primo de Rivera was a victim of the crisis, and that his fall signalized the advent of the Republic.

Soon after the collapse of the dictatorship a revolutionary committee, consisting of Liberals, Socialists, and other political groups, was formed with a view to setting up a Provisional Government as a step towards the restoration of a stable parliamentary constitution.

In a manifesto, issued to the Spanish people in December 1930, the Committee declared:

[1] It was the prevalence of these strikes in 1932–33 that led to a Conservative régime in November 1933.

"The men of the past and the present have begun a crusade against the men of the future to divert the action of popular justice which is furiously demanding historical responsibilities. . . . Force has been substituted for right, arbitrary action for law, licence for discipline. . . . We have sunk to the level of our present ignominy down the slope of such degradation. The country has no other way to save itself but that of revolution.

"We are not impassioned by the rising violence, the drama of a revolution; but the people's misery, the country's anxieties move us deeply. Revolution will always be a crime or madness where justice and right prevail; but it is right and just when tyranny dominates. . . .

"We are determined to overthrow the fortress in which is embattled the personal power of the monarchy, and establish the Republic on the basis of the national sovereignty represented by a Constituent Assembly.

"Meanwhile, we, fully conscious of our mission and our responsibility, assume the functions of the Public Power with the character of a Provisional Government."

The elections for municipal bodies in April 1931, with a view to reconstituting Local Councils on a democratic basis, gave a clear indication of the strong support in favour of the plan of the revolutionary committee. For over three months the country was governed by a Provisional Government, with Alcala Zamora as President. There was no legislative body during this period, but immediate steps were taken to adjust the electoral system to the new constitutional position A new electoral census was taken, and the voting age was lowered from twenty-five to twenty-three, so that all citizens over twenty-three, without distinction of sex or civil status, might be eligible to take part in the election. For every fifty thousand of population there was to be one deputy elected under the system of universal suffrage on a basis of proportional representation. The urban centres were given more equitable representation, and the total number of deputies elected to the Cortes was raised to four hundred and seventy-three.

The main issue presented to the enlarged electorate was the question of its approval or disapproval of the revolution. The country was divided into several political parties, with sharp differences in regard to constitutional and economic programmes. It was therefore necessary to proceed cautiously, so that the party conflicts should not wreck the first essential step towards the establishment of a republican constitution. The Socialist and Republican groups combined against the opposition, which consisted of the remnants of old political cliques, and won a decisive victory in the General Election held on June 28, 1931. The Constituent Assembly was convened on July 14th, and proceeded to draw up a Constitution for the Spanish Republic. It provided for a President and a unicameral legislature, the Cortes, which would elect the President. It was empowered to select a leader of the party in power as a Premier who would be responsible, in collaboration with his Cabinet (or Executive Body), for carrying out the policy of the Government. A Supreme Tribunal was set up for deciding upon issues that involved the operation of the instruments of the Republic. In conformity with the demands of certain provinces, provision was made for "permissive autonomy" within certain defined limits. This provision enabled Catalonia, Galicia and the Basque Provinces to set up autonomous Governments competent to administer provincial affairs, retaining their co-ordinating links with the Central Government. Article 18 states that "all powers not explicitly granted in the charter of an autonomous region shall be considered as reserved to the Spanish State." While the Constitution made Spain federative, it did not set out to establish a federal republic. It renounced war as "an instrument of national policy" and adhered to the principle of collective security as an effective means of maintaining the rights of the State. The Republic therefore declared its allegiance to the Covenant of the League of Nations and pursued a policy of strengthening "the defence of peace." Provision was made to reform the Army and to repeal those laws which had so long endowed the military with wide powers to interfere in politics.

In the sphere of social and economic legislation the Constitution sought to readjust the relations of State and Church by restricting the numerous privileges so long enjoyed by the latter under the patronage of the monarchy. It emphatically declared that the Spanish State no longer recognized any official Church, and would guarantee freedom of religious belief and practice to the individual. Education was to be free, compulsory and secular;

and the Church would not be permitted to exercise its prerogatives over education and other social services. The process by while the Church came to play an insidious rôle in the economic life of the people must needs be arrested. The Constitution therefore empowered the Government to adopt measures regulating Church property and forbidding religious Orders to engage in commerce and industry. But, in truth, the offensive against the Church was well planned and feebly executed.

Further provisions in the Constitution related to the rights of all citizens in civic and social life to freedom of speech and of the press, and to such liberties of action as would tend to develop "the national will."

Thus the new Constitution of Spain emerged from the Constituent Assembly with the essential characteristic features of a progressive democratic republic. It gave her a wide opportunity for the reorientation of her social and economic structure; it provided for measures that would be necessary for the nationalization of public utilities, and for bringing about drastic agrarian reforms; and it sought to adjust the relation of the State to the Church in a spirit of moderation. Indeed, the programme formulated by the Republic was hailed as a great step in advance, not only towards social and economic amelioration, but also towards laying the foundation of a State devoid of those serious handicaps which had hitherto obstructed every attempt at progress. The promise of substantial agrarian reform, the expropriation of property for social uses on payment of adequate compensation, the improvement of leasehold contracts, the protection of the industrial and agricultural proletariat, the introduction of minimum wages, the right of forming political associations and trade unions, and, above all, the separation of Church and State—all these items were received by the masses with a wave of optimist faith in the strength and stability of the Republic.

However, in facing crucial problems that required bold and deliberate action, the leaders showed hesitancy and even timidity. The Constitution, though replete with empty phraseology, gave the Republicans the necessary power to take determined steps towards breaking with Spain's feudal past; but the Government were "vacillating, irresolute and temporizing." The Republican leaders were, indeed, too liberal in their dealings with reactionaries and allowed the "feudal elements" to retreat *pour mieux sauter*. This is illustrated by their failure to solve the all-important question of agrarian reform.

The Government established an Institute of Agrarian Reform entrusted with the task of carrying out the programme of land settlement, so that the semi-feudal system of ownership might disappear within a reasonable period; but its activities, though sufficient to infuriate the landed interests, were yet totally inadequate to produce any favourable impression upon the peasantry. Months passed in the preliminary study of the agrarian situation, and expropriation began in respect of the large estates, in some cases with and in others without compensation. The compensation was paid by capitalizing the value of the land as stated in the assessments for taxation, at the rate of 5 per cent for incomes up to 15,000 pesetas, rising to 20 per cent for incomes of 200,000 pesetas and over. The expropriated lands were distributed to individual farmers or to associations of farm workers for collective farming, but from 1931 to 1933 only 40,000 hectares of land out of a total of 45 million hectares of cultivable land were divided among the landless agricultural labourers. Meanwhile all the reactionary groups combined to sabotage the work of the Institute. They held the key positions, and were able to influence the elections in 1933, despite universal suffrage, and the peasant masses, which had hoped much from the Government they put in power, began to grow restive. Indeed, the Agrarian Reform could not shake the power of the *Caciques*, a caste of overseers who, as landlords' agents, exercise a powerful influence over the rural population.

The Republican Government also failed to control the Army and the Civil Guard, and even tolerated the formation of paramilitary organizations, such as the Falange Española and the Requetes. These set on foot an intense campaign against the Republic, but the Government looked on and did almost nothing to arrest the risk of a Fascist insurrection. The Army, still exercising great influence, more as a political than as a military instrument, was a distinct threat to the Republic. It is true that the Government introduced a number of reforms designed to break the tradition of the Army's interference in political affairs, and required every officer to take an oath of allegiance to the Republic. But here again they failed to adopt the necessary disciplinary measures against the rebellious tendencies of the Army.

Then there was the Church, that formidable enemy of the Spanish people. The entire ecclesiastical hierarchy did all it could to wreck the Republic, and gave its support to the old bureaucracy, the landlords, and the Army, although a large body of the clergy revolted against the insidious relations between their Church and Fascism. It announced that the Roman Catholic Church would not obey that part of the Republican Constitution which threatened to reduce it to the position of a non-political and non-property owning body. The Constitution provided that "all religious denominations shall be considered as associations subject to special laws," and empowered the Cortes to dissolve religious Orders dangerous to the State. Notwithstanding these and other restrictive provisions in the Constitution, the Government approached the problem in a half-hearted manner, and fatal dissensions arose among its own parties.

Of course, any system of government which bears some resemblance to a Parliamentary democracy functions rather slowly. In the case of Spain the tendency became more acute because of the character and form of political re-alignment, and an additional difficulty arose from lack of experience on the part of the Executives. Faced with the problem of unemployment, they attempted, for example, to realize an ambitious programme of public works, which they launched without adequate investigations or well-considered plans. Although the public works cost the Government over 860 million pesetas, the benefit derived from them was largely confined to the cities.

Perhaps the most serious failure of the Government was its inability to settle economic disputes with wisdom and foresight, especially when the *agents provocateurs* of the reactionary forces were at work among the industrial proletariat. Cheap labour was the only advantage which Spain possessed over foreign enterprise, and this the Spanish capitalists wished to maintain even during the economic crisis. They therefore resisted the attempts of the workers to restore the scale of wages which they had received during the period of war-prosperity. While the Government gave vent to platonic expressions of sympathy for the workers, it had not the courage to restrain the capitalist clique which was seeking to build up the political power of the plutocracy.

We must, however, give the Republican Government due

credit for its great effort to carry out the work of reconstruction under the most difficult circumstances, especially in the field of education. Delivered from the hands of the Jesuits, the entire system of education was recast and extended to a wider community, while the State expenditure was increased from over 200 million pesetas in 1931 to about 300 million in 1933. Within the short period of two years nearly ten thousand primary schools, over seven hundred kindergartens, and a large number of training colleges were established throughout the country.

Another significant achievement consisted of the positive measures taken to stabilize the position of organized labour. As many as twenty-two out of thirty conventions recommended by the International Labour Office were ratified by the Government without delay. Various sources of labour exploitation, both private bodies and municipalities, were effectively controlled, giving the working class protection against the sinister intrigues of the propertied classes. Above all, the Government created appropriate machinery for arbitration between employers and employees (e.g. *Jurados mixtos, Tribunalos industriales*) and encouraged the formation of *bona-fide* Labour Associations, as a means of developing the spirit of self-reliance and fraternity among the workers.

To the Western democracies, Republican Spain appeared to be influenced by Communism and they interpreted its revolutionary programme as an attempt to set up a Soviet State. They viewed with great concern the victory of the People's Front at the election of February 16, 1936, and were inclined to approve of the rise of the reactionary forces. But the truth is that the Government formed after the election was a Liberal Government, with Manuel Azana as Prime Minister, and did not include a single member from the Socialist or Communist Parties. The first Cabinet in which these parties were represented was formed just about six weeks *after* the outbreak of the civil war.

It is outside the scope of this book to enter into the origins and causes of the civil war. It would suffice for our purpose to point out that the conflict was not due to the means and methods adopted in framing the Republican Constitution. The Constituent Assembly and the Constitution which emerged from it had no serious inherent weakness. Both the form and the spirit of the Constitution represented the earnest striving of progressive Spain to raise her political status to the level of the Western democracies. The Republicans even realized that Spain would never be able to fulfil her destiny if she were not rescued from the grip of feudalism. But, to quote a recent writer, "instead of once and for all sweeping away the economic foundations of feudalism in Spain, the politicians strove to provide water-tight evidence of their innocuousness. Once more they surrendered to the fatal illusion that it was possible for the Middle Ages and the new era to live side by side in a state of idyllic harmony. Spain paid dearly for this tolerance on July 18, 1936."[1]

Nevertheless, the lesson derived from this conflict cannot be lost to the makers of new Spain. It has shown that the political constitution of a country shrouded in the gloom of the Middle Ages and rent asunder by religious schism cannot normally function without effecting *revolutionary* changes in social and economic conditions, and that a slow machinery of parliamentary democracy does not seem to be appropriate for the purpose, especially when it has to face the cold, calculating and organized forces of reaction. It has shown that the task of liberating a people from the bonds of slavery demands something more than the co-operation of amateur politicians. The progressive political parties in Spain have now realized that the awakening of a nation is no more than a phantasm, an innocuous product of patriotism, a collective babbling of idealists, if there is no disciplined and invincible force of *action* behind the movement of liberation. Spain's constitutional struggle shows that *bloody* revolution does not lead to the realization of republican ideals. On the contrary, brutalities, illegal executions, and an orgy of violence against the Church have, we believe, weakened the moral basis of the Government's fight for freedom. Brute force can never serve the purpose of a true revolution. The defeat of reactionary forces would have been possible if the Constitutional Assembly in 1931 and the Cortes that emerged from it had acted with foresight and courage. While it is true that governments by the bourgeois majority are not readily induced to take decisive action in favour of the working class, the Republicans in Spain should have realized the grave risk of driving the masses to disillusion and despair. They roused them to expect radical changes in their social and economic relations, but utterly failed

[1] Arthur Koestler, *Spanish Testament*, 1937.

to control the means of production and distribution, which remained in the hands of private enterprises. They allowed the nation's finances to be controlled by its usurers, and turned deaf ears to Caballero's proposal to utilize the surplus millions of pesetas in the banks[1] for public works. While the main preoccupation of the peasantry was land reform, leading to the abolition of *Latifundia* (the system of large landed estates run by absentee landlords), the Government was largely concerned with the problem of conciliating the industrialists and the landed interests. Only after the election in February 1936, about six months before the Civil War, the Government sought to adopt popular measures with some degree of promptness; but things had gone too far, and the stage was well set for an armed conflict.

[1] While production was going down and the country was in the throes of economic depression, the banks were earning enormous profits, as the following figures show:—

Year	*Profit*
1928	83 million pesetas
1929	97 ,, ,,
1930	100 ,, ,,
1931	120 ,, ,,
1932	132 ,, ,,
1933	115 ,, ,,
1934	115 ,, ,,

Part Two

THE INDIAN NATIONAL DEMAND

Chapter Seven

INDIA REJECTS THE IMPOSED FEDERAL CONSTITUTION

I

The Government of India Act embodying a Federal Constitution was passed by Parliament in 1935. In a previous volume[1] I attempted to give an historical account of the circumstances which led up to the Act after prolonged discussion and deliberation over a term of years. There I have recorded India's opposition to the Constitution, which only made certain changes in the machinery of administration, while retaining the irresponsible sovereignty of imperialism. It bore no relation whatever to the demand of all sections of Indian public opinion, and left India in an anomalous position within the British Empire.

It should be noted that the series of Round Table Conferences and fact-finding Committees were held at a time when British parliamentary life was in confusion. The traditional political parties had lost their position, and the National Government had become somewhat like a *union sacrée*. The reactionaries of the Conservative Party, resenting the influx of 'liberal' ideas within their ranks, fought the Government policy, and succeeded in curbing the enthusiasm of its supporters. The Act emerged as an elaborate contrivance ingeniously provided with "safeguards and special responsibilities." The National Government assured the militant Conservatives that the fundamental position of Great Britain in India was secure, that the Act was an "experiment," and that the Constitution was based upon a compromise, without any risk of derogation of the British Sovereignty in India. From its very inception, the federal scheme thus carried with it the germs of its destruction. Not only did it deny India the status of a

[1] *The Making of Federal India*. James Nisbet & Co., 1936.

free nation, but it sought to effect a constitutional settlement by holding Round Table Conferences with members mostly drawn from the ranks of those who had such vested interests in India as require to be protected and consolidated by a powerful bureaucracy.

Perhaps one significant outcome of the interminable examination of Indian Constitutional proposals by the Imperial Government was that all sections of organized public opinion in India were cured of their illusion of attaining Dominion status through the Government of India Act, 1935. The Congress and other minor political parties favoured the procedure of Round Table Conference on the understanding that Dominion status was to be the basis of the Indian Constitution, but they observed that the expression "Dominion status" was scrupulously avoided in the conferences and committees, and in any pronouncement of His Majesty's Government subsequent to the statement of Lord Irwin (now Lord Halifax) in 1929, declaring that status to be the goal of British policy in India. The Act contained no reference to Dominion status. As a matter of fact, it was held by a large section of the British public that "not within humanly measurable distance of time could India attain Dominion status." The Indian nationals, irrespective of class or community, realized that the reins of political power must be seized through their own struggle for freedom. Sovereign independence is derived from the people, and political sovereignty can never be a gift: it has to be gained through struggle.

The inevitable result of the rejection of India's demand for a Constitution based even upon the status of a Dominion was that the Indian National Congress began to receive fresh recruits from all classes and committees. The swing of the political pendulum went against the Liberals and other sectarian parties, and the Government of India decided to revive not only the Ordinances of Lord Irwin, which were suspended for a few months of truce between the Viceroy and Gandhi, but also to issue a new series, in order to combat the increasing strength of the Congress.

But the Government of India underestimated the power and prestige of the Congress, which had not only advanced its demand for independence and for the right of the Indian people to frame their own Constitution without the interference of any external authority, but had taken steps to organize the masses. Under the stimulus of the Ordinances the entire National Movement acquired strength and courage to face the obstinate resistance of the Imperial power. When the time came for contesting the provincial elections under the new Constitution, it was shown that the Congress did not lack the dynamic force necessary to overcome both the weight of bureaucracy and the virulence of communalism.

Within the framework of the single Act there are provisions for both Federal structure and provincial Autonomy. Although they were interdependent, the reconstruction of the bureaucratic Central Government was postponed. Meanwhile certain administrative and legislative changes warranted by the introduction of provincial Autonomy were effected in 1936, and, as a result of the elections, seven out of eleven provinces returned the nominees of the Indian National Congress, and in two Provinces there was a Congress coalition. The Congress candidates, in fighting the provincial elections, openly avowed that the policy of the Congress was to oppose and combat the new Constitution.

Although the substance of power now vested in the provincial legislatures and executives was more real than that of the past, the Congress members realized that without popular control over the Federal centre the powers of provincial Autonomy would be reduced to non-essentials. But the Government hoped that the "pull of political office" would be more compelling than the adherence to the Congress ideals, and, indeed, interpreted the participation of the Congress in provincial elections as a surrender of its avowed policy of repudiation of the Government of India Act, 1935. However, the debates in the Assemblies of these Provinces under the Congress ministries showed unanimity in their opposition to the federal scheme. The Congress has no quarrel with a federal form of government. What is demanded is a genuine federation, in which sovereignty resides in the combined grouping of all units. In other words, the Federation must be national. Only a national Federation can conjure up forces for Indian unity.

The success of the Congress was, however, beyond the speculations of the Imperial Government; it had counted upon the strength of moderate political parties, and had hoped that the corroding influence of the religio-political strife which was so manifest in the Round Table Conferences would tend to foster partisanship. They failed to understand that the ferment of the national movement, working for over half a century, had developed unity of purpose, and that any status of India other than that of a sovereign independent State was manifestly impossible in the third decade of the twentieth century.

The results of the provincial elections made the Imperial Government cautious in taking a step towards inaugurating Federation which was to it nothing more than a device for strengthening its hold on India. The predominance of the Congress Party in the Federal Legislature would create a situation entirely different from that envisaged by the framers of the Constitution. The Congress might successfully break through all the reactionary buttresses designed by the Act. Since forewarned was forearmed, it was clear that the policy of the Delhi-Simla Coup was to "wait and see." The sterile effort to reconcile the basic concept of genuine federalism with mediaeval and feudal structures enshrined in the Indian States was then continued as a convenient plea for gaining time in bringing the Act to a logical conclusion. The Government knew from its past experience how Indian political parties reacted to the weariness arising from time-lag, and how disruptive hidden forces were likely to appear in the field of political struggle and succeed in creating confusion.

But the imposition of a Federal Constitution, cast in a mould suited to the Imperial Government, constitutes a negation of India's political freedom, and therefore all sections of organized public opinion are unanimous in condemning the proposed Federal scheme. It is this unanimity of opinion on fundamental issues that distinguishes the main currents of Indian political thought of to-day from those of the past. The fact that Parliament could ignore the opposition of all political parties in India is in itself a proof of Great Britain's determination to keep India under her tutelage. In the second Round Table Conference Gandhi declared that the mechanism of the Constitution as devised by the Imperial Government would only tighten the bonds which held India in subjection to imperialistic domination. A greater part of his countrymen now realize the truth of this declaration, and their unbending resolution to reject concessions which are only of momentary value and to secure freedom is becoming manifest. That Indian Federation is only a step towards Dominion status, as defined by the Statute of Westminster—that make-believe so dear to Indian Liberals—deludes no one. Even the National Liberal Federation is beginning to express doubts as to whether the Constitutional "gifts" offered by the Imperial Government will lead to the status of a sovereign State providing at the initial stage sufficient internal cohesion and organic strength between the federating units. The Liberals now protest against the "purdah" negotiations between the British Government and the Indian Princes, and realize the necessity of revising the Federal scheme drawn by the Government of India Act, 1935. The Moslem League has also raised its voice in protest, and regards the scheme as "a monstrous political fraud."

The Indian National Congress, the foremost political organization, has consistently declared that the Federal Constitution, as embodied in the Government of India Act, 1935, is wholly unacceptable to India, and that a Constituent Assembly "completely free from Imperialist influences" has alone the right to choose the Constitution India needs. In other words, India asserts her sovereign right not merely to determine the form and functions of the Government which is an essential instrument of the State, but also to change the character of the State itself. The result of the election was, indeed, "a plebiscite against the Constitution." "If there is any meaning in democracy," declared Jawaharlal Nehru, "then the Indian people have spoken so that even the dead might hear, and they proclaim that they will not have this Constitution."

The State is a political entity which is indivisible and immutable, and its sovereignty is by far its most essential feature. The struggle between Great Britain and India thus resolves itself into a struggle for the possession of sovereignty. We recognize that the Federal Constitution as devised by the Imperial Government does not in any way affect the character of the State, and that the changes to be effected in its government do not alter the location of sovereignty.

Willoughby expresses this idea in clear terms: "The one characteristic that is essential to the State, and serves to distinguish it *in toto genere* from all other human associations, is its possession of political sovereignty. By political sovereignty is meant, on the one hand, complete freedom from the legal control of any other power whatsoever, and, on the other hand, absolute and exclusive control over the legal rights and obligations of its citizens individually considered or grouped into larger or small associations."[1]

Thus the basis of our national demand is the inalienable political sovereignty of India. Her legislatures must acquire sovereign legislative power, and her allegiance to Great Britain must be based upon a settlement which recognizes unreservedly the principle that political sovereignty comes from the people. It is therefore not a question of better government, but of national government. Nor are we now concerned with the merits of different forms of government or of divergent ideologies. So long as the present ill-defined status continues, there can be no peace with India, and she will drift further apart from Great Britain.

The demand of the Indian National Congress is explicit in the following resolution, passed at the Haripura Session (1938) of the Congress:

> "The Congress has rejected the new Constitution and declared that a Constitution for India which can be accepted by the people must be based on independence, and can only be framed by the people themselves by means of a Constituent Assembly, without interference by any foreign authority. Adhering to this policy of rejection, the Congress has, however, permitted the formation in provinces of Congress Ministries with a view to strengthen the position of the Congress in its struggle for independence. In regard to the proposed Federation, no such considerations apply even provisionally or for a period, and the imposition of this Federation will do grave injury to India and tighten the bonds which hold her in subjection to imperialist domination. This scheme of Federation excludes from the sphere of responsibility vital functions of government.
>
> "The Congress is not opposed to the idea of Federation; but a real Federation must, even apart from the question of responsibility, consist of free units enjoying more or less the same measure of freedom and civil liberty, and representation by democratic process of election. The Indian States participating in the Federation should approximate to the

[1] W. W. Willoughby, *The American Constitutional System.*

provinces in the establishment of representative institutions and responsible Government, civil liberties, and method of election to the Federal Houses. Otherwise the Federation as it is now contemplated, will, instead of building up Indian unity, encourage separatist tendencies and involve the states in internal and external conflicts.

"The Congress therefore reiterates its condemnation of the proposed Federal Scheme and calls upon the provincial and local Congress Committees and the people generally, as well as the provincial Governments and Ministries, to prevent its inauguration. In the event of an attempt being made to impose it, despite the declared will of the people, such an attempt must be combated in every way, and the provincial Governments and Ministries must refuse to co-operate with it. In case such a contingency arises, the All-India Congress Committee is authorized and directed to determine the line of action to be pursued in this regard."

Yet in the face of this opposition to the imposed Constitution, the Viceroy continues to express his profound belief in the Federal Scheme, and the satellites of British bureaucracy agree among themselves that the repudiation of a Constitution evolved by the genius of the Imperial race, after protracted consideration, by "the mobs of India," should not be taken seriously. With that arrogant attitude towards Indian opinion, it is held "that the principles upon which the Act is based are not only inherently sound, but in harmony with the requirements of India. . . ."[1]

II

We reject the Federal Constitution not only because it does not meet the requirements of the changing needs of our national life, but because it does not endow the people with political authority. After all, to quote a penetrating remark of Lassalle, "The real Constitution is the actual relationships of power." Under the Federal Constitution the ultimate power—that is, law, force, sovereignty, all these attributes of a State—is vested in the Imperial Government.

It is of course true that certain concessions have been made to

[1] L. F. Rushbrook Williams, *What About India?* 1939.

Indians in the sphere of provincial autonomy; but a critical analysis of the Act would show that, if the Imperial Government have yielded on non-essentials, they have taken much care to strengthen their hold on essentials. Referring to the long-drawn-out controversy on Indian constitutional reform, a distinguished American correspondent in London wrote: "England's ruling classes are running true to form in giving their enemies a taste of power. England has once more used her familiar formula of surrendering the semblance of power in order to keep the reality in her own hands."[1]

But our opposition is not merely to the Federal Constitution and the structure it proposes to introduce in the machinery of the Government. In the first place, the Indian National Congress challenges the validity of the principle of framing the Constitution without a Constituent Assembly. The constitution which has received no sanction from the great majority of the people destined to live under it is like a house divided against itself. It cannot stand. It is a negation of democracy. "It is fixed as an obstinate principle in our rulers' minds," writes Mr. H. N. Brailsford, the eminent British publicist, "that God's Englishman must plan the house in which Indians are to live. Our Civil Servants will do the drafting. Our Parliament, clause by clause, will debate the Bill. The votes of white men responsible to the electors of Govan and Clapham and Cardiff will decide whether India shall have two chambers or one, a wide or a propertied franchise. . . . It is too late in the day for us to play Providence to this awakened nation. Indians will not submit to our paternal authority. They stand for 'self-determination'—the right to choose for themselves the type of government under which they shall rule themselves."

Secondly, constitutional independence such as we strive for is not an end but an indispensable means to the rational approach towards progressive adjustments in India's socio-economic relations. Without it we cannot succeed in tempering the rigidity of archaic social life and extricate ourselves from insufferable economic bondage. The imperial domination disturbed and finally destroyed the entire basis of socio-economic life and created disequilibrium in the field of production. The balance between agriculture and manufacturing industry was upset, and

[1] See *We Saw it Happen*, by Mr. Ferdinand Kuhn, 1937.

the handloom and the spinning-wheel, which were, as Marx puts it, "the pivots of the social structure," received a set-back. We are becoming conscious of the fact that unless the basic structure of our economic life is altered, democracy cannot function, and that British Imperialism will frustrate all chances of democracy in India. We realize also that the restriction of the range of Imperialism is a positive contribution towards world peace.

Thirdly, the particular variety of federation which the Act proposes to establish in India is not a true federation, but an ingenious constitutional device for impeding the growth of nationalism. It strengthens British Imperialism, stabilizes the autocratic and mediaeval Indian States, and encourages sectional interests. It does not in any sense recognize the sovereignty of the Indian people. That the Imperial Government, so accustomed to a centralized bureaucratic régime, should now be seriously concerned for the inauguration of a genuine federal structure in India evokes in us a mood of suspicion. We apprehend that behind the mask of formal unity displayed by this federalism there lurks the danger of aggravating the tendency toward separatism whose further development would be a menace to the organic unity of the Indian peoples. The growth of that unity is a reality; for, in spite of our communal differences, we are beginning to realize that the circumstances which separate us as communities are less effective to-day than those which unite us as Indians. And the present status of the Indian National Congress and the growth of mass movement, encourage us to believe that the problem of India, *considered as a whole*, would be a thousand times clearer than the problem of any communal and sectional interests.

We are not concerned here with the intricacies of the Federal Act, but the reasons for the universal condemnation of the proposal in India may be summed up as follows:

(1) The Act reasserts and consolidates the sovereignty of the Imperial Parliament and avoids any reference even to Dominion Status. Although the Act repealed the constitutional measure enacted in 1919, it retained its preamble, which declared nothing more than "the gradual development of self-governing institutions." This "legislative monstrosity" is truly likened unto "the preservation of the smile of the Cheshire cat after its disappearance."

(2) While in theory Federal Legislatures are responsible to the Executive through various ingenious and intricate devices, the Act empowers the Governor-General with authority similar to that of the head of a totalitarian State; and since it means the dictatorship of an alien government, not only does the Act assume an undemocratic character, but it perpetuates India's bondage to the Empire. Under the Act, the Governor-General has:

(*a*) Absolute control of Defence, Foreign Affairs, Currency, and Ecclesiastical matters, and of the Administrations of "Excluded Areas."
(*b*) Power to veto Bills passed by the Legislature.
(*c*) Power to withhold certain Bills from being introduced.
(*d*) Power to reserve a Bill for the signification of the King's pleasure.
(*e*) Power to veto financial decisions of the Legislatures.
(*f*) Power to issue Ordinances.
(*g*) Power to make laws independently of the Legislatures.
(*h*) Power to arrest discussion of any measure in the Legislatures.
(*i*) Power to act in defiance of the vote of the Legislatures.
(*j*) Power to suspend any part or the whole of the Constitution.

(3) The restrictions imposed upon even undemocratic legislatures are of absolute character, and can never be reconciled with the sentiments often expressed by responsible British politicians, that the Act would be a step towards the attainment of Dominion Status. No legislative action is possible without the previous sanction of the Governor-General or Governor. The Report of the Statutory Commission recommended that "the new Constitution should, as far as possible, contain within itself provision for its own development and that it should not lay down too rigid and uniform a plan, but should allow for natural growth and diversity." But this pious wish was not fulfilled! Introducing the Government of India Bill in the House of Commons, the Secretary of State for India (Sir Samuel Hoare) assured the Members that "this Constitution is a rigid Constitution and it can only be amended by future Acts of Parliament." All matters affecting the supremacy of Parliament over India are definitely

beyond the scope of Indian legislatures; nor may these bodies "alter, except as specifically provided, the Act itself, or any Order-in-Council under it, or any rules made under it by the Secretary of State, the Governor-General, or a Governor in his *discretion or in his individual judgment.*"[1] In addition to these limitations to legislative powers, the introduction of financial Bills, matters relating to Indian fiscal policy, the repealing of Ordinances, and other issues which involve the maintenance of law and order, require the prior sanction of the Governor-General or the Governor. We note also that the system of dual government known as dyarchy which produced so much chaos under the Government of India Act of 1919 is deliberately installed in the Federal structure.

(4) The Act retains the powers of the bureaucracy in a new guise as an essential co-ordinating authority of federating units. "We record our conviction," declare the Joint Select Committee, "that the existence of an authority in India armed with adequate powers, able to hold the scales evenly between conflicting interests . . . will be as necessary in the future as experience has proved it to be in the past." Therefore, it should be obvious that there can be no healthy development of the party system on national lines which may reconcile conflicting interests, and that the responsibility of holding the scales between them by an alien Government can be fruitful only in the direction of elaborating its Machiavellian designs.

(5) As regards the structures of the Federal legislatures to be set up by the Act, they are incompatible with any concept of democratic government. The Indian Princes are given the right to nominate one-third of the Lower House (125 out of 375) and 40 *per cent* of the Upper House (104 out of 260 members) of the Federal Legislatures. While their accession to the Federation is voluntary, the condition precedent to the inauguration of the Federal structure is that not less than half of the 104 seats of the Council of State must be filled by them. Since these representatives of the Indian States would not be chosen by the people, they would certainly add to the *bloc* of reactionary elements within the legislatures.

(6) On the plea of protecting the Moslem minority, the Constitution retains the communal electorate, with the result that

[1] Keith, *A Constitutional History of India*, 1936.

492 seats out of a total of 1,585 seats in the Provincial Assemblies are such that only Mohammedans can contest them and only Mohammedans can vote for them. This is a serious feature of the Constitution;[1] it is a negation of democracy, and disastrous to the realization of our ideal of unity and liberation. It would tend to aggravate the religious and social differences between the two great communities of India, and would certainly offer an interested third party a tempting opportunity of playing on their religious susceptibilities.

Ever since the introduction of communal representation by means of separate electorates in the Morley-Minto Reforms (1906), the Government have succeeded in intensifying antagonism between various Indian communities. It is common knowledge that the franchise policy thus introduced into Indian polity cuts across the whole principle of representative government. Yet the Government of India Act (1935) retains and extends the system both in the Federal and Provincial spheres.

(7) Under the Act, over three-fourths of the revenues of the Federal Government will be administered by the Governor-General, and the Federal Legislature will have no control over them. Defence would absorb over 60 per cent of Federal expenditure, and it is scheduled as one of the reserved items. In what sense could the Federal Legislature be regarded as a responsible body when military expenditure, salaries, and pensions of the Civil Service, charges on the public debt, and currency remain outside its control? Apart from these non-votable budget items, which cover nearly 80 per cent of the annual Federal expenditure, the Governor-General has the right of disallowing any decision of the Legislature in respect of the remaining 20 per cent. Similar provisions are imposed upon the concurrent provincial sphere.

(8) Then there are statutory provisions relating to commerce and industry which would certainly be applied to the maintenance of the predominant interests of British Imperialism. On both political and economic grounds, India cannot accept the principle of Imperial preference. The Ottawa Agreements (1932) had not proved advantageous to her industries, which needed

[1] "India's electoral arrangements make her Parliaments rather resemble a series of Mappin Terraces (of the London Zoo), where each species has its assigned habitat," writes Edward Thompson. (*Enlist India for Freedom!* Gollancz, 1940.)

protective tariffs; on the contrary, they handicapped India in the matter of arriving at satisfactory trade agreements with countries outside the Empire. Under the Federal Act, the interests of Indian commercial enterprises are made subservient to those of the British. The development of a mercantile marine is, for example, a necessity for India's economic welfare; but restric*tions imposed by the Government of India Act are obviously* designed to perpetuate the virtual monopoly now enjoyed by British shipping companies. The truth is that the British Government in India has the difficult task of reconciling the two quite incompatible objectives, namely, maintaining the interests of British trade there, and governing the country in the interests of its people. One of the special responsibilities of the Governor-General is to interfere in such measures as are likely to injure British commercial and industrial interests in India, but at the same time we are assured that he should be empowered to do all he can to further the economic interests of India. That these two policies cannot be reconciled is obvious to those who understand the purpose of British rule in India. The army of occupation, the maintenance of semi-feudal Indian States, the strengthening of the "steel frame" of Imperial services, the introduction of the system of communal electorate under the plea of protecting the minorities—all these are the accessories of the central policy of holding India for the benefit of Imperial interests.

(9) We have already mentioned that the Act does not provide India with the freedom of controlling her financial policy. It *perpetuates her financial dependence upon Great Britain. She is* a debtor country, and the need of capital for her economic and social development is urgent; but she must be able to borrow from the sources which may not encroach upon her political sovereignty. It cannot be denied that British investors who supply the capital in India are generally opposed to her attaining political freedom. Consequently their financial assistance, even for her economic development, is prejudicial to her future, and it is necessary that she should now be able to resist successfully further invasion by finance capitalism. Every loan issued in the City of London is a link in the chain which entangles Indian finance with the British. The allurement of Indian investments is maintained by the Imperial Government with a view to keeping India as a debtor country. All loans raised in the Metropolis, for

example, are exempted from Indian income-tax. Under the pretext of maintaining India's credit in the world money markets and with the object of meeting the financial obligations of the Central Government, the Governor-General is invested with special responsibilities of such wide range that ministerial responsibilities have been narrowed down to the pleasant task of giving advice if and when the Governor-General deigns to consult his ministers. We should add that the creation of a Federal Reserve Bank under the control of the Imperial authorities nullifies even the pretence of granting fiscal autonomy.

(10) The Act leaves the vital issue of defence of the country entirely under full Imperial control, but the costs of defence are charged as usual on the revenues of India. Although all political parties and all shades of public opinion in India demand that the man-power for the defence of the country should be organized on a broader basis, and that the Army of Occupation should give place to a National Army, the Act does not even mention the subject of Indianization, much less any provision for transferring the responsibility of defence to the Indian people. The question of sending Indian troops outside India rests with the Imperial Government, but as a concession to Indian sentiment, it has been announced that under normal circumstances the Assembly would be consulted!

(11) Closely related to the problem of defence is the control of India's foreign affairs. Under the Federal Act, it is to be left entirely in the hands of the Imperial Government. Her relations with foreign Powers are to be determined as before by Britain's own relations with them. India is thus bound by such terms of treaties with foreign States as may be agreed upon by the British Foreign Office, and she has no right to neutrality in the case of war declared by His Britannic Majesty's Government. Nor has India constitutional freedom to dispatch diplomatic agents even to her immediate foreign neighbours, or to carry on independent negotiations of any kind with them. Her political contact with the world is carefully insulated, and that is why there is no diplomatic corps in India's capital (New Delhi), while foreign consuls are permitted only at the seaports.

(12) Lastly, the Imperial services which constitute the highly expensive scaffolding of bureaucracy in India are jealously guarded against democratic control. The Act provides elaborate

safeguards to secure a "strong British element in the services," and to maintain their "sound traditions." The recruitment conditions of service, promotion, dismissal, pay and pensions--all these continue to be regulated by the Secretary of State for India.

We may conclude our brief survey of the Federal Act by citing the judgment of Professor Berriedale Keith on this "great Indian constitutional scheme." He writes: "For the Federal scheme it is difficult to feel any satisfaction. The units of which it is composed are too disparate to be joined suitably together, and it is too obvious that on the British side the scheme is favoured in order to provide an element of pure conservatism in order to combat any dangerous elements of democracy contributed by British India. On the side of the rulers (the Indian Princes) it is patent that their essential preoccupation is with the effort to secure immunity from pressure in regard to the improvement of the internal administration of their States. Particularly unsatisfactory is the effort made to obtain a definition of paramountcy which would acknowledge the right of the ruler to misgovern his State, assured of British support to put down any resistance to his régime. It is difficult to deny the justice of the contention in India that federation was largely evoked by the desire to evade the issue of extending responsible government to the Central Government of British India. Moreover, the withholding of defence and external affairs from federal control, inevitable as the course is, renders the alleged concession of responsibility all but meaningless. Further, it is impossible to ignore the fact that, if the State representatives intervene in discussions of issues in which the provinces are alone concerned, their action will be justly resented by the representatives of British India, while, if they do not, there may arise the spectacle of a government which when the States intervene has a majority, only to fall into a minority when they abstain. Whether a federation built on incoherent lines can operate successfully is wholly conjectural; if it does, it will probably be due to the virtual disappearance of responsibility and the assertion of the controlling power of the Governor-General backed by the conservative elements of the States and of British India."[1]

Yet the Government of India Act (1935)[2] is hailed as "the

[1] Keith, *A Constitutional History of India* (1600–1935), 1936.

[2] The Act contains 451 clauses and about 120,000 words. Several amendments have already been passed by Order-in-Council. No wonder Mr. Winston Churchill described it as "a gigantic quilt of jumbled crochet-work."

final and the most vital" of the constitutional changes, and Indian public opinion is invited to accept them as "the only practicable road to Indian union and Indian nationhood."

III

Our survey of the present constitutional position of India would be incomplete without a reference to what is known as Provincial Autonomy. It is regarded as an integral part of the Federal scheme, and its elaborately complex patterns are woven into the Government of India Act, 1935, to reconcile the principle of autonomy with an anomalous Federal polity.

The Governor's powers in the provincial sphere are as extensive as those of the Governor-General in the Federal centre. The Governor's "special responsibilities" include:

(*a*) The prevention of any grave menace to the peace or tranquillity of the Province.
(*b*) The safeguarding of the legitimate interests of minorities.
(*c*) The safeguarding of the legitimate interests of "persons who are or have been members of the public services and their dependents."
(*d*) The prevention of discrimination against British trade and commerce.
(*e*) The protection of the rights of any Indian State, and the rights and dignity of the Ruler thereof.
(*f*) The securing of peace and good government in the "excluded areas." (These are defined by Order-in-Council.)

He may also issue Proclamations by which he may

(*a*) Declare that functions specified therein will be exercised by him "in his discretion."
(*b*) Assume to himself all powers exercisable by any Provincial body or authority.
(*c*) Suspend part or the whole of the Act "relating to any Provincial body or authority."

With the Governor-General's concurrence, he may assume to himself all powers normally vested in the legislature. He may in matters involving his discretion or individual judgment issue ordinances or promulgate a "Governor's Act." He may withhold assent from a Bill or reserve it for the consideration of the Governor-General or return it to the Legislature suggesting amendments. He may prohibit discussion or asking of questions in the Legislature on:

(*a*) Any matter concerning an Indian State.
(*b*) Any matter concerning the relations between the King or the Governor-General and any foreign State or Prince.
(*c*) Matters concerning the tribal areas, except in relation to estimates of expenditure.
(*d*) The personal conduct of the Ruler of any Indian State.

In addition to these extraordinary and special powers of the Governors, there are several statutory provisions which render the real control and responsibility of provincial legislature ineffective. The British supervision of the machinery of law and order remains intact; in financial matters the legislature is "permitted a voice but no initiative"; and even rules of procedure in the legislature are regulated by the Governor. Theoretically the responsibilities of law and order are, for instance, vested in the elected representatives of the people; but when the question of releasing political prisoners was raised the late Lord Brabourne, then Governor of Bengal, assured the European Association that the ultimate power still remained with the bureaucracy. His Excellency observed: "You need not fear that my Government for the sake of any immediate or transitory political advantage will lend themselves to a course which will involve undermining the basic sanctions of law."

Or, to take another instance, the Congress Ministry of the United Provinces undertook several measures for the relief of the peasantry, which necessitated exploration of fresh sources of revenue. Accordingly, the Provincial Legislature passed the Employments Tax Bill, designed to impose a graduated tax on salaries in professions, but the imperial Government held the view that such an enactment was not within the competence of the Provincial Legislature. An amending Bill was passed by Parliament so as to remove all doubts about the scope of Item 46 of the Provincial Legislature List.

The truth is, provincial autonomy is in actual fact nothing more than a reminiscence of the old system converted into an administration in which Indians have been permitted to take a share. The safeguards and special powers provided by a Constitution framed without a mandate from the people and vested in an alien bureaucracy constitute a gross betrayal of democratic ideals, and are bound to impede the development of true responsible government. The assurance that they are not likely to be used in regard to constitutional activities deceives no one, and only those who have made an honest effort to work under the new Provincial Constitution can judge the extent to which these safeguards have nullified autonomy. It is like the story of a blind man who married a shrew. His parents chose to call her a rose, but their blind son replied, "I am no judge of colours; she may be a rose, for I feel the thorns daily."

The provincial elections under the new Constitution, to which we have already referred, threw much light on the position of the Indian National Congress *vis-à-vis* the reactionary forces. In April 1936, the Congress met in Lucknow and recorded the unanimous resolution rejecting the imposed Constitution but decided to contest the Provincial Elections, the results of which demonstrated the growing allegiance of the masses to the ideals set forth in the Election Manifesto. This Manifesto was issued under the authority of the Congress Parliamentary Board and it appealed to the voters to return the candidates on the basis of a programme which included:

(*a*) Opposition to, and rejection of the new Constitution.
(*b*) The calling of a Constituent Assembly, elected on a mass basis, for the purpose of determining the political and economic future of India.
(*c*) The establishment of National Independence.
(*d*) Economic measures for the immediate relief of the burdens of the peasantry, the industrial workers, and the masses generally.
(*e*) The abolition of untouchability.

The question of acceptance of office by the Congress candidates who were elected to the Legislatures was debated at a Convention held in Delhi in March 1937, and the decision was taken that it was in the interests of the National movement to accept office in provinces where they had a majority. The following oath was taken by them:

"I, a member of this All-India Convention, pledge myself to the service of India, and to work in the Legislatures and outside for the independence of India and for the ending of the exploitation and poverty of her people. I pledge myself to work under the discipline of the Congress for the furtherance of Congress ideals and objectives, to the end that India may be free and independent, and her millions freed from the heavy burdens from which they suffer."

The formation of Congress Ministries in eight provinces was indeed a move in the right direction; for, by adopting measures that would lighten the burden of the masses, the Ministries had not only prepared the ground for popular support, but had certainly bridged the gap between the people and the Administration.[1]

Measures such as revision of land tenure, a graduated tax on agricultural incomes, moratorium on peasants' debts, adoption of prohibition, promotion of village industries, intensive campaign against illiteracy—all strengthened the position of the Congress in the estimation of the masses. And they would bear testimony to the fact that the Congress Ministries made no discrimination and had worked alike in the interests of the peasants and workers of all communities.

In 1937, the Congress session was held in a village (Faizpur) in the Bombay Presidency. It adopted a comprehensive agrarian programme which included

(*a*) Rent and revenue reductions;
(*b*) Fixity of tenure;
(*c*) Exemption of uneconomic holdings from rent or land-tax;
(*d*) Abolition of all feudal dues, levies, etc.;
(*e*) A debt moratorium;
(*f*) Provision of common pasture lands and
(*g*) Recognition of peasant unions.

Since then, step by step, the National Movement has allied

[1] "It is a familiar sight," writes an observer, "to see peasant Congress workers from distant villages interviewing members of Legislative Assemblies and Ministers and insisting on being heard on particular points. They gather in large deputations in houses of Assemblies; they sit in the galleries listening to the debates, which are now in some provinces carried on mostly in the language of the people." (*The Tribune*, London, 1938.)

itself to the masses and has definitely established *effective* contact between them. In a country where the entire trend of the social hierarchy had been toward the maintenance of rigid class structure, it was an achievement which is likely to play a decisive rôle in India's struggle for freedom. After all, the fundamental character of that struggle is the liberation of the peasant, worker and lower-middle class from the grip of a socio-economic system inconsistent with true democratic concepts.

Within the last few years activities of very great importance have also come to the fore, participated in by some of the ardent political workers of the Congress. These activities embrace such organizations as the *Kisan Sabha* (Peasant League) and the Trade Unions. It is these that constitute the "left wing" of the Congress and it is chiefly through their influence that the Congress is emerging from the narrow outlook of the liberal intellectuals. Through these organizations the Indian masses are becoming conscious of their power and it is widely recognized that the real source of strength of the National Movement lies in "the sum total of activities of the great masses of the people themselves."

The "right wing" of the Congress, composed of various groups of the bourgeoisie, drawn from divergent social categories, retains its faith in liberal democracy and seeks to control the mass movement by advocating measures of economic and social reforms calculated to bring in an era of social justice for all classes of the Indian peoples. They realize the need of overcoming the inertia of the masses but consider that the calamity of revolution can be staved off by diverting the revolutionary tendencies into *restraining channels.*

But it must be remembered that both the wings are in complete accord with the basic ideal of the Congress and that diversity of opinion based upon a fundamental concord in political objective is not an unwholesome phenomenon in a national movement. The Trade Unions, the Peasant Leagues and the All-India Students' Federation are in full sympathy with the national demand and appeal to all radical elements in the country to prepare themselves for a bitter struggle in the event of Britain refusing India the right of convening a Constituent Assembly.

With the growing tempo of the national movement the most widely varied sectional groups are being gradually drawn into the Congress fold. The Moslem organizations (except the Moslem

League), the Depressed classes, the Indian Christians, the Indian States Peoples' Association—all these bodies are now allied to the National Congress. It has a membership exceeding five millions. Its plenary sessions are attended by at least 100,000 people drawn from all the variegated strata of Indian social life. It is not easy even for the sympathetic foreigner to interpret aright the rôle of such a heterogeneous assembly in the evolution of Indian Nationalism. Indeed, the history of the Indian National Congress shows that the spirit of renaissance in India is both co-operative and creative: it synthesizes the forces that touch her life but does not antagonize them; it is through the working of this spirit that the positive aspects of our national endeavours are becoming manifest. It would therefore be erroneous to assume that the Congress was a class organization and irresponsive to the will of our divergent people; nor should we regard it as just a powerfully organized political party. Its influence in National life is undoubtedly greater than its numerical strength and the circumstance of conflict with an alien bureaucracy enhances rather than diminishes its prestige.

For over two years the Congress Ministries functioned in eight provinces where there was a Congress majority in the Assemblies; but it was not long before the Congress came into open conflict with the Government of India. As a protest against the policy of sending Indian troops abroad without the consent of the Central Legislative Assembly, the Congress Party refrained from attending its session. India learned about these troop movements from overseas sources. Meanwhile the gathering of war-clouds in Europe brought fresh complications, and the Congress Ministries had to resign office. We shall consider these developments in the following chapter, but it may be noted here that the blame for the political deadlock is conveniently laid at the door of the "Congress High Command." Our complacent rulers proclaimed from the Olympian heights that the inherent weakness of the new Constitution would be overcome only by the acceptance of the "doctrine of gradualness."

Meanwhile all the political parties in India were continuing their opposition to the Government of India Act, 1935. The situation reminds one of the story of a clergyman scolding his son for pulling the cat's tail, to which the son replied: "I'm just holding the cat's tail, Daddy, but the wretched cat is pulling it!"

To the Congress the issue became increasingly clear. No State can be organically related to the community unless the normal attributes of sovereignty are vested in it by the people themselves. It is only then that the State can achieve democratic conditions and fulfil its proper function. Therefore the opposition of the Congress to the New Constitution imposed on India arises out of the fundamental question as to the residence of sovereignty. The annual session of the Congress at Tripuri (1939), attended by nearly one hundred thousand men and women, reiterated the country's determination to achieve independence and have a Constitution framed for a free India through a Constituent Assembly elected by the people on a basis of adult franchise, without interference from foreign authority. The resolution called on Congress organizations, provincial Governments, and the people generally to prepare themselves for a nation-wide struggle.

Chapter Eight

THE CONSTITUTIONAL DEADLOCK CONTINUES

I

If the failure of the new Constitution to evoke any enthusiasm in India came as a surprise to British Liberals, the fact that the Federal scheme had aroused fierce controversy on detail even among those on whose support the Government had relied was a source of disappointment to them. Things have not run "according to plan" and the plan was to placate the Indian propertied classes, to protect the semi-feudal Indian States and to intensify inter-communal rivalries, so that all these reactionary elements might well constitute a formidable opposition to Indian nationalism.

Nearly a decade passed by in deliberations on claims and counter-claims of various organized interests, while the frame of the Constitution was being hammered out. In the commissions, conferences and committees the minorities were encouraged to wrangle over the safeguarding of their interests; landowners, money-lenders, lawyers, mill-owners and other propertied classes were grouped around the bargaining table, both to protect their existing privileges and to secure more in the future government of the country; the British commercial bodies, not known to have been enamoured of the granting of even a measure of self-government to India, gave their support to the Federal Act on the understanding that their interests would in no way be jeopardized; the Indian Princes signified their consent to lend stabilizing forces to the new constitutional structure *provided* their position in regard to the maintenance of "internal sovereignty" of the States was improved, and their privileges, rights and dignities remained unimpaired; and finally, the Imperial Government was prepared to bring about changes in the character and composition of the Indian Constitution, looking upon the transfer of partial responsibilities to Indian legislatures as the Duke of Wellington did upon the Reform Bill—"ready to take the damned thing, and let it pass; because the King's Government must be carried on."

Strengthened by the conviction that Britain's rule in India had been made secure by a closer allegiance of all reactionary elements, the national demand for a Constituent Assembly was dismissed rather petulantly by the Imperial Government. It had hoped that the installation of Congress Ministries in the provinces would overcome the dynamism of the popular movement, the development of which it could not view with equanimity and sympathy. Its apparent toleration with regard to Congress governments, compelled by the force of circumstances, was not enough, and it failed to realize that India was no longer interested in "the see-saw between (as an American writer puts it) Indian demands and British conciliation."

Meanwhile the declaration of war (September 3, 1939) brought the demand for a Constituent Assembly to the forefront of Indian politics. Two days before the declaration, Parliament hurriedly passed an amendment of the Act providing that the executive authority of the Central Government should be extended to the provincial sphere, and that the Central Legislature should be empowered to enact such laws as were ordinarily within the powers of the Provincial Legislatures. The Amendment was given retrospective effect as from April 1, 1937. And in exercise of the power thus vested by it, the Governor-General forthwith promulgated the Defence of India Ordinance. The Ordinance and the Rules under it came into being without the consultation of the Provincial Governments, although they affected the normal field of the Provincial Legislature. As regards preparations for the Federal scheme, the Viceroy announced its suspension with the assurance of retaining federation "as *our*[1] objective." While Indian public opinion considered that this opportunity should have been taken to abandon the scheme completely, the Imperial Government relied on the witty epigram: "Bad schemes are sometimes successful, but abandoned ones never."

Simultaneously with the declaration of war in Britain, the Viceroy proclaimed that India was at war with Germany. The Indian National Congress at its plenary session (March 1939) expressed its entire disapproval of British Foreign Policy which had "consistently aided the Fascist Power and helped in the destruction of democratic countries." Recognizing that war was imminent and that the Government should not be allowed to take steps which might lead to India's entanglement in a war, the

[1] Italics are mine.

All-India Congress Committee declared (May 1, 1939) the determination of Congress "to oppose all attempts to impose a war on India and use civilian resources in a war without the consent of the Indian people." Whereas Canada and the Union of South Africa took their own decision on participation in the war after consulting their respective legislatures, and Eire, Britain's closest neighbour, declared her neutrality, the Government of India committed India to war without even an informal consultation with the representatives of the Indian people. They had no voice in the gravest decision that can be taken by a nation. Wise statesmanship might have avoided such a blatant and indefensible challenge to Indian susceptibilities; but the truth is that India is a British possession, and her rulers are careful not to create precedents which may be interpreted as recognition of India's sovereign rights. However, in his message to the people of India, exhorting them to join Britain in the prosecution of the war, the Viceroy observed:

> "It is clear beyond any question from what has happened that Poland has had to face the same fate that Czechoslovakia had to face a year ago. Confronted with the demand that she should accept the dictation of a foreign Power in relation to her own territory and her own subjects, Poland has yet stood firm."

Indeed, statements from the British governing class setting forth Britain's war aims seemed to have given the impression that the struggle was for the recovery of liberties of those peoples that had been deprived of their independence by Germany. In face of persistent opposition to India's claim for independent status, such statements become nothing but a cloak of hypocrisy. Therefore the Indian National Congress raised the question of India's freedom to achieve freedom, endorsing Gandhi's pronouncement that "the freedom of India is necessarily included in the war aims."

On September 14, 1939, the Working Committee of the Indian National Congress issued a unanimous statement clarifying its position in regard to the war imposed upon India. It is a comprehensive document which may well be reproduced here in full:

> "The Working Committee have given their earnest consideration to the grave crisis that has developed owing to the

declaration of war in Europe. The principles which should guide the nation in the event of war have been repeatedly laid down by the Congress, and only a month ago this Committee reiterated them and expressed their displeasure at the flouting of Indian opinion by the British Government in India. As a first step to dissociate themselves from this policy of the British Government, the Committee called upon the Congress members of the Central Legislative Assembly to refrain from attending the next session. Since then the British Government have declared India to be a belligerent country, promulgated Ordinances, passed the Government of India Act Amending Bill, and taken over far-reaching measures which affect the Indian people vitally, and circumscribe and limit the powers and activities of the provincial governments. This has been done without the consent of the Indian people whose declared wishes in such matters have been deliberately ignored by the British Government. The Working Committee must take the gravest view of these developments.

"The Congress has repeatedly declared its entire disapproval of the ideology and practice of Fascism and Nazism and their glorification of war and violence and the suppression of the human spirit. It has condemned the aggression in which they have repeatedly indulged and their sweeping away of well-established principles and recognized standards of civilized behaviour. It has seen in Fascism and Nazism the intensification of the principle of Imperialism against which the Indian people have struggled for many years. The Working Committee must therefore unhesitatingly condemn the latest aggression of the Nazi Government in Germany against Poland and sympathize with those who resist it.

"The Congress has further laid down that the issue of war and peace for India must be decided by the Indian people, and no outside authority can impose this decision upon them, nor can the Indian people permit their resources to be exploited for imperialist ends. Any imposed decision, or attempt to use India's resources, for purposes not approved by them, will necessarily have to be opposed by them. If co-operation is desired in a worthy cause, this cannot be obtained by compulsion and imposition, and the Committee cannot agree to the carrying out by the Indian people of orders issued by external authority. Co-operation must be between equals by mutual consent for a cause which both consider to be worthy. The people of India have, in the recent past, faced great risks and willingly made great sacrifices to secure their own freedom and establish a free democratic State in India, and their sympathy is entirely on the side of democracy and freedom. But India cannot associate herself in a war said to be for democratic freedom when that very freedom is denied to her, and such limited freedom as she possesses taken away from her.

"The Committee are aware that the Governments of Great Britain and France have declared that they are fighting for democracy and freedom and to put an end to aggression. But the history of the recent past is full of examples showing the constant divergence between the spoken word, the ideals proclaimed, and the real motives and objectives. During the war of 1914–18, the declared war aims were preservation of democracy, self-determination and the freedom of small nations, and yet the very Governments which solemnly proclaimed these aims entered into secret treaties embodying imperialist designs for the carving up of the Ottoman Empire. While stating that they did not want any acquisition of territory, the victorious Powers added largely to their colonial domains. The present European war itself signifies the abject failure of the Treaty of Versailles and of its makers, who broke their pledged word and imposed an imperialist peace on the defeated nations. The one hopeful outcome of that Treaty, the League of Nations, was muzzled and strangled at the outset and later killed by its parent States.

"Subsequent history has demonstrated afresh how even a seemingly fervent declaration of faith may be followed by an ignoble desertion. In Manchuria the British Government connived at aggression; in Abyssinia they acquiesced in it. In Czechoslovakia and Spain, democracy was in peril and it was deliberately betrayed, and the whole system of collective security was sabotaged by the very Powers who had previously declared their firm faith in it.

"Again, it is asserted that democracy is in danger and must be defended, and with this statement the Committee are in entire agreement. The Committee believe that the peoples of the West are moved by this ideal and objective and for these they are prepared to make sacrifices. But again and again the ideals and sentiments of the people and of those who have sacrificed themselves in the struggle have been ignored and faith has not been kept with them.

"If the war is to defend the *status quo*, imperialist possessions, colonies, vested interests and privilege, then India can have nothing to do with it. If, however, the issue is democracy and a world order based on democracy, then India is intensely interested in it. The Committee are convinced that the interests of Indian democracy do not conflict with the interests of British democracy or of world democracy. But there is an inherent and ineradicable conflict between democracy for India or elsewhere and Imperialism and Fascism. *If Great Britain fights for the maintenance and extension of democracy, then she must necessarily end imperialism in her own possessions, establish full democracy in India*, and the Indian people must have the right of self-determination by framing their own Constitution through a Constituent Assembly without external interference, and must guide their own policy. A free democratic India will gladly associate herself with other free nations for mutual defence against aggression and for economic co-operation. She will work for the establishment of a real world order based on freedom and democracy, utilizing the world's knowledge and resources for the progress and advancement of humanity.

"The crisis that has overtaken Europe is not of Europe only but of humanity and will not pass like other crises or wars, leaving the essential structure of the present-day world intact. It is likely to refashion the world for good or ill, politically, socially and economically. This crisis is the inevitable consequence of the social and political conflicts and contradictions which have grown alarmingly since the last Great War, and it will not be finally resolved till these conflicts and contradictions are removed and a new equilibrium established. That equilibrium can only be based on the ending of the domination and exploitation of one country by another, and on a reorganization of economic relations on a juster basis for the common good of all. India is the crux of the problem, for India has been the outstanding example of modern imperialism and no refashioning of the world can succeed which ignores this vital problem. With her vast resources she must play an important part in any scheme of world reorganization. But she can only do so as a free nation whose energies have been released to work for this great end. Freedom to-day is indivisible and every attempt to retain imperialist domination in any part of the world will lead inevitably to fresh disaster.

"The Working Committee have noted that many Rulers of Indian States have offered their services and resources and expressed their desire to support the cause of democracy in Europe. If they must make their professions in favour of democracy abroad, the Committee would suggest that their first concern should be the introduction of democracy within their own States in which to-day undiluted autocracy reigns supreme. The British Government in India is more responsible for this autocracy than even the Rulers themselves, as has been made painfully evident during the past year. This policy is the very negation of democracy and of the new world order for which Great Britain claims to be fighting in Europe.

"As the Working Committee view past events in Europe, Africa and Asia, and more particularly past and present occurrences in India, they fail to find any attempt to advance the cause of democracy or self-determination or any evidence that the present war declarations of the British Government are being, or are going to be, acted upon. The true measure of democracy is the ending of Imperialism and Fascism alike and the aggression that has accompanied them in the past and the present. Only on that basis can a new order be built up. In the struggle for that new world order, the Committee are eager and desirous to help in every way. But the Committee cannot associate themselves or offer any co-operation in a war which is conducted on imperialist lines and which is meant to consolidate imperialism in India and elsewhere.

"In view, however, of the gravity of the occasion and the fact that the pace of events during the last few days has often been swifter than the working of men's minds, the Committee desire to take no final decision at this stage, so as to allow for the full elucidation of the issues at stake, and the real objectives aimed at, and the position of India in the present and the future. But the decision cannot long be delayed as India is being committed from day to day to a policy to which she is not a party and of which she disapproves.

"The Working Committee therefore invite the British Government to declare in unequivocal terms what their war aims are in regard to democracy and imperialism and the new order that is envisaged, in particular, how these aims are going to apply to India and to be given effect to in the present. Do they include the elimination of imperialism and the treatment of India as a free nation whose policy will be guided in accordance with the wishes of her people? A clear declaration about the future, pledging the Government to the ending of Imperialism and Fascism alike will be welcomed by the people of all countries, but it is far more important to give immediate effect to it, to the largest possible extent, for only this will convince the people that the declaration is meant to be honoured. The real test of any declaration is its application in the present, for it is the present that will govern action to-day and give shape to the future.

"War has broken out in Europe and the prospect is terrible to contemplate. But war has been taking its heavy toll of human life during recent years in Abyssinia, Spain and China. Innumerable innocent men, women and children have been bombed to death from the air in open cities, cold-blooded massacres, torture and utmost humiliation have followed each other in quick succession during these years of horror. That horror grows, and the violence and the threat of violence shadow the world and, unless checked and ended, will destroy the precious inheritance of past ages. That horror has to be checked in Europe and China, but it will not end till its root causes of Fascism and Imperialism are removed. To that end the Working Committee are prepared to give their co-operation. But it will be infinite tragedy if even this terrible war is carried on in the spirit of Imperialism and for the purpose of retaining this structure which is itself the cause of war and human degradation.

"The Working Committee wish to declare that the Indian people have no quarrel with the German people or the Japanese people or any other people. But they have a deep-rooted quarrel with systems which deny freedom and are based on violence and aggression. *They do not look forward to a victory of one people over another or to a dictated peace, but to a victory of real democracy for all the people of all countries and a world freed from the nightmare of violence and imperialist oppression.*

"The Committee earnestly appeal to the Indian people to end all internal conflict and controversy and, in this grave hour of peril, to keep in readiness and hold together as a United Nation, calm of purpose and determined to achieve the freedom of India within the larger freedom of the world."

The statement was unanimously endorsed by the All-India Congress Committee on October 10th, in a resolution which added that "India must be declared an independent nation and present application must be given to this status to the largest possible extent."

II

To world public opinion and to the British people in particular, the question raised by the Indian National Congress—"a body that is able to make or mar India's contribution to the world," as *The Manchester Guardian* put it—was made abundantly clear, although the statement we have just quoted appeared vague and unreal to the rulers of India. "If Britain is fighting to save democracy," writes *The Manchester Guardian*, "and establish a new world order, India would gladly join in the struggle; but, if the war should turn out to be aimed at the defence of imperialist possessions, India could take no part in it. Thus, the Congress invites the British Government to declare their aims regarding democracy and imperialism, and state how these aims will be applied to India now."[1]

But the response from the Imperial Government was not forthcoming. The Viceroy's interviews with Congress leaders began about a month after the declaration of war, although his Excellency saw Gandhi at an earlier date. "As a friend of the

[1] *The Manchester Guardian*, October 3, 1939.

British," declared Gandhi, "I appeal to English statesmen that they will forget the old language of imperialists and open a new chapter for those who have been held under imperial bondage."

The Parliamentary debates on India *vis-à-vis* the question asked by the Congress, however, elicited a few curt remarks, or phrases without precise definition. Lord Zetland, then Secretary of State for India, thought that the "conditions affecting the political relations between the two countries had so far been expressed in abstract terms." Lord Snell, leader of the Opposition in the House of Lords, maintained that "it was necessary that they should not over-estimate the seriousness of the attitude which the Congress Party had thought it right to assume. It was natural that they should wish to take advantage of this crisis to further their own political claims. These claims were not new. They were part of a very old programme and were now being merely re-stated." Lord Salisbury remarked: "What has shocked us in this country is that these Indian leaders have thought fit to use the international situation in order to promote a further step towards self-government."

Here we must refute the charge that the time chosen for pressing our national demand for a Constituent Assembly is calculated to embarrass the Government at a time when Britain is engaged in a life-and-death struggle. Nor does that demand fall under the category of political bargaining. As a matter of fact, this concrete demand was put forward by the Congress in their Election Manifesto in 1934 as the only alternative to the White Paper on the Indian Constitution laid before Parliament in that year. It would be a misreading of the spirit of the Indian struggle to assume that it seeks to gain its objectives by methods not in conformity with the ideal of non-violence (*Ahimsa*). Political subterfuges and evasions, the stirring up of malign and mischievous propaganda, and Machiavellian designs—all these symptoms of aggressive nationalism are held under strict discipline by the Congress. On the other hand, Gandhi's advice to the Congress that Britain's difficulty should not be an occasion for launching civil disobedience is interpreted as being a sign of internal weakness of the National Movement. At any rate, India cannot suspend her struggle, for she realizes that she cannot gain her independence for the asking, or by the mere assurances of a post-war settlement.

But this accusation of taking advantage of the war situation was not heard when the Dominion Ministers clamoured for the full recognition of the Dominions as autonomous sovereign States during the war of 1914–18. Besides, it is in the light of a crisis that one may gain insight into the causes of conflict. If Britain is fighting for her own existence, our independence from alien rule is also a matter of life and death to us.

In the hope of appeasing the political tension, the Viceroy issued a statement[1] which bore no relation whatsoever to the questions raised by the Congress. In answer to its invitation for a clear declaration of British war aims, he announced that "His Majesty's Government have not themselves yet defined with any ultimate precision their detailed objectives in the prosecution of the war," and quoted the following words of the late Mr. Neville Chamberlain, then Prime Minister:

> "We are seeking no material advantage for ourselves. We are not aiming only at victory, but looking beyond it to the laying of a foundation of a better international system which will mean that war is not the inevitable lot of every succeeding generation."

There was no reference to the Constituent Assembly, but His Excellency reaffirmed his belief "in the essential soundness of the federal aspects of the Act of 1935," and reiterated that the pledge given to India in the preamble of the Act of 1919 should make India's constitutional position in relation to Britain "clear beyond the shadow of a doubt." After stating that the goal of British policy was to confer Dominion Status on India, His Excellency said:

> "At the end of the war His Majesty's Government would be very willing to enter into consultations with the representatives of several communities, parties and interests in India and with the Indian Princes with a view to securing their aid and co-operation in the framing of such modifications (to the Government of India Act, 1935) as may seem desirable."

Meanwhile the closest association with the Executive Council of the Government of India in India's contribution to the war effort would be secured by the formation of a "consultative

[1] Cmd. 6121.

group" over which his Excellency would himself preside and which would be summoned at his invitation.

All this, however, was symptomatic of Britain's determination to retain her *status quo* in India. Through a series of crisis-interviews[1] the Viceroy had discovered "marked differences of outlook, markedly different methods, and markedly different solutions for the problems," and, in pursuance of the principle of counterpoise, he raised the communal issue against the demand of the Congress. While the British Conservative Press hailed this imperialist manœuvre as a mark of the Government's deep concern for the protection of the interests of minorities, the Congress leaders realized that their hope of co-operation with the Government was being frustrated by this total disregard of the national demand.

"It would have been better," writes Gandhi, "if the British Government had declined to make any declaration whatsoever. The long statement made by the Viceroy simply shows that the old policy of 'divide and rule' is to continue. So far as I can see, the Congress will be no party to it; nor can the India of the Congress conception be a partner with Britain in her war with Herr Hitler. The declaration shows clearly that there is to be no democracy for India if Britain can prevent it."

The Working Committee of the Congress in a resolution declared that "the viceregal statement is an unequivocal reiteration of the old imperialist policy" and "it cannot possibly give any support to Great Britain, for it would amount to an endorsement of the imperialist policy which the Congress has always sought to end. As a first step in this direction, the Committee call upon the Congress Ministers to tender their resignations."

Thereupon eight out of the eleven provincial Governments resigned, and as no other ministries could be formed, the Governors assumed the government of their respective provinces by Proclamation issued under the provisions of Section 93 of the Government of India Act, 1935. In other words, those provinces are now under the autocratic rule of British bureaucracy in India.

[1] The noble Marquess interviewed fifty-two persons in succession and they included leaders of every kind and calibre. After this, he issued a statement.

III

While the postponement of the Federal scheme caused no heart-burning even among those who were enamoured of its conception, the suspension of so-called provincial autonomy in the greater part of India represented nothing less than a serious political deadlock. It would not look well to go back to the old bureaucratic form of government, and in the hour of crisis even the passive revolt of the people might be a fertile source of trouble.

At this juncture the Imperial Government revived the magic phrase "Dominion Status," and reiterated the interpretation placed in 1929 by Lord Irwin as Viceroy on the preamble of the Act of 1919, that "the natural issue of India's progress as there contemplated is the attainment of Dominion Status." But it also revived in us the memory of fierce opposition in Parliament to that interpretation, which nearly precipitated a first-class political crisis. On that occasion, Lord Birkenhead, then Secretary of State for India, assured the House of Lords in the following terms: "No sane man could assign any approximate period for the date on which we could conceive India attaining Dominion Status. No one had the right to tell the people of India that they were likely in any near period to attain to Dominion Status."[1]

We have already mentioned that there is no reference to the goal of Dominion Status in a Preamble to the Government of India Act, 1935. The explanation of this omission was given in *The Times*. It writes:

> "Dominion Status is not susceptible of definition in a precise constitutional document. . . . Dominion Status has carried so many different shades of meaning at different times, and is applied to-day to so many varieties of government, that it would be hopeless to attempt to define the phrase with common agreement even in the preamble to a Parliamentary Bill."[2]

Now, on the outbreak of war, through sounding Indian public opinion, the Viceroy realized that Indian Liberals had still faith in this "undefined and indefinable" goal of Dominion Status: they only demanded that Dominion Status for India should be of

[1] Debate, House of Lords, November 5, 1929.

[2] *The Times*, January 25, 1935.

the same character as is set forth in the Statute of Westminster (1931) and that its advent should not be postponed to some indefinite period.

But His Excellency was not authorized to make a clear pronouncement in regard to Dominion Status for India, and therefore his statement, already referred to, contains the following sentence. His Excellency writes: "I am convinced myself, if I may say so with the utmost emphasis, that, having regard to the extent of agreement which in fact exists in the constitutional field, and on this most difficult and important question of the nature of the arrangements to be made for expediting and facilitating the attainment by India of her full status, there is nothing to be gained by phrases which, widely and generally expressed, contemplate a state of things which is unlikely to stand at the present point of political development the test of practical application, or to result in that unified effort by all parties and all communities in India on the basis of which alone India can hope to go forward as one and to occupy the place to which her history and her destinies entitle her."

I leave the English reader to ponder over the composition of this Viceregal sentence, but, as Dr. Thompson rightly says, it "struck Indian opinion, after the first outburst of sheer exasperation, as very, very funny, and the air was cleansed by happy laughter."

However, with the semblance of sincerity, the Imperial authorities continued to use the expression "Dominion Status" in relation to the future constitutional development of India, and declared that the attainment of that status would be assured only if Congress and the minorities and the Princes came to an agreement. Thereupon His Majesty's Government would be "ready to consider the re-opening of the scheme of the Act of 1935 as soon as practicable after the War with the aid of Indian opinion."[1] His Excellency the Viceroy modified his previous proposal for a "consultative Committee," declaring "the readiness of His Majesty's Government, if certain conditions were secured, to associate Indian opinion in a still closer and more responsible manner with the conduct of war by a temporary expansion of the Governor-General's Executive Council."

All these proposals, which evaded the main issue, raised by

[1] The Viceroy's Address, January 10, 1940.

Indian national demand, had no basis even for a political truce. The Government are opposed to the idea of a Constituent Assembly because it would mean the surrender of their own prerogative to devise a constitution for India. Should India be allowed to determine her political destiny without British interference, it would mean the recognition of India's sovereign rights. The British ruling class is not prepared to admit such a claim, for the advent of a real social democracy in India would certainly mean the dissolution of the system under which that sub-continent has been a valuable imperial asset.

The refusal to concede such a demand is, of course, natural on the part of the Government. Instead of declaring that it is its firm policy to prolong "effectual control of Indian life and progress" in close alliance with the reactionary elements in India, it poses problems whose real solution cannot be achieved so long as an alien Government exists as the arbiter of Indian destiny; it raises the communal issue, claiming that "the onerous duties of distributing justice" between the minority communities in India rest with the Imperial Government; and they exhibit a deep concern for the future of the semi-feudal Indian States. "It would be honest to say," writes Gandhi, "that the British desire to hold India yet awhile. There will be nothing wrong in such a desire. India is a conquest. Conquests are not surrendered except when the conquered successfully rebel, or when under an awakened conscience the conqueror repents of the conquest, or when the conquered territory ceases to be a profitable concern."

To return to the "promise" of Dominion Status. In Chapter IV the circumstances under which the three daughter countries of Great Britain acquired Dominion sovereignty have been discussed. They have not been regarded in a real sense as colonies of the British Empire, and the relations between their European inhabitants and the mother country are based on what Germans call the *Blutgemeinschaft* (community of blood). Even then they have not been promoted to the status of Dominions without a struggle. Indeed, revolt in Canada preceded Federation; the uprising of the Bendigo miners led to the demand for autonomy in Australia, while the Union of South Africa followed the forcible annexation of two small Republics against their will. Or, take the case of Ireland, as we have seen in Chapter V, the struggle developed into a serious conflict. For over seven hundred years the English rule had created a situation which had to be disentangled, though not by "peaceful" evolution; nor was her present political status the outcome of the "inevitability of gradualness." We should also remember that Ireland's geographical position, and consequently the strategic safety of Britain, were decisive factors in the settlement of the Irish problem.

Besides, it is not an exaggeration to say that one of the keystones in the arch of the British Empire has always been, and continues to be, the most rigid and uncompromising colour bar, and that the theory of imperialistic rule is based upon the myth of white supremacy. The evidence of this may be gathered from the conditions of political and social disabilities imposed upon non-European "members" living within the British Empire.

However, the precise implications of Dominion Status for India have given rise to much controversy. The left wing of the Congress, for example, interpreted *Swaraj* not as Dominion Status but as Independence for India, the view which Mr. Gandhi submitted in the Lahore Congress (1929). It is clear to Indian nationalists that Dominion Status under the Statute of Westminster is not identical with Independence. On the other hand, an idealistic interpretation of the expression was given in a speech at Faridpur (1924) by the late Mr. C. R. Das, who said:

> "No nation can live in isolation; Dominion Status, while it affords complete protection to each constituent composing the great Commonwealth of Nations, called the British Empire, secures to each the right to realize itself, develop itself and fulfil itself.... Therefore it expresses all the elements of *Swaraj*. To me the idea is specially attractive, because of its deep spiritual significance. I believe in world-peace, in the ultimate federation of the world.... The great Commonwealth of Nations called the British Empire—a federation of diverse races, each with its distinct life, its distinct civilization, its distinct mental outlook—if properly led, is bound to make a lasting contribution to the great problem that awaits statesmen, the problem of knitting the world into the greatest federation the mind can conceive, the federation of the human race. . . Independence to my mind is a narrower ideal than *Swaraj*."

Some of the imperial apologists assert that India has already attained Dominion Status in spheres inter-imperial and international. Here the confusion arises out of a failure to understand the distinction between status and function. India enjoys Dominion Status, as Mr. Winston Churchill truly observed, for ceremonial purposes, but she cannot claim the sovereignty implicit in that status. "Why is it," he explained in a speech, "that the principles of government and lessons of history which we have learnt in our experience with the great self-governing Dominions, which we have learnt in Canada, in South Africa and in Ireland, apply only in a limited degree to India? It is because the problem of Indian government is primarily a technical one. In India far more than in any other commmunity in the world moral, political and economic considerations are outweighed by the importance of technical and administrative apparatus."[1]

Be that as it may, India is not lingering on the doorstep of her ruler, waiting to be promoted, as a recent writer[2] puts it, "to a higher stage in the imperial hierarchy." That stage does not imply a break with the political tradition of imperialism. India demands freedom to decide her own destiny and to take her share in the evolution of a new world order. In her case, as distinct from that of the Dominions controlled by the descendants of European races, "Dominion Status" appears as a euphemistic expression of British tutelage. It should also be borne in mind that the passage of the Statute of Westminster (1931) did not free the Dominions from the financial control of the City of London. An independent political status without the full power of economic control gives rise to a chimerical situation and cannot be tolerated.

Whatever may be the future of the Dominions in their relation to the finance capitalism of Britain, India must "cut adrift from the financial domination of the City of London." While fiscal autonomy is the very essence of self-government, it is not merely the question of India's financial entanglements with Britain or of India's power to hold the reins of financial control in her own hands which concerns us. The entire process of the exploitation of India by British finance, trade, industry and administration represents the central concept of imperialism, whose devastating

[1] Our Duty in India, speech, Albert Hall, March 18, 1931.
[2] V. K. Menon, *Why Must India Fight?* 1940.

effect upon our life and progress is implicit in the concept itself. Our struggle is to terminate this association with a system which has kept India in a subservient position, and which devises ingenious means and methods of imposing a Constitution with the semblance of a democratic form but devoid of the basic sanction of the will of the people. India demands the fully democratic method of a Constituent Assembly elected by adult suffrage, empowered to frame a Constitution suitable to the requirements of the country. Dominion Status is, for India, racially unnatural, politically risky in terms of foreign entanglements and wars, administratively expensive and ideologically unacceptable because India refuses to be associated with British imperialism. "Maturer reflections have led me to think," writes Gandhi, "that Dominion Status cannot suit India's case." That is also the considered judgment of the Indian National Congress.

In an address to the Benares University Convocation, Sir Maurice Gwyer, Chief Justice of India, found an occasion to attack the concept of a Constituent Assembly for India. One of his remarks deserves our attention. He said:

> "It is of the essence of a democratic Constitution (and I am concerned with no other) that ultimately, and after full discussion and deliberation, the popular will shall prevail; and no more effective political expedient has yet been discovered to achieve this result than that of counting votes. But it remains a *political expedient* and is *not* to be elevated into a *moral principle*. The democratic machine would scarcely be workable without majority decision in some form; but it works because those whom it may affect are content to live under it, and they will only be content when they are confident that the expedient will not be employed to do them injustice, and because the majority of to-day may become the minority of to-morrow."[1]

We need not pause to consider Sir Maurice's conception of democracy. It would suffice to point out that the fundamental basis of our struggle for freedom is self-determination, which stands as the opposite of imperialism. Our goal is more precious than a "political expedient" and its realization does involve a moral principle.

[1] Italics are mine.

IV

To return to the constitutional stalemate. We have seen that even the semblance of a constitutional régime was suspended *sine die*, and the Viceroy was granted statutory authority, which made him a virtual dictator. The passing of a Bill "to make emergency provision in respect to the government of India and Burma" by Parliament has not increased, to say the least, India's faith in British democratic ideals.

Adept in the art of manœuvring for gaining tactical advantages, the Government of India held out the bright prospect of industrial progress under the stimulus of war, so that the hope of economic prosperity among the Indian capitalists and bourgeoisie might effectively offset the growing strength of political demand. The policy pursued by the Viceroy may be summed up as follows:

(1) To present the organized political parties with variants of the original proposal for bringing their representatives within the orbit of the Central Government;
(2) To start the manufacturing of war material on a large scale, employing the Indian arsenal as well as Indian private firms, and thus rally Indian capitalists and bourgeoisie to the side of the Government;
(3) To strengthen the reactionary buttresses of the imperial edifice in India by all possible means; and lastly
(4) To suppress the activities of the Indian National Congress and allied national organizations.

The Viceroy again modified his proposal, offering to set up an all-Indian Executive with extended powers. New members of his Executive Council would be chosen by him from various political groups, and they would be empowered to act not as mere advisers, but as ministers in charge of departments of the Central Government, responsible not to their parties or to the Legislature, but to him. There would also be established a War Advisory Council on an all-Indian basis containing representatives of the Indian States.

These proposals, and the eloquence with which they were offered to India, left the main constitutional issue untouched, but the Imperial Government declared their intention to allow "the modification or fundamental reconstruction of the existing Act," provided the Indian leaders assisted the Empire in the prosecution of the war. The modified and provisional proposal of the Congress Executive to form a National Central Government commanding the confidence of the elected members of the Legislative Assembly was rejected on the usual plea that the Congress, though the largest single party in India, with the most efficient political organization at its disposal, did not represent all important elements in India's national life. Indeed, the rejection of the proposal of a Provisional National Government at the Centre unmistakably indicates the unwillingness of the Imperial Government to part with power it wields in India.

The truth is that the Congress had raised the most crucial constitutional issue, namely, the transformation of the essentially undemocratic Viceroy's Executive Council into one responsible to the Central Legislature. This elementary principle of a democratic Constitution could not, of course, be conceded by the Imperial Government now engaged in another war in defence of democracy!

Following the development of the war in the Middle East, a fresh effort was made to secure a war-time settlement, and the initiative now came from the Indian Liberal politicians. Sir Tej Bahadur Sapru, the doyen of the moribund Liberal Party, and his colleagues, hoped to solve the constitutional difficulty inherent in the modified Congress proposal by asking for the creation of a Viceroy's Executive Council consisting entirely of non-official Indians. The proposal implied the transfer of the portfolios of Defence and Finance from British to Indian hands, and therefore it was rejected with the pontifical advice, from the Secretary of State for India to Sir Tej, that he should comprehend the necessity of reconciling the policy of the Moslem League with his proposal, and work unceasingly for a united front which would bring the contending parties together.

And so the deadlock persists. The Viceroy declared: "There is nothing more we can do than we have done."

After the collapse of France and the entry of Italy into the war as the ally of Germany, it became necessary to mobilize India's war machine and her war industries. The Imperial Government sent a mission to survey the possibilities of expanding the production of war material. The mission discovered that there existed the potential sources of industrial progress in India, and that she could indeed turn out numerous items of war material which would be needed for the British war effort. Eventually a conference of Empire delegates was summoned, inviting the representatives of the Governments of Australia, New Zealand, the Union of South Africa, Rhodesia, the East African Colonies, Palestine, Burma, Malaya and Hong-Kong. It was termed "The Eastern Group Supply Conference," and its aim was to ensure the supply of the Eastern armies and garrisons by a co-ordinated plan for the production of war material in the Empire, east of Suez.

The Viceroy opened the proceedings by reading a message from the Prime Minister (Mr. Winston Churchill), who hailed as a fresh encouragement this "assembly of all our Governments in the Eastern Hemisphere to plan a more effective integration of their resources." The British Press welcomed this integration of effort as "characteristic of the vitality of the British Commonwealth," and the fact that the Conference should be held in India was regarded as a step towards "a new stage in British political evolution."

But the promise of economic prosperity consequent upon the diversion of the productive energies of India to the production of instruments of destruction evoked no enthusiasm among Indian nationalists. To them this is an imposed war, and the National Congress insists on India's right to carry on propaganda against the exploitation of men and resources for war effort. Following Gandhi's declaration in favour of civil disobedience, the Government of India launched an organized attack on the National movement, and thus the Indian deadlock deepened into a crisis.

But repressive measures are no prophylactic against the determined will of a nation to gain an independent sovereign status. Unmindful of the moral and material consequences of using "the argument of force" in settling the disputes between the Government and the people, a large-scale repression was directed against the people. Once again the whole machinery of Law and Order has been set in motion against the rank and file of the national movement with all the power and precision of a totalitarian régime. The assault is not upon the Indian National Congress alone, but all the reactionary forces are mobilized to control the activities of the Trade Unions, the *Kisan Sabhas* (Peasant Leagues), and similar politico-economic bodies closely related to the mass movement.

The main target is, however, the Congress. Prisons are being filled with outstanding national leaders, and with men and women who were once premiers and cabinet ministers in the provinces under the Congress Ministries. Pandit Jawaharlal Nehru was sentenced to four years' rigorous imprisonment on charges "arising out of speeches delivered by him which were calculated to hinder the progress of India's war effort." Maulana Abul Kalam Azad, President of Congress, was also sentenced to 18 months' imprisonment under the Defence of India Rules. In addition to several Congress workers, some of the leading members of the All-India Women's Conference were imprisoned for refusing to obey the dictatorial régime.

The Government of India thus moved on from confusion to chaos with the inevitable result of creating an unbridgeable gulf between it and the people; for it is an illusion that repressive measures can have any success in crushing the spirit of Indian nationalism. On the contrary, imprisonments, flogging, curtailment of civil liberties, suppression of the Press—all these have no terror for the people. They only show that the inherent contradictions in the circumstances of India's dependence upon British imperialism are bound to break out into such open conflicts. Each act of repression[1] represents the dialectic of the Indian struggle; each attempt to subordinate national interests to those of our present rulers provides a lesson for the masses; and each phase of imperialist oppression impels all the isolated but progressive forces of the country to alliance. The spontaneity of this alliance may well be a preparatory stage to the calling of a Constituent Assembly.

V

By the middle of 1941, the trend of events in the Middle East and the pressure of a great body of public opinion in Britain to find a way out of "the regrettable deadlock" in India induced the

[1] "But let it be granted that freedom may be crushed, and man be so bound down, that they do not dare to utter a whisper, save at the bidding of their rulers; nevertheless, this can never be carried to the pitch of making them think according to authority, so that the necessary consequences would be that men would daily be thinking one thing and saying another, to the corruption of good faith, that mainstay of Government, and to the fostering of hateful flattery and perfidy, whence spring stratagems, and the corruption of every good art." (Spinoza, *Tractatus Theologico-Politicus.*)

Imperial Government to reopen the possibility of a "provisional accommodation." It did not, however, attempt a new approach to the problem and proceeded with the expansion of the Viceroy's Executive Council by the addition of five non-official Indians who were willing to co-operate in the conduct of the war. As a result of these changes the Viceroy's Executive Council for the first time contains a majority of Indian non-official members, but it should be remembered that the Viceroy's Council is *not a Cabinet* and that he can overrule its decisions, subject only to the Secretary of State for India in Whitehall.

The other plan was the creation of a War Advisory Council under the title of the National Defence Council. It consists of twenty Indians from British India and nine from Indian States. The Council meets at intervals under the presidency of the Viceroy and receives statements on the progress of the war. The object of this body, to quote an official statement, "is to associate representatives of Indian opinion with the war effort and through its members to obtain a reflection of the views of local and functional interests, and to increase local interest in war activities."

With these achievements the Government of India sought to create a myth that India was united behind its policy and that the influence of the Congress Party was rapidly becoming negligible. It had hoped that as a result of the imprisonment of its leaders, there would be a feeling of frustration and even discontent within the Congress Party, and that public opinion in India would favourably react to Government's war effort.

But those who were in touch with the realities of the situation felt the urgency of taking some definite steps towards resolving the present deadlock. On November 18, 1941, Mr. N. M. Joshi, the nominated Labour representative in the Central Legislative Assembly, submitted a resolution recommending the release of political prisoners in India; but the Home Member stated that the Government of India were not in a position to commit themselves or the Provinces to any decision on this matter which needed further careful consideration. Meanwhile the war had nearly reached the gates of India and therefore on December 3rd the Government of India "reached the conclusion that those civil disobedience prisoners whose offences have been formal or symbolic in character can be set free."

But the release of the prisoners made no difference either to the policy of the Congress or of the Imperial Government. The decision, declares Mr. Gandhi, "cannot evoke a single responsive or appreciative chord in me. If the Government of India were confident of the full support of India in the war effort, the logical conclusion would be to keep the civil disobedience prisoners in custody because they produce a jarring note. The only meaning I can attach to their release, therefore, is that the Government of India expects the prisoners to have changed their opinion regarding their self-invited solitude. I am hoping the Government will soon be disillusioned." While Mr. Amery came to the conclusion that "there is no immediate solution that we can bring, for the simple reason that there is no temporary interim step forward which does not run the risk of prejudging, at any rate in Indian eyes, the ultimate solution," Pandit Jawaharlal Nehru stated in clear terms that "not even the most far-reaching promises of what will happen when the war ends will lessen the people's distrust of the British Government. It is the present that counts."

As regards taking a share wholeheartedly in the prosecution of the war, it is recognized that in view of the re-alignment of forces set up, first by the entry of the Soviet Union, and later of China, into the struggle, it is no longer possible to take up a negative attitude to it. The people of India welcome the Anglo-Soviet Alliance; they are deeply moved by the heroic courage of the Chinese people in defending freedom; and they are eager to render *real and effective* help to all who are fighting against fascist aggression; but this can only be possible in the circumstances of her own freedom.

The focus of Indian nationalism is thus clear: the Indian people must have the right to frame their own Constitution and their own form of government through the agency of a Constituent Assembly. Only then will Indo-British relationship be real as between two free nations.

The question is often asked, whether it would be possible to find a peaceful solution of Indian deadlock. At present the Indian National Congress and the Imperial Government are working at cross purposes; for what India demands cuts across the whole basis of imperialist designs, and what the Imperial Government declares to be its obligations and duties militates against the goal of India—an independent, democratic sovereign State.

But a peaceful solution may yet be possible if the British

democracy, with a Government controlled by genuine democratic elements in the country, becomes closely allied with the movement for India's liberation. When we soberly consider how the democratic forces of Britain, rescued from the anarchy of capitalism, and India, freed from imperial bondage, might co-operate in laying a new foundation of their relations, to their mutual benefit, it is hard to believe that the bitterness of the present situation will be allowed to continue. The Indian National Congress has, by its declarations, given ample evidence of its desire to establish a close alliance with the democratic forces in Britain. What is not fully realized is that the Indian struggle is not against British but against *foreign* rule. It has been made abundantly clear that the time for "freedom" by instalments is over, and nothing less than India's status as a free nation can ever satisfy the demand of Indian nationalism. By virtue of its position, the Imperial Government may succeed in encouraging sectional interests, and have persuaded some public men to accept the proposal for expanding the Viceroy's Executive Council, a body not responsible to the Central Legislature, and for establishing a War Advisory Council in order to assist Great Britain in her war efforts; but this has not contributed an iota towards the termination of the deadlock. On the contrary, the attempts to ignore the national demand by the gibe that the Congress "has once more entered the political wilderness" constitute a signal for the revival of intense agitation, and could by no means be helpful to Britain at war under the world circumstances of to-day.

I believe that the progressive and democratic public of Britain realizes that in the midst of the present European crisis India's demand for independence comes as a challenge to their professed faith and conviction. Both Fascism and Imperialism are the "conjoined enemies of the spirit of liberty." India's right to self-determination constitutes a demand, not for the assertion of an abstract aspiration of growing nationalism, but for fundamental changes in the entire circumstances of the life of the peoples of India. Indeed, the growth of the Indian national movement has already advanced to a stage when it would be perilous to attempt to ignore its demand, or to evade it by raising irrelevant issues. "To the degree," writes Laski, "that we refuse India what is essential in statehood for her national freedom we impoverish the spiritual well-being of the world."[1] India in bondage cannot make an essential contribution to the peace of the world; nor can Britain's avowed faith in freedom be vindicated if India is retained against her will within the Empire as a strategic and economic necessity for Britain.

The fact that our struggle for freedom is devoid of racial bitterness is interpreted as "instinctive acceptance" of the Imperial Government by the people of India. "The tragedy is," writes *United Empire*, "that there is no real anti-British feeling in India on a large scale. In spite of all the oratorical fervour of certain politicians, the average Indian has a warm regard for the rule under whose auspices he has been safe for many years, and in which he has had absolute freedom of thought and religion—a matter of the utmost importance to Indians. The Muslims are a 100 per cent in favour of Britain and the Allies."[2] Such a statement only betrays ignorance of the tenacity of the national movement in India. It is symptomatic of that complacent attitude towards India, so common among her present rulers and the British bourgeoisie, which arises from the belief that they can retain their hold on the defenceless peoples of that sub-continent by virtue of the strength of an organized imperial bureaucracy.

But the absence of anti-British feeling in our determination to be freed from the yoke of British imperialism is neither a sign of weakness nor a proof of "instinctive acceptance" of an alien rule. On the contrary, it is characteristic of those moral principles to which the national movement owes its allegiance. We cherish no hatred against the British people, and we desire an effective partnership with Britain emerging anew from her present conflict with the Fascist Powers, but without her own freedom India cannot lay an abiding foundation for re-establishing such an alliance. "India wants to forget," writes Pandit Jawaharlal Nehru, "the past of conflict and stretch out her hand in comradeship. But she can only do this as a free nation on terms of equality."

Most of our rebellious Congress leaders cherish faith in the British people, and whenever any grievances agitate their minds they think of sending deputations to England, address letters to the democratic British Press, and there are those who, even in the midst of extreme humiliation, swear by the Englishman's love of freedom and liberty. "Our representatives must go to England,"

[1] H. L. Laski, *The Danger of Being a Gentleman*, 1939. [2] April 1940.

cried the late Mr. C. R. Das in 1924, "and tell the British people that the men on the spot are no longer to be trusted. . . . I refused to believe that England has sunk so low to-day that her sons will form themselves into an association for the express purpose of crushing the legitimate aspirations of the people of India."

Now, this faith in the British tradition of free democratic ideals is perhaps the only valuable asset Britain still has in India. If that lingering faith is lost, if all the features of imperialism are tenaciously retained in India under the pretence of ushering in the "dawn of freedom," if Britain's answer to India's demand for freedom is savage repression in order to crush the vitality of the national movement, it will then be impossible to avoid a major conflict with Britain. Obsessed with the idea of being able to maintain the *status quo* of imperialism in India against the will of the people, our present rulers see nothing inconsistent in their methods of negotiation. To them negotiations represent an effort to have their own plan accepted intact, and if they find that the leaders of the national movement for India's liberation are not submissive to the will of the Imperial Government, they are accused of sedition!

To-day the Empire is engaged in a grim struggle. Although one cannot safely predict its ultimate consequences, I believe that the present war is the eve of revolutionary changes in Britain, and that *New* Britain would be prepared to liquidate the dismal legacy of imperialism in India. It would then be recognized that free association with independent India is essential not only for the reconstruction of Britain, but also for her becoming a true instrument in the making of a democratic Commonwealth of Nations.

But I believe that a declaration *now*, while Britain is at war, of her decision to concede the Indian National demand for a Constituent Assembly would convince the world of the sincerity of her faith, in the defence of which she professes to have entered into the present struggle. The moral effect of such a declaration would be incalculable. It would exonerate Britain of the charge of a blatant hypocrisy, the charge which cannot be refuted by vague promises to the people of India, or by the Imperial Government's championship of democratic claims in declarations, debates and charters.

The latest pronouncement of democratic ideals declared from a dramatic setting is to be found in the Atlantic Charter. It is the Joint Declaration of the President of the United States of America and the Prime Minister, Mr. Winston Churchill, and enunciates certain common principles on which they base their hopes for a better future of the world. Article Three of this Charter reads as follows: "They respect the right of all peoples to choose the form of government under which they will live; and they wish to see sovereign rights and self-government restored to those who have been forcibly deprived of them."

There has been a good deal of discussion as to the reasons why two Governments felt it necessary to make such a declaration of principles at this time. Most commentators believe that the initiative in preparing the declaration came from President Roosevelt; but we need not pause to consider the trend of the Anglo-American politics that may have necessitated such a clear-cut statement of war and peace aims, or to examine the plethora of interpretations put to it. For our purpose it is interesting to note that a large section of the public on both sides of the Atlantic raised the question how would the Charter be applied to India where the demand for political freedom was met by imprisoning thousands of Indian nationalists.

About three weeks later the answer to this question came from Mr. Winston Churchill himself, who stated in his speech in the House of Commons that "the Joint Declaration does not qualify in any way the various statements of policy which have been made from time to time about the development of constitutional government in India, in Burma, or any other parts of the British Empire. We had in mind primarily the restoration of the sovereignty, self-government and national life of the States and nations of Europe now under the Nazi yoke, and the principles which would govern any alterations in the territorial boundaries of countries which may have to be made. That is quite a separate problem from the progressive evolution of self-governing institutions in the regions and peoples who owe allegiance to the British Crown."

While the Prime Minister's interpretation disappointed Indian liberals who cherished the belief that this war was a common struggle for the freedom of all subject peoples, it caused no surprise among the rank and file of the Indian national movement. Indeed, Mr. Churchill's statement clarified the war aims of the

Imperial Government in so far as India was concerned and clearly revealed what British policy stood for when he announced that the Atlantic Charter would be applied to Germany's *Mittel Europa* but not to India and the other non-European countries of the British Empire.

Since a considerable volume of opinion in Britain became gravely concerned about India's reactions to the Prime Minister's statement, the Secretary of State for India thought it necessary to elaborate it, showing why the principles of the Atlantic Charter could not be applied to India's future political status. After characterizing the clamour for such interpretation of the Charter as "a typical instance of loose thinking," Mr. Amery reminded the members of the Manchester Luncheon Club that the Charter gave no indication as to whether India was to be regarded as one people or several; nor did it say by what method the form of government was to be decided; and that the Charter laid down no procedure, no time-table. But the example of his own logical thinking was to be found in his own question when he asked: "Would any one suggest that the framing of any new form of government in pursuance of the Atlantic Charter could take place anywhere without provision for the fulfilment of *pre-existing obligations*."[1]

Be that as it may, Indian nationalists must read with a smile rather than in temper such explanations from British politicians who are myopic in their vision and take slow count of the March of Events[2] in the world of to-day. One can only hope that there are champions of freedom in Britain who realize that by denying India freedom to achieve her freedom, they would stifle their own cause as well as the moral ideal of humanity.

Assuming that the democratic Government of Britain is disposed to concede the Indian national demand, and to allow the representatives of the peoples the freedom to frame a Constitution for India, there should be an Order-in-Council authorizing them to summon a Constituent Assembly. The existing Constitution should then be suspended, and the present Governments, both

[1] Italics are mine.

[2] Speaking about the Indian political situation ten years ago, Mr. Churchill observed: "If I am alone I am going to receive shortly an ally—a very powerful ally—an ally whom I dread—an ally with a sombre title—his title is The March of Events. The march of events in India will be grim and may possibly be rapid." (Speech before Constitutional Club, March 26, 1931.)

central and provincial, should be declared provisional during the period of transition. "If there is an honourable settlement," writes Gandhi, "the Constituent Assembly will meet in the presence of the British, but without any interference from them. If there is no settlement, it will meet after a successful rebellion, in which case India will have made herself ready to face any emergency."[1] It is for Britain to choose whether India will be allowed to form a Constituent Assembly with Britain's goodwill and co-operation, or whether she must be forced to engage in a bitter struggle in order to attain her freedom.

India's demand is not an incoherent challenge. It comes from the masses, who realize that their choice lies between servitude and freedom, and that freedom is more precious than the so-called "Pax Britannica." The workers and peasants are innocent of the malevolent designs and intrigues of sectional interests sedulously fostered by the bourgeoisie in alliance with reactionary forces. It would indeed be a folly to under-estimate the psychological reflex of the influence of the Indian National Congress upon the masses. To-day they are not incapable of breaking the chains that rob them of free and rational existence.

[1] *Harijan*, February 17, 1940.

Chapter Nine

A CONSTITUENT ASSEMBLY FOR INDIA

I

The concrete demand for a Constituent Assembly for determining India's political destiny was first made in the Election Manifesto of the Congress on July 29, 1934; but its concept was implicit in India's opposition to the Government of India Act, 1919. In the preamble to that Act, it was declared that "the time and manner of each advance (towards the progressive realization of responsible government in British India) can be determined only by Parliament, upon whom responsibility lies for the welfare and advancement of the Indian peoples." In other words, the responsibility for the successive stages of development of self-government in India must rest on Parliament and on Parliament alone. As we have seen, the Preamble of the Government of India Act, 1919, which denies the Indian people the right to frame their own Constitution without external interference, is retained in the Act of 1935.

Indians of all political persuasions and creeds realized that the so-called Reforms of 1919 did not contain a vestige of freedom, that the system of the constitutional structure known as "Dyarchy" designed by the Act would be unworkable, and that the promise of responsible government was unreal. In 1922, soon after the inauguration of the Reforms, Gandhi observed:

"Let us see clearly what *Swaraj* (independence) together with the British connection means. It means undoubtedly India's ability to declare her independence if she wishes. *Swaraj*, therefore, will not be a free gift of the British Parliament. It will be a declaration of India's full self-expression. That it will be expressed through an Act of Parliament is true. But it will be merely a courteous ratification of the declared wish of the people of India, even as it was in the case of the Union of South Africa. Not an unnecessary adverb in the Union Scheme could be altered by the House of Commons. The ratification in our case will be of a Treaty of which Britain will be a party. Such *Swaraj* may not come this year, may not come within our generation. But I have contemplated nothing less. The British Parliament, when the settlement comes, will ratify the wishes of the people of India as expressed not through the bureaucracy, but through her freely chosen representatives." Here the *modus operandi* of a Constituent Assembly is stated in clear terms.

In 1924, as the leader of the Swaraj Party in the Legislative Assembly—the then Parliamentary wing of the Congress—the late Pandit Motilal Nehru demanded a representative convention for the revision of the Act and for the establishment of a genuine responsible government in India. He argued that a representative convention alone should have the responsibility of framing a Constitution, and it was this Constitution that would safeguard the rights of the people. His proposal was accepted by a large majority in the Assembly, 76 members voting for and 43 against.

The official response to this demand was true to the traditions of British Imperialism in India. Sir Malcolm Hailey (now Lord Hailey), then the Home member of the Government of India, opposed the demand, and displayed much dialectical skill in drawing a distinction between "responsible government" and "Dominion Status." After expressing much concern about the problem of the minorities, he ridiculed the political judgment of the Indian Nationalists, who thought that "when the day of independence dawned, communal difficulties would disappear in the bright sunshine of the new freedom."

But the struggle for this "new freedom" continued, and a year later the Legislative Assembly again voted for the acceptance of the national demand of a representative convention to frame the Constitution of India. The procedure suggested was similar to that adopted by the Dominions: a Convention of accredited representatives would draft a Constitution; it would then be approved by the Legislative Assembly, and finally it would be submitted to the Imperial Parliament to be embodied in a Statute. The Government could not accede to the demand.

The exigencies of circumstances, however, led the Imperial Government to appoint an Indian Statutory Commission with British personnel chosen by Parliament. Its appointment was a challenge to India's right of self-determination, and her protest could find expression only in an organized boycott successfully carried out by the Indian nationalists against the Commission.

It became increasingly clear to them that the Imperial Government had no intention of respecting the inherent right of the Indian people to decide their own Constitution in accordance with their own needs, and that the Statutory Commission was just another attempt to create confusion between contending political parties. It was indeed designed, to use Lord Birkenhead's own words, as "a useful bargain-counter or for further disintegrating the Swarajist Party." "We have always relied," writes the late Lord Birkenhead (then the Secretary of State for India) to the Viceroy, Lord Irwin, "on the non-boycotting Moslems, on the depressed community, on the business interests, and on many others, to break down the attitude of boycott. You and Simon must be the judges whether or not it is expedient in these directions to try to make a breach in the wall of antagonism, even in the course of the present visit."[1]

The boycott of the Statutory Commission was, however, embarrassing to the Government, for as a natural result the labours of the Commission were entirely divorced from the realities of the political situation. In 1927 the National Congress authorized the Working Committee, in consultation with other political organizations, "to draft a Swaraj Constitution for India on the basis of a Declaration of Rights" and to place the same before an All-Parties' National Convention.

The Convention produced a Report (known as the Nehru Report) outlining the framework of a Constitution for India somewhat on the model of the Canadian Constitution. The Congress, in its plenary session in December 1928, decided to adopt the Report *provided* the British Parliament accepted the proposal in its entirety within a definite period not exceeding one year. Neither Parliamentary Indian debates nor Viceregal pronouncements on the Congress demand held out any hope of its acceptance, and after a futile interview with the Viceroy, Lord Irwin, on December 23, 1929, the leaders of the National Congress knew exactly where they stood in regard to a peaceful settlement of the constitutional issue.

And so the Congress met in Lahore and passed a Declaration of Independence.[2] The scheme outlined in the Nehru Report was now abandoned, and the policy of His Majesty's Government clearly demonstrated that it did not propose to take any steps

[1] Birkenhead, *The Last Phase*, 1935.

[2] Appendix X.

whatsoever which might even imply recognition of India's right to determine her political destiny. The content and nature of her political status must be dictated and finally determined by the Imperial Government. Therefore the *modus operandi* proposed by the All-Parties' National Convention, which was similar to that which had operated in the Dominions, and which did not mean a surrender of Parliamentary sovereignty, was unacceptable to them.

But the demand for a Constituent Assembly for India is insistent, and constitutes the major political issue between India and Britain. It is not a demand that has merely arisen from the opposition to the Government of India Act, 1935. It dates, as we have seen, from the introduction of the Reforms of 1919. The Congress has consistently maintained that the responsibility of framing a Constitution for India must rest with the accredited representatives of the people themselves, and that "any alternative will lack finality."

The persistent refusal of the Imperial Government to respond to the Indian political demand has, however, helped to clarify the concept of a *real* Constituent Assembly for India. It is now apparent that neither the proposal for a conference after the present war, to frame a Dominion Constitution for India—a proposal which is a sop to the *amour propre* of Indian liberals—nor the Viceregal promise to set up "a body representative of principal elements in India's national life in order to *devise the framework*[1] of the new Constitution" would result in what Gandhi envisages as an "honourable settlement" between India and Britain. Those friends of India in Britain who desire an "imaginative settlement" with India assert that formal changes cannot be rushed through in this war emergency. But they do not realize that the Indian national demand is not for any changes or for a share in responsibility within the existing administrative structure. What is wanted is an explicit declaration from the Imperial Government in favour of a Constituent Assembly. A real Constituent Assembly must have sovereign rights, must derive its authority from the people electing it, and must be able to exercise its plenary powers *without any external interference*. There is no middle course for a settlement with India.

[1] Italics are mine.

II

In the first part of this book we have traversed a wide field of inquiry into the working of Constituent Assemblies in different countries. Their convocation, in most cases, was preceded by revolutionary circumstances arising from the conflict between the old and the new régime. Excepting in the case of North America and of Eire, the struggle for freedom had no relation to those peculiar problems that arise as a consequence of a *foreign* rule. None of the other countries we have mentioned was faced with the aggregation of forces that had been assembled by a foreign Power for the purpose of retaining and consolidating its interests. The Constituent Assemblies in these countries were concerned with the issues thrust upon the nation by the inner dynamics of democratic forces. They aimed at the control of the substance of their *own* government.

India's struggle falls under a different category. She is a colony —"the pivot of the British Empire and the brightest jewel in the British Crown." The fundamental issue in her struggle is therefore independence, and the national demand for a Constituent Assembly implies the surrender of the political sovereignty of the Imperial Government to the people's representatives.

But what lessons can we derive from the experiences of those Constituent Assemblies to which reference has been made in the earlier chapters? The function of a Constituent Assembly is concerned with the struggle for power, and therefore, historically speaking, it comes into existence by force, charged with the problem of legalizing the essentially illegal fact of revolution. But owing to the fact that the earliest Constitutional Assemblies arose to deal with the new problems consequent on the rise of nascent capitalism, the classic models on which subsequent Constitutional Assemblies were to be based were of a bourgeois or middle-class nature. They represented the new class that had come to supersede the old feudal order, a class of merchant traders and bankers, with a sprinkling of intellectuals to whom the old order could offer but a limited appeal.

At the time of first emergence of bourgeois strength, during the century between 1688 and 1789, the issue was simple and clear enough. On the one side a dying feudalism, an unlimited autocracy, on the other, the rise of a new economic force, bringing with it a new social order. In the English, American and French Revolutions of this period, therefore, the new, strong and unrivalled ideology of bourgeois democracy was able to evolve, unfettered, and with great rapidity, the new mechanism which was to legalize the passing of political power from a dying to a growing class.

In Britain, the Whig Settlement of 1688 endured, with hardly a break, right up to the accession of George III in 1760. In North America the victory of progressive capitalism over the reactionary feudal slavery of the South remained secure until the outbreak of the Civil War of the 1860's, consequent on the despairing struggle of the obsolete economy of the Confederate States against a more highly developed system in the North, constantly reinforced by the steady stream of new States created in the Middle West. Even in France, despite the local and temporary social revolution of the Jacobins in Paris and a few other great cities of the Republic, the new order secured a permanent hold on the machinery of the State with the triumph of the Directory, a triumph which steadily moved from strength to strength, despite the advent of First Consul and Emperor, of Bourbon and Orleanist.

In all cases the basic formula was identical. An electorate, restricted to the upper class, was to produce a temporary body charged with the drafting of a scheme of government in which political power was to remain in the hands of the same type of people.

A change occurs with the evolution of bourgeois democracy in the British Dominions. The first British Empire had been lost because the Mother Country had attempted to exploit her white Colonies as purely subject territories, unrepresented and unconsulted. From the time of the Durham Report on Canada a new technique was slowly evolved. The Colonies were still to play the rôle of producers of raw materials and consumers of British manufactures, but the lesson of past experience were drawn upon. Limited self-government was allowed, although the existence of such a statute as the Colonial Laws Validity Act shows how niggardly was the spirit in which the concession was made.

Britain at this period could still afford to be generous to her white colonials, both because of the vast disparity in wealth and population between the Mother Country and her overseas dependants, and also because of the virtual world monopoly enjoyed at this time by British manufacturers. With the emergence of the Imperialist phase of Capitalism, however, the entire basis of the position was changed. The rise of Germany and of the United States as world Powers coincided with a growth in economic power of the white Colonies, now fast approaching the stage of adult Dominion Status. The governing class in the Dominions, however, still remained the bourgeoisie, whose industrial development was still financially tied to the City of London. The First Imperialist War of 1914–18 led to an intensified growth of independent capitalist structures within the political boundaries of the four main Dominions of Canada, Australia, New Zealand and South Africa, due in great part to the restrictions on overseas trade inherent in large-scale naval warfare. The Imperial Conference became a sort of Constitutional Assembly of the British Empire, and was the parent of that loosely-drafted Statute, the Statute of Westminster. The Dominions became politically autonomous, but still remained economically dependent. The amicable relations existing between two governing classes of similar type quickly came to an end, however, with the election of a Socialist Government in New Zealand in 1936. The first clash had occurred between the forces of democratic socialism and the now outworn bourgeois democracy, and though the outbreak of the Second Imperialist War in 1939 postponed the struggle, on terms exclusively favourable to the old order, the fact remains on record that the first clash has occurred between the new, rising power of Socialism and the now moribund and reactionary force of Imperialism.

It therefore appears that the era of "peaceful, typically British" evolutionary reform has now passed, never to return. It was solely the product of exceptional historical circumstances that no longer exist. In the future we must look, in these days of imperialist crisis, when the old order of increasing capitalist exploitation is breaking down, to the birth of a new and solid economic basis, superseding the now obsolete forms of bourgeois democracy, just as bourgeois democracy, progressive in its origins, superseded a decaying and obsolete feudalism in Europe.

It follows that the old machinery of bourgeois democracy, the Constitutional Assembly as we have hitherto known it, is also obsolete, and incapable of dealing with a situation radically different from the past. The period of flux of the last twenty years provides the key to the question why the old form of Constitutional Assembly has in general failed in Europe as a whole. The Constitution of Weimar paid no attention to economic realities, and its apparent perfection collapsed before the first onslaught of reactionary forces; the Irish Free State of the 1922 Treaty is rapidly disintegrating into the all-Ireland Eire of de Valera; the Spanish Republic fell before the blows of foreign and domestic reaction because it refused to attempt a serious solution of the agrarian problem; while the comparatively successful record of the Turkish Republic is due to the ruthless laicization of a theocratic feudalism by Mustapha Kemal.

The epoch of imperialist hegemony is passing rapidly away, and a new force is coming to the surface of the modern world—the force of Socialism. The Constituent Assembly, as the emergency device of the capitalist bourgeoisie, is obsolete. It must represent the will of the people, and its aim must be the acquisition of political sovereignty for the benefit of the people. In the form which it has taken in the Russia of to-day, that of government by a representative Congress elected by the Soviets of workers, democracy shows signs of life. There the co-operation of all races and creeds in the interest of their own freedom has become a reality. The sources from which lack of unity and resistance to a National State arise and create confusion have been overcome by democratic alliance between the workers and peasants.

The function of the Constituent Assembly is, in the main, to frame a Constitution for India; but any attempt to produce a *perfect* Constitution, or to elaborate its form with all legal niceties, is to be deprecated. During a transitional stage, when the affairs of a nation are inevitably in a state of flux, it is both inopportune and unwise to attempt anything more than a declaration of the form of government aimed at and a brief definition of functions which would pave the way for the ultimate construction of that government. It is enough if the members of the Constituent Assembly realize that a pseudo-democratic Constitution can never solve our basic problems; for it is designed only to protect and foster the power of vested interests. While the main purpose of the Assembly would be the framing of a Constitution, it would lay down a number of Organic Laws relating to political, social and economic problems. It would be empowered to issue an irrevocable Declaration of Fundamental Rights and would register its decision to protect the interests of all recognized minorities. It would formulate the principles governing India's relations to other countries of the world, and finally it would take steps towards adjusting certain interests which the British Government has acquired in India.

Our goal is to create a State which can be *organically* related to the community; it must derive its power from the will of the people, and it must, in brief, be a national State. The Constitution of such a State should include all the elements that are essential for the development of Statehood. It should therefore be obvious that we cannot have a national Government in an alien State; or a national State under an alien Government. As regards the general mechanism of that State, the Constituent Assembly is likely to be confronted with divergent views and plausible theories. Here the essential principle of guidance should be, in my judgment, that nothing is to be allowed to undermine the growth of national unity. The advice which Mazzini gave to the leaders of Italian independence might well be chosen as a motto for the Indian Constituent Assembly. Denouncing the Machiavellian designs concealed beneath the Federal scheme, he bade his countrymen: "Never to rise in any other name than that of Italy, and all Italy." The argument that the homogeneous character of the population is essential for a national State is not valid; for it is possible to create a multi-national State with a heterogeneous population on a broad foundation of democratic Socialism. That the diversity of peoples is no handicap to the evolution of a unified State is shown by the Union of Soviet Socialist Republics.

We will now consider some of the basic problems that must be faced in India in order to secure a *peaceful* course for the convocation of a Constituent Assembly.

III

In response to almost every argument relating to the Indian demand for independence, our rulers remind us of grave communal differences, which, they declare, would break out into open revolt as soon as the control of an "impartial" Imperial Government was relaxed. We may therefore give some consideration to this problem of safeguarding the interests of our national minorities.

In its present aspects the problem is the creation of the imperial strategists. Since the Morley-Minto Reforms (1909) there has been a great accentuation of religious asperities between the two great Indian communities, the Hindus and the Moslems, owing to the practice of making "a religious belief the cause of advantage in the political field." On the introduction of separate Moslem electorates, an official expressed his jubilation in a letter to Lady Minto. He wrote: "I must send Your Excellency a line to say that a very very big thing has happened to-day. A work of statesmanship that will affect India and Indian history for many a long year. It is nothing less than the pulling back of sixty-two millions of people from joining the ranks of the seditious opposition."[1]

The policy of using separate electorates as an effective counterpoise to the Indian national demand was pursued with zeal in the Reform Bill of 1919, which resulted in the creation of further fissures among the Indian communities. On that occasion the bureaucracy in India declared with one voice: "If we must have reforms, let us divide the voters as much as possible: *divide et impera*." This advice was followed with Machiavellian ingenuity during those years of commissions, committees and conferences, and finally during the framing of the Constitution itself.

Lord Birkenhead once wrote to the Viceroy (Lord Reading): "To me it is frankly inconceivable that India will ever be fit for Dominion self-government." In another letter to Lord Reading's successor, with reference to the successful boycott of the Statutory Commission, he says: "I should advise Simon to see at all stages important people who are not boycotting the Commission, particularly Moslems and the depressed classes. I should widely advertise all his interviews with representative Moslems. The whole policy now is obvious: it is to terrify the immense Hindu population by the apprehension that the Commission is being got hold of by the Moslems, and may present a report altogether destructive of the Hindu position, thereby securing a solid Moslem support, and leaving Jinnah high and dry."[2]

Mr. Ramsay MacDonald writes in his *Awakening of India*:[3]

[1] *Diary*, Lady Minto.
[2] Lord Birkenhead, *The Last Phase*, 1935.
[3] *The Awakening of India*, by J. Ramsay MacDonald.

"Sinister influences have been, and are, at work on the part of the Government; that Mohammedan leaders have been, and are, inspired by certain British officials, and that these officials have pulled, and continue to pull, wires at Simla and in London, and of malice aforethought sow discord between the Mohammedan and Hindu communities, by showing to the Mohammedans special favours."

Writing in 1927, in *The Times*, Lord Olivier (Secretary of State for India in the first Labour Government) observed: "No one with a close acquaintance with Indian affairs will be prepared to deny that on the whole there is a predominant bias in British officialdom in favour of the Moslem community, partly on the ground of closer sympathy, but more largely as a make-weight against Hindu nationalism."

In his book *Must England Lose India?* Lieutenant-Colonel Arthur Osburn asks: "Would the chief of the Indian secret service or political service be able truthfully to deny that his department has never used or condoned the use of *agents-provocateurs* and that he had never followed Lord Curzon's example and 'kept others quarrelling' ?" To a very large section of Indians this is a pertinent question.

With remarkable frankness, Sir John Maynard, a retired member of the Executive Council of the Punjab, writes: "It is, of course, true that British authority could not have established and could not now maintain itself but for the fissiparous tendency, of which the Hindu-Moslem antagonism is one manifestation. It is also true that the mass rivalry of the two communities began under British rule. Persecuting rulers made their appearance from time to time in the pre-British era, levying tribute on unbelievers or punishing with fanatical zeal the slaying of kine. But the Hindu and Moslem masses, before they had eaten of the tree of knowledge and had become religion-conscious, worshipped peacefully side by side at the same shrine."[1]

But all this is easily understandable. From the point of view of an alien Government, any symptoms of unity between the two dominant Indian communities may be regarded as ominous. Not long ago in Peshawar—Moslem city—when the Garhwali high-caste Hindu mercenaries refused to fire on the turbulent Moslems, the incident created a stir among our rulers. Mr. Winston Churchill

[1] *Foreign Affairs* (New York).

once told the House of Commons the policy which the Government should adopt in regard to the Indian Communal question. He said: "There is a Roman motto, 'Divide and rule'.[1] We have unanimously decided that that is an improper motto for us to follow, but not let us fall into the opposite system—combine and abdicate. That indeed would be a great danger and a very great error into which we might very easily fall."[2] Is not there then some truth in the assertion that the lack of understanding between the two great Indian communities has been fostered by British administrators?

In this connexion, it may be profitable for us to turn to another part of the British Empire, where the maintenance of conflicting religious groups has been encouraged under a cloak of hypocrisy. An Irish author observes: "One thing experience has proved, and that is, that written guarantees and safeguards for minorities are useless, and even injure the minorities they profess to protect. By emphasizing the racial or religious foundation of the minority, by emphasizing the antipathy of that religious or racial foundation to the main body, these guarantees help to sharpen the differences rather than to assuage them."[3]

The total lack of understanding of British policy in India deludes a section of Indian public opinion into believing that the British Government may "play the part of composers" in communal antagonism. But it is not clear why they should be regarded as the harbinger of communal and political harmony in India when such a development would further strengthen the demand for independence.

Now, it would serve no purpose to dilate further upon the policy of the Imperial Power, which is designed as an effective safeguard against Indian national integration. In any case, as Gandhi puts it, "the burden of solving the tangle rests not on Britain but on the Constituent Assembly." The problem of minorities exists in most organized Governments, but it does not preclude them from attaining an independent political status. Our task now is to remove such irritants as may have been lodged in the national life through the system of communal

[1] Lord Elphinstone, Governor of Bombay, in a minute, dated May 4, 1859 (about two years after the Mutiny), wrote "*Divide et impera* was the old Roman motto, and it should be ours."

[2] *Hansard*, June 27, 1932.

[3] J. Devane, *Isle of Destiny*. 1937.

electorates. This inherited obstacle must be removed from our political life. The mischief is not irreparable; for there is a significant change in the outlook of the young members of all communities. They are beginning to realize the grave danger of strengthening the hold of an alien rule over them if the path of achieving harmony amongst themselves is to be obstructed by Communal Representation in the political system of India. The old intrigue of bureaucracy can no longer delude the majority of the Moslems.

As a matter of fact, the official creed of the Moslem League is Independence. Three years ago, in one of its sessions, it declared as follows:

> ". . . We want India to be free and want that freedom enjoyed by every community. Our quarrel with the Congress has been with regard to the correct use of political power which is coming into Indian hands. But it (the quarrel) must not be interpreted to mean, as is sometimes done, that we can ever oppose political progress. Moslem public opinion is solidly in favour of full freedom as will be apparent when the time comes. Their quarrel with the Congress is a domestic matter and must not be used as an argument by British imperialists to block political advance. If this is done, disillusionment must follow. . . . Throughout the Moslem world Islam stands for liberty and freedom. Love of freedom is ingrained in a Mussalman and he could neither be intimidated nor be manœuvred into saying: 'Let me and my countrymen remain slaves. I would prefer slavery to freedom.'"

And yet we must recognize the fact that a conflict of communal interests exists, and that it threatens to destroy the ideals of equal and common citizenship in a State. But when we probe into its root cause, it becomes apparent that the basic trouble lies in the maladjustments of economic relations. Communal ferments are usually produced by the oppression of a host of parasites living in rural and industrial areas among the 90 per cent majority of our population. This majority is not as yet fully organized for the purpose of defending its interests and demanding its rights. Most of its members are in a static phase of civilization, utterly remote from any effective movement through which social justice may be secured. They are not aware of the fact that communal cliques spring from the social, economic and political systems which constitute the machinery of coercion and exploitation.

But it is well to remember that the circumstances of poverty and misery have awakened a considerable section of the illiterate mass to a consciousness of the need of asserting their rights. Indeed, one of the most encouraging manifestations of Indian national life to-day is the growing spirit of revolt among the peasants and workers. They are rapidly overcoming the inertia of centuries and are anxious to seize opportunties for improving their mode of living. Once the process of drawing the masses into the orbit of the national movement is further accelerated, the minority problem will have dwindled into insignificance. Once we gain their active support in the national struggle, the opposition of the bureaucracy, with its legions of indigenous reactionary forces, can be faced with courage and confidence. We have seen how the problem of minorities has been solved in the U.S.S.R., by uprooting the economic sources of antagonism between national groups and by safeguarding their rights to cultural autonomy.

In the declaration of Fundamental Rights, emphasis must be laid upon the basic interests of the masses. The Indian National Congress has enumerated these Rights as follows:

(1) Rights of free expression of opinion, free association and combination and peaceful assembly.
(2) Freedom of conscience and religion.
(3) Neutrality of the State in regard to all religions.
(4) Culture, language and script of minorities to be protected.
(5) Universal adult suffrage.
(6) No discrimination in regard to public employment or any trade or calling.
(7) All citizens to have equal rights and duties in regard to State institutions and others dedicated by private persons for the use of the general public.
(8) Equality before the law.

While it is true that Congress has repeatedly assured the minority communities that their rights will be securely protected in drawing up the Constitution of India, it has not as yet succeeded in allaying the fear of these communities. An intensive educative campaign is therefore necessary to convince them that it is to the interest of the nation that every possible fissiparous tendency must be rectified if we are to become the arbiters of our own destinies. The protection they now enjoy, owing to the perpetuation of separate communal electorates, stands discredited because it perpetuates India's bondage and does not serve their *ultimate* interest. It should be driven home to all communities that "the objective of the Congress is an independent and united India where no class or group or majority or minority may exploit another to its own advantage, and where all the elements in the nation may co-operate together for the common good and the advancement of the people of India. This objective of unity and mutual co-operation in a common freedom does not mean the suppression in any way of the rich variety and cultural diversity of Indian life, which have to be preserved in order to give freedom and opportunity to the individual as well as to each group to develop unhindered according to its capacity and inclination."

I believe *definite* proposals for agrarian reform and for the control of usury should be placed before the nation. After all, social systems rest on economic systems. The multiplicity of vested interests in land has brought about inexpressible confusion in the Indian economy, and so long as the Indian bourgeoisie are allowed to create a social and economic incubus the enfranchised electors in rural areas cannot be persuaded to believe either in the Declaration of Rights or in the power of the vote. "Why carry men to the top of a mountain, thence to show them the domain that belongs to them, when afterwards one must take them down and place them in the political order, where they will find themselves limited at every turn?" cried Victor Malouet, a member of the States-General. Unless and until the fundamental basis of the economic life of all communities is transformed in a manner appropriate to our democratic aspirations, the problem of minorities will remain unsolved with us. It is not merely a question of the proper regimentation of economic life, but our task is to *integrate* the diverse and even conflicting aspects of civilization and culture that have sprung up within our borders. We must be ready for a plain and unequivocal answer to the problems of social solidarity, bearing in mind that our demand for freedom always evokes prophetic declarations of the danger of racial antagonism and the disaster of social upheaval, not only from our imperial rulers, but also from the comity of nations. It is now our responsiblity to show that racial diversity can never be a handicap to political independence.

It should be possible to include in a manifesto for the election of the Constituent Assembly such concrete measures of land reforms as would eliminate many evil usages and privileges which are fruitful sources of communal friction. The *real* enfranchisement of the people must be accompanied by certain radical changes in the economic structure, and if to all the communities they become a reality, the clamour for special representatives in order to safeguard the rights and interests of the masses will cease In our communal controversy it is not fully realized that the only thing that matters is freedom—freedom fron subjugation and freedom to pursue without fear the economic and cultural development of all peoples of India.

We are not concerned here with the details of summoning a Constituent Assembly. What is important to bear in mind is the fact that this body must be *national*, and that there can be no compromise in regard to the retention of communal representation which in the judgment of our rulers is "an inherent necessity of the situation."[1] If it be necessary to accept the existing communal constituencies at the initial stage of convening the Constituent Assembly, the Assembly must proclaim the system as a source of disintegration of the very foundation of democracy. It must rigidly exclude a religious nomenclature basis of representation from Indian political life and it must lay stress upon the similarities and not the differences between communities.

IV

Perhaps the most formidable bulwark of British rule in India is to be found in the feudal autocracies maintained by what Lee Warner calls "the protected Princes of India." We have seen how the high priests of British imperialism sought to consummate the marriage of British India with these States under the new Constitution, assuring the world that they were creating an organic federation, to India as a whole. While every possible concession

[1] L. S. Amery, *The Forward View*, 1935.

was made to accommodate the rulers of States within the so-called Federal sphere, both the rulers themselves and their imperial masters totally ignored the people of the States as an entity with a *status quo*. The result is that the peculiar characteristic of this new-fangled form of federation is based upon the States to be federated, and *not* upon the peoples of the federation. Furthermore, so long as the constitutional relations between the Princes and the people of British India are subject to any intervention of the "Paramount Power," it would not be possible to work out the fundamental conditions of a genuine Indian federation.

Although the feudatory Princes are apprehensive of what may happen to their secured position if the principles of democracy become operative in British India, I believe they would eventually come to submit to the will of the people, once it was realized that their destiny could no longer be fulfilled by remaining under the tutelage of a foreign Power. Most of them realize now that it is not to their credit to have to ask an alien Government to assure their power and prestige within their own territories. This dependence is fraught with incalculable peril both to the Princes and to the peoples of the States. When an English admiral offered to defend Victor Emanuel I from French invasion, he answered: "Do you take me for one of your Indian Nabobs?" The King was well aware of the price which the weak have to pay for protection by the strong.

Now, the Indian States distributed throughout the sub-continent occupy collectively an area of 690 thousand square miles as against the 886 thousand square miles of British India. While the total population of British India is about 285 millions, the figure for the Indian States approaches 90 millions. But their classification in accordance with size, population and revenue shows that the majority of them fall under the category of estates. Over 450 of these are each less than 1,000 square miles in area, and only eight States have a revenue of over a crore of rupees. Those States with areas as large as England or France would come within the framework of the Constitution as autonomous units on the same basis as the provincial units in the future government of the country.

As an illustration of the forces that are operating within the States, we reproduce here a resolution passed by the All-India States' Peoples' Conference at its annual session in February,

1939. It says: "It is the considered opinion of the Conference that only those States which have a population exceeding 20 lakhs souls or revenue exceeding 50 lakhs rupees can maintain the standard of administration necessary and suitable for being workable units for the purpose of uniting with the Provinces in a scheme of a Free and Federated India and therefore all States not coming within the above category should be amalgamated, either singly or by groups, with the neighbouring Provinces for the purpose of administration, with suitable provisions for the reasonable rights and privileges of the rulers concerned."

The administration of the States is autocratic, although in some States attempts have been made to introduce a semblance of representative government. Even here political rights are conceded more as a concession than as a just and legitimate right. In the language of a distinguished Indian Liberal, we may say: "Many of the rulers have not yet begun to realize that the Princes are for the people and not the people for the Princes." It is to be deplored that some of the Princes and their councils of ministers have resorted to repressive measures almost identical with those that are adopted in British India in order to suppress the voice of the people. Those who still look to our princely houses for leadership in the making of New India ask themselves if this creation of internal scission can serve the interest of the States even when they are assured of protection by the "paramount power." The policy of thwarting the natural expression of political consciousness is unwise, and will certainly injure the relationship, not only between the Princes and their peoples, but between the two Indias.

The ominous prospect of India being torn into further fragments led Mahatma Gandhi to sound a note of warning. He writes:

> "The almost simultaneous awakening in the various States is a very significant event in the national struggle for independence. It will be wrong to think that such awakening can be due to the instigation of one person or a body of persons or any organization. It is just possible that the Haripura Resolution of the Congress put the people of the States on their mettle, and they realized as never before that their salvation depended upon their own labours. But, above all,

it is the time-spirit that has brought about the awakening. It is to be hoped that the Princes and their advisers will recognize it and meet the legitimate aspirations of the people. There is no half-way house between total extinction of the States and the Princes making their people responsible for the administration of their States and themselves becoming trustees for the people, taking an earned commission for their labours.

"I am responsible for the policy of non-interference hitherto followed by the Congress. But with the growing influence of the Congress, it is impossible for me to defend it in the face of injustice perpetrated in the States. If the Congress feels that it has the power to offer effective interference, it will be bound to do so when the call comes. And if the Princes believe that the good of the people is also their good, they would gratefully seek and accept the Congress assistance. It is surely in their interest to cultivate friendly relations with an organization which bids fair in the future, not very distant, to replace the Paramount Power—let me hope by friendly arrangement. Will they not read the writing on the wall?"

This is indeed a timely warning from one who has a deep comprehension of the entire rhythm of our national movement. Feudalism is based upon fear. Our feudal Princes are not fully conscious of the decay of the system under which they have so long taken shelter, and which they guard so jealously, in the belief that under the protection of the paramount power it would be possible to resist the impact of new social forces. They are ill-advised to offer obstinate resistance to the legitimate demands of the people, and they should know that the only way to avert the cataclysm of anarchy is to understand the exigencies of social changes. They do not seem to realize the underlying motive of the British preference for the maintenance of feudalism. The survival of the fetters of feudalism constitutes a bondage both for the Princes and the peoples. In the world of to-day the traditional feudal pattern is an absurd anachronism, and its retention is derogatory to the entire spirit of true aristocracy. The fact that the majority of the States do not conform to the essentials of a progressive and civilized administration represents a state of affairs which can no longer be tolerated. Nor can the rulers remain blind to the fact that repressive measures will never succeed in crushing the people's spirit when it demands social justice and freedom.

At any rate, the conflict accompanying the inevitable breakdown of feudalism in the Indian States and the growth of political consciousness of the peoples living within these territories are factors which cannot be ignored without a grave risk. The peoples of the States are now eager to take a legitimate share in administrative affairs; they are organizing public opinion in favour of truly representative forms of government within the States, but even now they show profound attachment to the Princely Houses. It is only this spirit of loyalty that impels them to warn the Princes of the threatening catastrophe inherent in clinging to the outworn tradition of autocracy to the advantage of British imperialism. The masses are weary of servitude, but their plea for social and economic justice is still within the bounds of moderation; yet signs of revolt in the Indian States are becoming manifest, and the reliance upon the British military power for safeguarding the interests of the Princes may prove illusory. One is reminded of Mirabeau's warning: "Ah, Madame, if this game of blindman's buff is played too long, it will end in a general catastrophe!"

I am of opinion that the Indian States' participation in the Constituent Assembly may be effected through the Peoples' Association. An appropriate committee of the Constituent Assembly should be empowered to negotiate with the States not represented by the Peoples' Association; but no coercion is contemplated if any of the States chooses to withhold its co-operation with the Assembly. It should even be made clear that neither the Indian National Congress nor the States' Peoples' Association has any intention of depriving the Princes of their privileges so far as they are consistent with India's claim to freedom and with the rights of free citizenship. In the uncertainties of a transition period nothing should be done to widen and perpetuate the schism between the two Indias. While every section of organized opinion in the States stands for political liberty, the Princes themselves must realize that history does not stand still, especially when the people are conscious of their legitimate rights. Once the freely elected Constituent Assembly acquires *power* and consolidates its prestige, it may succeed in bringing about new political alignments with the Indian States. Meanwhile, the elected representatives of the States' Peoples' Association should be active participants, not only in the work of the Assembly, but in all movements for national regeneration throughout India. It is through increasing co-ordinated activities with the peoples of the States that the two Indias must move towards national integration. It is through the accession of strength of the Indian States' Peoples' Association that Indian Princes will be cured of that self-delusion of moral inertia which makes them seek protection of "Paramount Power."

V

One of the essential conditions for the practical realization of a truly representative Constituent Assembly is Adult Franchise. Hostile critics of the Indian national demand repudiate the conception of a Constituent Assembly on the ground of illiteracy alone, and declare that it would be impossible in India to adopt a reasonable scheme for adult franchise. Others raise the question of the heavy cost of setting up electoral machinery, and one also hears the parrot cry that social circumstances obtaining in the continent of India are wholly unfavourable for the election of a Constituent Assembly by a system of adult franchise.

But all these criticisms betray a lack of comprehension of the growing strength of the Indian mass movement. Indeed, slowly but surely, it is the masses who are driving the National Movement onward, impelling it to adopt a line of action which has already prepared, to some extent; the conditions of success for democratic methods in approaching Indian problems; it is they who are making a considerable section of the Indian bourgeoisie increasingly aware of the snares and delusions of British imperialism; and it is their accumulated strength that constitues the real force behind India's struggle for freedom. Universal Adult Franchise is one of the means of mobilizing that force, and of making democracy healthy. "A healthy democracy," to quote an epigram by a French savant (Romain Rolland), "is never better protected than by itself."

Those of us who have had intimate contact with the Indian masses must admit that illiteracy itself is no handicap to their perception of political realities, and that they are usually endowed with a fund of common sense. Illiteracy does not mean ignorance, and the Indian masses are intelligent enough to be able to exercise judgment in affairs that concern them. "Illiteracy by all means does not imply," observes the Indian Franchise Committee, "that the individual is not capable of casting an intelligent vote in elections within the range of his own knowledge and experience. An Indian villager, like a peasant all over the world, is a fairly enlightened person."

Moreover, the Indian rural population is not entirely unfamiliar with electoral procedures; for in the villages throughout the greater part of India the village council and its headman are elected by ballot. These councils, we should remember, represent an indigenous system of local government. Villagers are usually tolerant of one another's caste and creed. Among them, unless it is deliberately fostered from outside, communal antagonism seldom arises, and therefore they would welcome a system of franchise which is devoid of communal bias.

But one must admit that the use of the franchise in a modern Constitution is something with which they are unfamiliar, and the suffrage cannot be properly exercised if they are unable to read or write. Illiteracy undoubtedly fosters electoral corruption, and gives rise to certain technical difficulties in the management of polling booths or the recording of votes. It is undoubtedly a serious handicap.

Yet it should be realized that the restricted suffrage is more susceptible of electoral corruption than the universal suffrage. Aristotle was of opinion that in the majority of cases the crowd is a better judge than any individual whatever, and that it may be conceded the right of deliberating upon public affairs with admirable discernment. He wrote: "A large quantity is always less corruptible, as is for example a large volume of water; and in the same way a majority is less easily corrupted than a minority."

We must further remember that it is for the rectification of illiteracy, communalism, economic servitude and social backwardness that India demands her freedom. The real health of her national being depends upon her sovereign rights to be the mistress of her own destiny.

In support of the proposal for the election of a Constituent Assembly on a very broad franchise Gandhi made an observation which deserves our attention. He writes: "There is a risk always in every big experiment, but in my opinion it is the least in the proposed method. Underlying the proposal is the faith that the *majority of candidates will be enlightened and selfless workers, in* that the elections will be concentrated on political education on a stupendous scale. There is no question of tyranny of numbers. There is undoubtedly the risk of ignorant voters being betrayed into a wrong choice. Nevertheless, the decision will be the verdict of the people. Discussion in the press and on the platform cannot replace the elective method. . . . What is wanted is not necessarily a wise but a representative decision."[1]

As a working arrangement at this stage, the present electorate may be doubled in order to approach the broad basis of adult suffrage. The size and distribution of the present electorate are given in the following table:

TABLE SHOWING THE NUMBER AND DISTRIBUTION OF THE PRESENT ELECTORATE IN BRITISH INDIA

Provinces of British India	*Population (according to the Census of 1931)*	*Present Electorate for Legislative Assembly*
Assam*	8,622,000	815,000
Bengal†	50,114,000	6,695,000
Bihar*	32,372,000	2,412,000
Bombay*	18,044,000	2,609,000
Central Provinces and Berar*	15,323,000	1,741,000
Madras*	45,326,000	6,437,000
N.W. Frontier*	2,425,000	247,000
Orissa*	6,905,000	520,000
Punjab†	23,581,000	2,686,000
Sind*	3,887,000	639,000
United Provinces*	48,409,000	5,335,000

* Congress Provinces. † Non-Congress Provinces.

N.B.—Electorate for Central Legislative Assembly at the last election, held in 1934, was 1,416,000.

I may now venture to offer a few suggestions regarding certain preparatory measures for summoning a Constituent Assembly.

In the first place, a strong representative Executive Committee, consisting of members elected from all recognized political

[1] *The Harijan*, February 3, 1940.

parties and Peoples' Associations, should be formed in each province, and it should be empowered to take such steps as are necessary for preparing the ground for calling a National Constituent Assembly into being. While the Committee must be representative, care should be taken not to make it unwieldy. It is with these representative provincial Committees that would lie the responsibility of settling the preludes and preliminary details. They would draw up plans for the electoral campaign on the issue of summoning a National Assembly, and would set up the necessary organizations for election. The actual conduct of the elections should be in the hands of these Committees.

Secondly, it is of the utmost importance that a nation-wide and intensive propaganda should be carried on with a view to explaining the meaning and purpose of the Constituent Assembly. The Village Councils (*panchayets*), the Trade Unions, the Peasant Leagues (*Kishan Sabhas*), the Indian States' Peoples' Association, the Spinners' Organizations, and all other recognized national institutions, have to be mobilized for this single purpose of making the masses aware of the issues involved in the struggle for freedom to achieve constitutional freedom. Selected workers from these organizations should be specially recruited and trained for the work of propaganda under the direction of provincial Committees. It should be made clear to the peoples that the real conception of a National Assembly for securing the independence of the country, to quote Pandit Jawarharlal Nehru, "is a dynamic one. It does not mean a body of people, or a gathering of able lawyers, who are intent on drawing up a Constitution. It means a nation on the move, throwing away the shell of its past political and possibly social structure, and fashioning for itself a new garment of its own making. It means the masses of a country in action through their elected representatives." What is essential is that the peoples should be made to realize that the authority of the Assembly proceeds from them, and that no sectional interests should be allowed to rob the Assembly of its value and significance in India's struggle for freedom.

Thirdly, simultaneously with the formation of provincial Committees, a National Preparatory Commission, consisting of members elected on the basis of a quota system from each provincial Committee, should be set up with a view to carrying on such negotiations as are necessary for the convocation of a Constituent Assembly. This central body would undertake to appoint, if necessary, any person or persons of international repute whose advice on certain specific problems might be of assistance to the deliberations of the Assembly. It would, in consultation with provincial Committees, draw up a Constitution, together with Fundamental Laws, and determine the time and place for summoning the Constituent Assembly.

Lastly, after the approval of the Draft Constitution by the plenary sessions of the Constituent Assembly, it should be made available in the principal Indian languages, and be given the widest possible publicity through the press and the platform. The Constitution should contain a Declaration not only of the *rights* of every citizen, but also of his duties towards India's struggle for freedom. For a period not exceeding six months, the Draft should be open to nation-wide discussion, and all recognized national institutions, affiliated to Peoples' Movements (e.g. The Trade Unions, the Kishan Sabhas, etc.), are to be invited to submit amendments and addenda to the Draft Constitution.

After scrutinizing these proposals, the Constituent Assembly would proceed with the revision of the Draft. The Constitution as framed and passed by an absolute majority of the members composing the Assembly would then be the subject of a Treaty between India and Britain.

VI

After having agreed upon the fundamental principles of the Constitution of India, the Constituent Assembly should continue to remain in full session for a period during which it would direct such measures as are necessary to prepare the essential conditions of success for setting up the new Constitution. Special tribunals may be appointed in order to ascertain the terms of an equitable settlement with the Imperial Government in regard to defence, finance, Indo-British trade, and other matters concerning the future relations between India and Britain. Admittedly these represent many difficult problems, but they are by no means peculiar to India, and they have had to be solved by all nations in their march towards freedom and democracy.

One of the vital problems for settlement with Britain is the defence of India. Having reduced the country to a state of helplessness through pursuing a persistent policy of emasculation of the people, our rulers find reasons to retain their army of occupation. They argue that without the help of the British military strength India cannot protect herself from external aggression, that their withdrawal from India would result in abandoning the country to chaos and internecine struggle, and that there can be no such thing as self-determination for a people who cannot defend themselves.

We have no space here to expound the deliberate policy so pertinaciously followed by the British, in denying the people their right of defending their own country. It was not until 1917 that the exigencies of circumstances induced His Majesty's Government to remove the bar which had hitherto prevented the admission of Indians into the commissioned ranks of His Majesty's Army. Until then only the "Viceroy's Commission" was thrown open to Indian soldiers, although they represented more than double the strength of the total British forces in India. The army is mercenary. Every care is taken to isolate Indian soldiers from the general population, and every possible measure is adopted to prevent the growth of solidarity among them. And the Indian Legislature has never been entrusted with the control of the military policy, although the military expenditure is a dominating factor in India's financial situation. It absorbs the bulk of the revenue and puts a severe strain upon the country: it has risen from £20 millions before the world war to £41 millions at the present day.

The truth is that the British Government in India has no intention of changing its time-honoured policy in regard to the defence of India. On the contrary, this is now being closely linked up with the general military policy of Great Britain in defence of imperial interests. That is why, in the Act of 1935, matters relating to Defence and External Affairs are reserved under the Governor-General of India. After all, whoever controls Finance, Foreign Affairs and Defence controls the political future of the country. The defence forces at the disposal of the Government of India comprise a standing army of approximately 55,000 British and 160,000 Indian troops, backed by a large reserve. There are some eight squadrons of the Royal Air Force; and a naval squadron guards the coastline.

Towards the end of 1938, an Expert Committee under Admiral

Lord Chatfield was appointed to investigate the military and financial aspects of the defence problems. The work of the Committee was, however, interrupted by the menace of war in Europe, but Lord Chatfield was able to make certain specific recommendations in regard to mechanization, coastal and frontier defences, air-raid precautions, and financial relations with the Imperial Government. As early as September 13, 1938, the Government announced that British battalions had been transferred from the Indian to the Imperial establishments, and His Majesty's Government made a free gift of 33½ crores (£5 million sterling) and a loan of 11¾ crores of rupees to India to modernize the equipment and organization of the defence forces in India. Since 1933 Britain has also been contributing an annual grant of £1,500,000, and it is now proposed to increase this by £500,000.

But we must have a clear comprehension of the Imperial policy that now inspires the Government to consider the limitations of the resources available in India and to lighten her burden of military expenditure. In 1933, at the time of the Round Table Conferences, the Garran Tribunal enunciated the principle that "the broad lines of division between Indian and Imperial responsibility for defence should be that India assumed responsibility for the 'minor danger' of the maintenance of internal security and protection of her frontiers and that Great Britain assumed responsibility for the 'major danger' of an attack by a great power upon India, or upon the Empire through India."

However, Lord Chatfield's Committee held the view that "the Forces maintained by India should be adequate not merely for the narrower purposes of purely local defence," but also to assist in maintaining what it described as "India's external security"; and further, "that India should acknowledge that her responsibility cannot in her own interests be safely limited to the local defence of her land frontiers and coasts." His Excellency the Commander-in-Chief in India, Sir Robert Cassels, put the case in simpler language when he said in a broadcast address:

> "Look eastwards, and think what would happen to India if Malaya and its great fortress of Singapore were to fall into the hands of an enemy. The British fleet would thereby lose its great base in the East, and the whole eastern coastline of India from Calcutta to Madras would become liable to raid

and bombardment by sea and air. The loss of Malaya might well also mean a serious threat to Burma. Napoleon once said when he occupied the Low Countries that he had in Antwerp a pistol pointed at the heart of England. Burma in hostile hands would be a pistol pointed at the heart of Bengal.

"Look westwards to the Red Sea and Egypt. So long as Egypt, our ally, is free and independent and able with our help to check the movement of a hostile Power, the Indian Ocean and the shores of India are likely to remain immune from attack from that direction. In other words, it might be said that it is vital to the interests of India that Egypt and Aden should never fall into hostile hands. In the conditions of the world situation as it has developed in recent years, the places which I named have become of the first importance to the defence of India and must be considered to be her outposts. Eastwards we have Singapore, Malaya and Burma; westwards Egypt, Aden and the lands of the Persian Gulf. If these were to be lost to India's friends, India would be directly threatened."

In other words, India's frontiers must be extended to all points from Gibraltar to Singapore, from Afghanistan to the Sino-Burmese border, and if possible to the moon! As a corollary to this policy, the Imperial Government declares "the governing principle" of sharing in a joint responsibility for India's external security, and Lord Chatfield's Committee observes that "in accordance with the principles on which the relations between the Governments of Great Britain and of India have been based, the Government of India must be responsible for the administration of all the Armed Forces situated in India for the purpose of local and external defence, and must, therefore, have full financial control over the expenditure necessary for their maintenance."

Now, this policy of retaining the control of India's defence in its own hands and of co-ordinating it with that of the imperial defence is a positive proof that the Imperial Government has no intention of allowing India to develop as a sovereign Power. Obviously, India cannot attain an independent status and exercise her sovereignty if she has to depend on Britain for defence. It is argued that this dependence upon Imperial strength for the defence of India is a necessity for her safety, and that the political aspect of the problem can be solved by a *partial* transference of its responsibility to the Indian legislature. South Africa, Australia and New Zealand are equally dependent on Britain, but their national defence is now under the authority of their own ministers. Their military establishments are under the control of the Dominion Governments, where facilities are freely provided for imperial needs without derogating in any way from the constitutional freedom enjoyed by them.

But the problem of the national defence of India, free from British tutelage, has to be approached from a different angle. At the moment, three-quarters of India's armed strength is abstracted from the people at large and jealously guarded as the mercenary appendage of British troops. Such a conception of defence of India cannot but be described as "an euphemism for the defence of British imperial interests." An army blended and identified with the people is alone invincible. The secret of Soviet Russia's heroic resistance lies in the fact that the Red Army belongs to the people and that, unlike the peasant masses of the Tsar, the soldiers of the Soviet Union, like the Troopers of Cromwell, know what they fight for and love what they know. Only a national army can be fortified with the spirit of true defence. Therefore, India must have a free hand in organizing a *national* army in accordance with her own needs and purposes. While her army must no longer remain as an integral part of the British Army, she may enter into an agreement with the Imperial Government under which British officers would lend their services to India as an ally for a period not exceeding ten years.

At all events, India must be in a position to resist external aggression without the protection of the British army or navy, if her independent status is to become a reality. The process of forming a *national* army in which military traditions survive will not be difficult. India has all the resources necessary for building up war industries—already she has become a colossal arsenal—and she may easily acquire any number of devilish machines if their possession becomes necessary for gaining an independent status.

India has no quarrel with her neighbours. Free from the entanglements of British foreign policy, she would willingly participate in a system of collective security with them. She desires a closer union with the peoples of China, the Soviet Union, Afghanistan and other Asiatic countries. She would take a share in forming world opinion in favour of disarmament, and throw her full weight into the policy of discarding the principle of force in international relations. For over a quarter of a century the leaders of the Indian National Congress have consistently instructed the nation to realize what the Atlantic Charter declares to-day, that "all of the nations of the world, for realistic as well as spiritual reasons, must come to the abandonment of the use of force." And they are in complete accord with General Wavell's recent pronouncement: "Think what a world we could make if we put into our peace endeavours the same self-sacrifice, the same energy, and the same co-operation as we use in the wastefulness of war."

VII

We now come to the problem of arriving at a final settlement of British financial claims on India. If India is to have a really independent political status, it is essential that she should free herself from the financial domination of the City of London. But here we at once come up against those "certain obligations which the British Government cannot renounce," although the letter[1] from which this quotation is taken declares that "the British people are irrevocably resolved to give India full political freedom." The Viceregal statement, issued on August 8, 1940, announced that His Majesty's Government were in sympathy *with the claims of Indians to frame India's political Constitution*, and "wished to see it given fullest practical expression, subject to due fulfilment of the obligations which Great Britain's long connection with India imposed upon her, and for which His Majesty's Government cannot divest themselves of responsibility."

Now these obligations are essentially financial. Following the transformation of a trading corporation into a ruling power, Britain in India entered into a phase of an expanding imperialism. The beginning of her imperialist venture may be traced to the prodigious exploitation of Drake and other corsairs. Drake never

[1] In December, 1940, nine members of Parliament, drawn from three major political parties, issued an appeal to India with a view to winning the co-operation of the Indian National Congress in the Empire's war effort.

disclosed the value of his exploits when his squadron overtook the *cacofuego* (the Spanish treasure ships) whose ballast was chiefly silver ores, and no correct estimate could be made of this great fortune. The other source of wealth was the slave trade. With the accumulation of wealth began the formation of trading companies, one of which laid the foundation of British rule in India.

Referring to Drake's adventures Professor Keynes writes: "Queen Elizabeth was a considerable shareholder in the syndicate which had financed the expedition. Out of her share she paid off the whole of England's foreign debt, balanced her Budget and found herself with about £40,000 in hand. This she invested in the Levant Company, which prospered. Out of the profits of the Levant Company, the East India Company was founded; and the profits of this great enterprise were the foundation of England's subsequent foreign investment." Calculating the accumulation of compound interest, Keynes found that "every £1 Drake brought home in 1580 had now become £100,000. Such is the power of compound interest."[1]

The East India Company launched its career in A.D. 1600—five years after the Dutch. The trade of the Company flourished, and new varieties of men known as the London merchants came to exercise a considerable power both in political and commercial spheres. In 1635, Sir Josiah Child estimated that "there were more merchants to be found upon the Exchange worth each £1,000 and upwards, than were in the former days, viz. before 1600, to be found worth one hundred pounds each." Capital began to accumulate, and the Bank of England was incorporated in 1694.

The East India Company had established a number of trading centres in Surat (1612) on the west coast, in Bengal, and in Madras. Swarms of commercial adventurers of various nationalities began to pour into the country, and as the struggle for commerce grew, this powerful trading corporation fully exploited its advantageous position and established the Company's régime in India.

But the régime of the Company had to be consolidated by wars and expeditions, the cost of which was debited to Indian revenues. Whenever it failed to balance its budgets, owing to the heavy expenditure involved in these military adventures, or to inade-

[1] J. M. Keynes, *Essays in Persuasion*.

quate revenues, it had recourse to borrowing. By 1858 the debt of the Company amounted to £71,557,369. The Parliamentary investigation, known as the Welby Commission, admitted that "the permanent debt of India, whether raised here or in India, amounted, on April 30, 1842, to £33,577,414. On April 30, 1857, immediately before the Mutiny, it amounted to £51,327,958, an increase of 53 per cent in fifteen years. April 30, 1862, marks the close of the Mutiny expenditure, and the permanent debt had then risen to £97,037,062, an increase in twenty years of nearly 190 per cent."

In 1857, when the Imperial Parliament assumed the full authority of the Government of India, it took over the total debt of the Company and paid a substantial amount to the proprietors of the East India Stock. Since then various imperialist adventures have been undertaken, and the burdens of the heavy expenditure thus incurred were also laid upon the shoulders of the Indian people.

We are not concerned here with a detailed analysis of the public debt of India, but a few items of the expenditures from which this debt arose may be cited in support of the Indian demand for an equitable financial settlement with Britain.

The East India Company's exploits in Afghanistan, Burma, China, Persia and Natal involved a total cost of £35 millions; the cost of suppressing the Revolt of 1857 was over £40 millions; and a sum of over £37 millions was paid by Parliament for redeeming the Company's capital and dividends. Thus, India's legacy of debt from the régime of the East India Company amounted to over £112 millions in 1858.

Between 1858 and 1914, the British Government waged several wars and directed many military expeditions in pursuance of the policy of imperialist expansion: the Bhutan war (1863), the Abyssinian war (1867), the Perak Expedition (1875), the Afghan war (1879–81), the Egyptian Expedition (1882), the North-Western Frontier wars (1882–92), the Burmese war (1886), and the Sonkim Expedition (1896); and the cost of all these operations, amounting to about £65 millions, was added to the so-called public debt of India.

In the world war (1914–18) India's free contribution was over £112½ millions (150 crores of rupees), but the sum of about £250 millions was charged to the Indian Exchequer. It is but fair that India's claim to be relieved of the burdens of debt arising out of wars and expeditions should now be settled by an impartial tribunal.

India has no *national* debt because the debt has not been contracted with the consent of the Indian people. The loans[1] raised by the Secretary of State for India in London, or by the Government of India, constitute the Public Debt of India. The Finance member put the total debt on March 31, 1924, at approximately 917.53 crores of rupees.[2] The amount is, however, on the increase, and at the end of the financial year 1935 the figure stood at 1,239 crores. This works out as a debt of £3·32 per head of the population, whose per capita income does not exceed £6, or about 2s. 3d. a week. These loans are usually opened for subscription only in the London money market, and are held mostly by British investors. Since the last war, when Britain had to sell about 25 per cent of her foreign investments, the Indian loans issues are being made available to the Indian money market.

India must, of course, accept full liability for her financial obligations to Britain arising out of loan capital utilized for the development of public works. The redemption of debt, the payment of "Home Charges," the adjustment of British vested interests other than public debt, and the future of British trade in India—all these questions should be settled by negotiation and eventually by Treaties and Pacts.

But it may be argued that no ruling class ever voluntarily abdicated its power, and that any hope of a peaceful solution of the problems concerning financial adjustment between India and Britain is entirely illusory. The recent policy of entering into partnership with the Indian capitalists and bourgeoisie, and of reducing India's sterling debt[3] under the stress of the present war, cannot possibly lead to her financial independence. On the contrary, it is designed to make the imperial structure "immeasurably stronger." It is to be remembered that the financial

[1] It is estimated that India is the second imperial "partner" who has the largest share of borrowed capital from the City of London guaranteed by the State. In addition to State loans, there is the capital of British companies from which British investors receive substantial dividends.

[2] One crore = £750,000.

[3] Since the war the Government of India has acquired Indian securities in sterling estimated at some 311 crores of rupees (over £230 millions) in payment for the munitions and war services.

policy of the Government of India is dependent upon an excess balance of exports in order to meet India's financial commitments in London and to maintain the exchange. Under these circumstances the peril of a bitter conflict is real, for the aim of Indian nationalism is to sever India's connection with a system of government which represents the financial and vested interests of British and other foreign investors.

Yet the peril can be averted. Both the parties should be prepared to accept arbitration, bearing in mind that so long as the factors emerging from India's financial entanglements with Britain dominate the relations between the two countries, there can be no prospect of a peaceful settlement of constitutional issues. The fulfilment of the hope of an equitable financial adjustment with India depends upon Britain and Britain alone.

Will the democratic leadership in Britain have the strength and vision to resist the conspiracy of all the reactionary forces, and allow the Indian people the freedom to pursue their own destiny in their own way, or must India be forced to tread the path of violence in order to reach her goal of independence? Would not such a conflict be a contingent threat to British democracy? Would not the "argument of force" be a clear transgression of democratic principles for the vindication of which Britain is now at war? And how could she take a leading rôle in the making of a "New World Order" unless she herself abandons her attempts to retain imperialist domination in India? These are the questions to which the people of Britain must find honest answers.

VIII

Meanwhile the leaders of the national movement for India's liberation must increasingly guard themselves against the intrusion of disruptive forces within each of its component parts. The circumstances of political servitude are liable to give rise to internecine strife, and it is against this danger that we must rouse the sense of our individual and common responsibility. "When everything is at stake," wrote Hazlitt, "dear and valuable to man, as man; *when there is but the one dreadful alternative of entire* loss, or final recovery of truth and freedom, it is no time to stand up on trifles and moot points; the great object is to be secured first, and at all hazards." The longer we tolerate India's subjection to a foreign yoke, the greater will be the complexities of our struggle for freedom. Without freedom we shall not succeed in arresting some of the potent causes of national deterioration.

But I believe Indian nationalists are fully conscious of the dimensions of the struggle, and the clarity of purpose with which the Indian National Congress has steered its course in recent years should encourage us to sink all our minor differences in order to reach the goal. The criticism that the predominance of the Congress High Command would lead to Party dictatorship is not valid; for it is necessary to overcome that corrosive individualism which militates against the formation of a united front in our present struggle. Nothing but confusion can result from unco-ordinated struggle against imperialism. Only a unitary authority can assess and adjust the competing claims of all national groups and only a unitary authority can assert the right to throw off foreign yoke. Above all, we must always bear in mind the immeasurable suffering of the masses under the organized exploitation of the all-powerful alien bureaucracy in alliance with the Indian bourgeoisie. When the malignant disease of poverty is destroying the soul of the people, and when we realize that the task of leading the masses of the people forward to the goal of social justice can be performed only by the acquisition of political sovereignty, it would be a criminal folly on the part of those who have any claim to leadership if the struggle for a freely elected Constituent Assembly were to be frustrated by the failure to subordinate both personal and sectional interests to those of the people. All other issues must fade into insignificance before the central objective of political power and its consolidation. Indeed, political liberty is the only basis of national unity.

Harrington's appeal to the people of England in the seventeenth century may be aptly addressed to the leaders of the Indian national movement who demand a Constituent Assembly.

"Excellent Patriots, if the people be sovereign, here is that which establishes their prerogative; if we be sincere, here is that which disburdens our souls, and makes good all our engagements; if we be charitable, here is that which embraces all parties; if we would be settled, here is that which will stand and last for ever. If our religion be anything else but a vain boast, scratching and defacing human nature or reason, which, being the image of God, makes it a kind of murder, here is that empire whence justice shall run down like a river, and judgment like a mighty stream."[1]

It is a happy omen for India that her struggle for freedom should have approached a decisive stage at the threshold of a new epoch. It has already released such forces that can effectively challenge the obsolete *status quo* and at the same time offer great possibilities for renewing the structure of civilization. Vast changes are taking place within the continent of Asia, and India cannot be left in bondage, with the largest conglomeration of subject people on earth. Her contribution as an independent sovereign power would be of great significance in the making of a New Order in Asia, and as a *voluntary* ally of Britain she would be a source of strength and stability to the new democracy of the British Commonwealth. The task of reconciling the principles of nationalism with those of internationalism must rest on independent India. She would willingly allow such circumscription of national sovereignty as may be required of her in setting up any new International Order.

But if the leaders of the Indian struggle fail *now*, through infirmity of will, in realizing the goal of independence; if they fail to merge all the minor issues in this fundamental objective; if they break down under the stress of the Machiavellian designs of a powerful alien bureaucracy, so deeply entrenched in the country; if the conspiracy of all the reactionary forces in India—the Princes, the communalists and the bourgeoisie—is designed to prolong India's subjection to foreign domination, even then, the struggle will continue. After all, as an Irish poet (Æ) observed, "The mighty British Empire is not outside the pale of the Government of the Cosmos, and the mills of God did come to the Roman Empire, to the Chaldean and other Kingdoms."

Finally, a word to the critics of the Indian national movement. A correct appraisal of this struggle against the present social and political systems is possible only from the point of view of the masses who are beginning to be conscious of the limitations and inconsistencies of bourgeois democracy. They realize that the task of changing the fundamental conditions of their life and labour must rest with them. It is from them comes the democratic impetus to the Indian struggle, and once they are determined to endow the nation with the life-giving power of freedom, nothing

[1] Harington, *Oceana* (1656).

could deflect their minds from the paramount issue confronting a revolutionary epoch. And the suppression of the Will of the People can but liberate a spiritual energy, and the eternal dispensation of the Time-spirit cannot be frustrated by violence.

> "Pilgrims pass from age to age on the road of Time uneven with the rise and fall of races.
> It resounds with the thunder-roar of Thy wheels, Thou Eternal Charioteer.
> Through the wrecks and ruins of kingdoms
> Thy conchshell sounds breathing life into death.
> Victory to Thee who guidest people to their purposes,
> Victory to Thee, Builder of India's destiny."[1]

[1] From a National Song composed by Rabindra Nath Tagore.

Chapter Ten

POSTSCRIPT

A great part of this book was in page proof when the Prime Minister (Mr. Churchill) announced the decision of the War Cabinet to send one of its members to India with a plan for a "just and final solution" of India's constitutional status. A brief survey of events leading to this decision may be of interest.

On the eve of Japan's entry into the war, the Government of India was advised to liberate some of the leaders of the Indian National Congress, in the hope that the extension of the war in the Far East might persuade them to lend their support in the war effort. The release of political prisoners did not, however, indicate any new approach to the constitutional problem; consequently "a fresh orientation of Congress opinion" was not made possible. The All-India Congress Working Committee observed that neither the profession of freedom and democracy nor the perils and catastrophes that had come in the wake of the war had effected any change in the attitude of the British Government towards India's claim to independence. "While there has been no change in British policy towards India," runs one of its resolutions, "the Working Committee must nevertheless take into consideration the new world situation that has arisen by the developments of the war in the world and its approach to India. The sympathies of Congress must inevitably lie with peoples who are the subjects of aggression and who are fighting for their freedom, but only a free and independent India can be in a position to undertake the defence of the country on a national basis and be of help in the furtherance of the larger causes that are emerging from the storm of war.

"The whole background in India is one of hostility and mistrust of the British Government, and not even the most far-reaching promises can alter this background, nor can a subject India offer voluntary or willing help to arrogant imperialism, which is indistinguishable from Fascist authoritarianism."

At this juncture, thirteen leading non-party leaders (Moderates) sent an appeal to Mr. Churchill, then in Washington, urging him to find, in the light of the war emergency, an interim solution of the present constitutional impasse, and they themselves put forward certain proposals which they believed would be regarded by all sections of Indian political parties as representing intermediary steps towards India's constitutional goal. The Prime Minister was asked to "realize the urgent necessity of transforming the entire spirit and outlook of the administration of India, and to make a declaration that India will no longer be treated as a dependency ruled from Whitehall, and that her constitutional position and powers will be identical with those of other units of the British Commonwealth."

The proposals may be briefly summarized as follows:

(*a*) The conversion and expansion of the Central Executive Council into a truly National Government consisting entirely of non-officials of all recognized parties and communities and in charge of all Portfolios, subject only to responsibility to the Crown.

(*b*) The restoration, in Provinces, now ruled autocratically by Governors in accordance with Section 93 of the Government of India Act, of popular governments broadly based on the confidence of the different classes and communities; or failing this, the establishment of non-official Executive Councils responsible to the Crown as proposed for the Centre.

(*c*) The recognition of India's right to direct representation, through men chosen by the National Government, in the Imperial War Cabinet (should such a body be set up), in all Allied War Councils wherever established, and at the Peace Conference.

(*d*) Consultation with the National Government on precisely the same footing, and to the same extent as His Majesty's Government consult Dominion Governments in all matters affecting the Commonwealth as a whole and India in particular.

But the Prime Minister, who consistently preserved "an ominous silence, except to deny the validity of the Atlantic Charter as regards India," took nearly two months to send even a formal reply to the appeal of these Indian "moderates." They had, however, the opinion of the Secretary of State for India (Mr. Amery), who stated in the House of Commons that in these proposals he was unable "to discover any satisfactory response to the Viceroy's recent appeal for unity and co-operation in the face of the common danger."

Meanwhile the menacing situation had developed by the fall of Singapore and by the Japanese advance into Burma. Mr. Churchill declared: "India is threatened," and British public opinion asked for a fresh effort to gain the loyal co-operation of the Indian National Congress and the Indian people in the prosecution of the war.

We now turn to the British War Cabinet's plan for India. Its nature was not revealed by the Prime Minister, but it was declared to be "a constructive British contribution" towards a settlement of the constitutional deadlock in India. As an explanation of the failure to announce the terms of this settlement in an official declaration, he observed: "We must first assure ourselves that *our scheme*[1] would win a reasonable and practical measure of acceptance, and thus promote the concentration of all Indian thought and energies upon the defence of the native soil. We should ill serve the common cause if we make a declaration which would be rejected by essential elements in the Indian world, and which provoked fierce constitutional and communal disputes at a moment when the enemy is at the gates of India."

Sir Stafford Cripps, the Lord Privy Seal, volunteered to act as an envoy for the purpose of holding personal consultation with leaders of the Indian National Congress and other sectional political groups, in order "to procure," to quote the words of the Prime Minister, "the necessary measure of assent, not only from the Hindu majority, but also from those great minorities, amongst which the Moslems are the most numerous and *on many grounds pre-eminent*."[1]

After disclosing the details of the draft Declaration first to the members of the Viceroy's Executive Council, and subsequently to all the principal Indian leaders personally, Sir Stafford made it public. The War Cabinet's plan for satisfying "the constitutional aspirations of India" is as follows:

> (*a*) Immediately upon the cessation of hostilities, steps shall be taken to set up in India, in the manner described hereafter, an elected body charged with the task of framing a new Constitution for India.

[1] Italics are mine.

(*b*) Provision shall be made, as set out below, for the participation of the Indian States in the constitution-making body.

(*c*) His Majesty's Government undertake to accept and implement forthwith the Constitution so framed subject only to:—

(i) the right of any Province of British India that is not prepared to accept the new Constitution to retain its present constitutional position, provision being made for its subsequent accession if it so decides.

With such non-acceding Provinces, should they so desire, His Majesty's Government will be prepared to agree upon a new Constitution, giving them the same full status as Indian Union, and arrived at by a procedure analogous to that here laid down.

(ii) the signing of a Treaty which shall be negotiated between His Majesty's Government and the constitution-making body. This Treaty will cover all necessary matters arising out of the complete transfer of responsibility from British to Indian hands; it will make provision, in accordance with the undertakings given by His Majesty's Government, for the protection of racial and religious minorities; but will not impose any restriction on the power of the Indian Union to decide in the future its relationship to the other Member States of the British Commonwealth.

Whether or not an Indian State elects to adhere to the Constitution, it will be necessary to negotiate a revision of its Treaty arrangements, so far as this may be required in the new situation.

(*d*) the constitution-making body shall be composed as follows, unless the leaders of Indian opinion in the principal communities agree upon some other form before the end of hostilities:—

Immediately upon the result being known of the provincial elections which will be necessary at the end of hostilities, the entire membership of the Lower Houses of the Provincial Legislatures shall, as a single electoral college, proceed to the election of the constitution-making body by the system of proportional representation. This new body shall be in number about one-tenth of the number of the electoral college.

Indian States shall be invited to appoint representatives in the same proportion to their total population as in the case of the representatives of British India as a whole, and with the same powers as the British Indian members.

(*e*) During the critical period which now faces India and until the new Constitution can be framed His Majesty's Government must inevitably bear the responsibility for and retain control and direction of the defence of India as part of their world war effort, but the task of organizing to the full the military, moral and material resources of India must be the responsibility of the Government of India with the co-operation of the peoples of India. His Majesty's Government desire and invite the immediate and effective participation of the leaders of the principal sections of the Indian people in the counsels of their country, of the Commonwealth and of the United Nations. Thus they will be enabled to give their active and constructive help in the discharge of a task which is vital and essential for the future freedom of India.[1]

The plan which is based upon the aims and policy as set forth in the Viceregal statement made on August 8, 1940, is now elaborated into two main parts: one relates to the future and the other to the effective participation in the present war. India is to enjoy after the war the blessings of Dominion status defined in the terms of the ancient Balfour Declaration, and she would be allowed to draw up her constitution by an all-Indian constitution-making body subject to the conditions stipulated in the plan. In other words, there is no question of recognizing the principle of popular sovereignty, and the constitution-making body will have to function within the limitations imposed upon it by the Imperial Government. In their plan they tamper with the people's right of self-determination and lay down, for instance, the condition that the Indian States[2] are to nominate about one-third of the consti-

[1] Cmd. 6350.

[2] The rulers of the Indian States will, however, have the option of remaining outside the proposed Indian Union.

tution-making body. In the resolution rejecting the draft plan, the Congress Working Committee states:

> The complete ignoring of ninety millions of people in the Indian States, and their treatment as commodities at the disposal of their Rulers, is a negation both of democracy and self-determination. While the representation of an Indian State in the constitution-making body is fixed on a population basis, the people of the State have no voice in choosing those representatives, nor are they to be consulted at any stage while decisions vitally affecting them are being taken. Such States may in many ways become barriers to the growth of Indian freedom, enclaves where foreign authority still prevails, and where the possibility of maintaining foreign-armed forces has been stated to be a likely contingency and a perpetual menace to the freedom of the people of the States as well as of the rest of India.

While a sovereign Constituent Assembly might have found ample accommodations in the democratic process for the fundamental political prerogatives of all communities, the constitution-making body as proposed by the British War Cabinet's draft declaration contained such elements as would imperil the development of a free and united India. The risk of fomenting communal and sectional interests and of giving rise to such circumstances as may lead to the political partition of India is inherent in the British plan. It enshrines the principle of counterpoise, perpetuates communalism, and follows up the technique of playing upon the fears and prejudices of each minority of the Indian communities.

The Congress Working Committee rejects the plan of breaking up India, and states:

> The acceptance beforehand of the novel principle of non-accession for a Province is also a severe blow to the conception of Indian unity and an apple of discord likely to generate growing trouble in the Provinces, and which may well lead to further difficulties in the way of the Indian States merging themselves into an Indian Union. Congress has been wedded to Indian freedom and unity and any break of that unity, especially in the modern world when peoples' minds inevitably think in terms of ever larger federations, would be injurious to all concerned and exceedingly painful to con-

template. Nevertheless the Committee cannot think in terms of compelling the people of any territorial unit to remain in an Indian Union against their declared and established will. While recognizing this principle, the Committee feel that every effort should be made to create conditions which would help the different units in developing a common and co-operative national life. Acceptance of this principle inevitably involves that no changes should be made which would result in fresh problems being created and compulsion being exercised on other substantial groups within that area. Each territorial unit should have the fullest possible autonomy within the Union consistently with a strong National State.

The proposal now made on the part of the British War Cabinet encourages and will lead to attempts at separation at the very inception of the Union and thus create great friction just when the utmost co-operation and goodwill are most needed. This proposal has been presumably made to meet the communal demand, but it will have other consequences also and lead politically reactionary and obscurantist groups among the different communities to create trouble and divert public attention from the vital issues before the country.

But all these proposals concerning the future constitutional status have not inspired animated discussions. The sonorous phrases of the Balfour Declaration, the promise of Dominion Status after the war, and even the recognition of the right of secession implied in the British War Cabinet's plan evoked no enthusiasm among representative Indian leaders. On the contrary, the mere reiteration of promises of post-war intentions was futile, and only served to increase doubts and suspicions. All parties were agreed that what concerned them was the formation of a Provisional National Government *now*, which would function as a Cabinet replacing the Viceroy's Executive Council. The dominant political issue is the location of popular sovereignty, and it involves a shift of the *actual* power from the Viceroy and his Executive Council to a National Government enjoying the confidence of the principal political parties. The formation of a responsible coalition government[1] within the framework of the

[1] The Coalition Ministry in Bengal shows the practicability of effective co-operation between the two major political parties. The Moslem Premiers of Bengal and Sind and their Ministries are supported by Hindu members of the respective Legislatures.

existing constitution would have resulted in an interim settlement of the present deadlock. Not only would it have provided a broad basis of agreement between all parties, but it would have been regarded as an earnest of the Imperial Government's intentions in regard to the future plan.

Now, as to the immediate issue: Since the main purpose of Sir Stafford Cripps's mission was to secure India's active and voluntary co-operation in the prosecution of the war, the question of Defence permeated the greater part of his efforts at arriving at a settlement. The negotiations were therefore centred around the clause (*e*) of the draft declaration.

From the very outset of these negotiations, the Congress enunciated the axiomatic truth that "popular resistance (to an invader) must have a national background and both the soldier and civilian must feel that they are fighting for their country's freedom under National leadership." Draft alternative formulas[1] on Defence, elaborated and submitted to the Congress leaders, did not meet the case, and they stated their reasons for the non-acceptance of such alternatives in the following words:

> At any time Defence is a vital subject; during war-time it is all-important and covers almost every sphere of life and administration. To take away Defence from the sphere of responsibility at this stage is to reduce that responsibility to a farce and nullity, and to make it perfectly clear that India is not going to be free in any way and her Government is not going to function as a free and independent Government during the pendency of the war.

Those who have any deep understanding of the Indian National Movement as a whole, and of the determination of the people of India to achieve no other political status save that of an independent sovereign State, could have predicted the failure of Sir Stafford Cripps's mission as soon as the plan which formed the basis of his negotiations was made known. At the close of three weeks' discussions with the political leaders, two major parties, and every sectional group functioning as an integral part of the Indian National Movement, rejected the draft Declaration of the British War Cabinet. Thereupon Sir Stafford Cripps announced that it had been withdrawn, and thus the situation in regard to

[1] See Cmd. 6350.

the constitutional controversy remained as it was before he undertook his mission.

The negotiations have, however, served to clarify the attitude of the Imperial Government towards the Indian National demand for independence. By their unanimous rejection of what *The Times* describes as "this frank and unreserved British offer of independence to India," Indian leaders have demonstrated the vitality of the Indian struggle for constitutional freedom. They have also made it clear to the people of India that this struggle can be carried on effectively only upon a united national basis. There is no divergence of opinion among the leaders of all communities upon the fundamental political issue, namely, *freedom to achieve freedom*; but this agreement alone cannot be the precondition of a successful Constituent Assembly. It is imperative that the primary postulate in its convocation must be the full recognition of the legitimate rights of the minority communities. We must now approach the problem of summoning the Constituent Assembly with renewed emphasis on the principle of guaranteeing essential functional freedoms to them.

But leaders of all communities and social groups must remember that the peasants and workers are the people of India, and that the Constituent Assembly would fail to achieve its purpose if it were dominated by the propertied classes and vested interests. In setting up an appropriate machinery of representation in the Constituent Assembly, whose composition must be essentially democratic, we must guard ourselves against all fissiparous and disruptive elements that may be encouraged to obstruct the way to democratic decisions. The draft Declaration of the British War Cabinet and the experience of the negotiations with the Lord Privy Seal should make the Indian leaders increasingly aware of this danger.

Finally, no time should be lost in making preparations for the convocation of the Constituent Assembly. The creation of a solid democratic front in India would, I believe, rally the progressive elements in British national life to the side of the Indian National Movement. I am convinced that British public opinion is much in advance of rigid official policy, and it is prepared to approach the constitutional problem of India in a new perspective of the world situation. I believe also that it is widely realized in Britain that the essential prerequisite to that approach is to remove those conventional ways of imperial rule which cumber the path of an entirely new relationship between India and Britain. There is now much evidence of a mood of fellowship with India, and one can, indeed, hope that *the people of Britain* will stand by India in her struggle for constitutional freedom. Without this hope, there can be no faith in British democracy, and without that faith we cannot lay the new foundations of an enduring partnership between free India and democratic Britain.

APPENDICES

I. The Virginia Bill of Rights, June 12, 1776.

II. Declaration of Independence, July 4, 1776.

III. *Déclaration des Droits de l'Homme et du Citoyen*, August, 1789.

IV. The Statute of Westminster, 1931.

V. Declaration of the Irish Republic, January 21, 1919.

VI. Extracts from the Constitution of the Union of Soviet Socialist Republics, 1936.

VII. Extracts from the Programme of the Turkish Republican Party, May, 1935.

VIII. Extracts from the Constitution of the Weimar Republic, August 11, 1919.

IX. Extracts from the Constitution of the Spanish Republic, December 9, 1931.

X. The Declaration of Independence of India at the Plenary Session of the National Congress at Lahore, 1939.

Appendix I

THE VIRGINIA BILL OF RIGHTS, JUNE 12, 1776

(This famous Declaration of Rights, adopted by the Virginia Convention of 1776, exerted a very wide influence both in this country and in France.)

A declaration of rights made by the representatives of the good people of Virginia, assembled in full and free convention; *which rights do pertain to them and their posterity*, as the basis and foundation of government.

1. That all men are by nature equally free and independent, and have certain inherent rights, of which, when they enter into a state of society, they cannot by any compact deprive or divest their posterity; namely, the enjoyment of life and liberty, with the means of acquiring and possessing property, and pursuing and obtaining happiness and safety.

2. That all power is vested in, and consequently derived from, the people; *that magistrates are their trustees and servants*, and at all times amenable to them.

3. That government is, or ought to be instituted for the common benefit, protection, and security of the people, nation, or community; of all the various modes and forms of government, that is best which is capable of producing the greatest degree of happiness and safety, and is most effectually secured against the danger of maladministration; and that when any government shall be found inadequate or contrary to these purposes, a majority of the community hath an indubitable, unalienable and indefeasible right to reform, alter or abolish it, in such manner as shall be judged most conducive to the public weal.

4. That no man, or set of men, are entitled to exclusive or separate emoluments or privileges from the community, but in consideration of publick services; which, not being descendible, neither ought the offices of magistrate, legislator or judge be hereditary.

5. That the legislative and executive powers of the State should be separate and distinct from the judiciary; and that the members of the two first may be restrained from oppression, by feeling and participating the burthens of the people, they should, at fixed periods, be reduced to a private station, return into the body from which they were originally taken, and the vacancies be supplied by frequent,

certain, and regular elections, in which all, or any part of the former members to be again eligible or ineligible, as the laws shall direct.

6. That elections of members to serve as representatives of the people in assembly, ought to be free; and that all men having sufficient evidence of permanent common interest with, and attachment to the community have the right of suffrage, and cannot be taxed or deprived of their property for publick uses, without their own consent, or that of their representatives so elected, nor bound by any law to which they have not, in like manner, assented for the public good.

7. That all power of suspending laws, or the execution of laws, by any authority without consent of the representatives of the people, is injurious to their rights, and ought not to be exercised.

8. That in all capital or criminal prosecutions a man hath a right to demand the cause and nature of his accusation, to be confronted with the accusers and witnesses, to call for evidence in his favour, and to a speedy trial by an impartial jury of his vicinage, without whose unanimous consent he cannot be found guilty; nor can he be compelled to give evidence against himself; that no man be deprived of his liberty, except by the laws of the land or the judgment of his peers.

9. That excessive bail ought not to be required, nor excessive fines imposed, nor cruel and unusual punishments inflicted.

10. That general warrants, whereby an officer or messenger can be commanded to search suspected places without evidence of a fact committed, or to seize any person or persons not named, or whose offense is not particularly described and supported by evidence, are grievous and oppressive, and ought not to be granted.

11. That in controversies respecting property, and in suits between man and man, the ancient trial by jury is preferable to any other, and ought to be held sacred.

12. That the freedom of the press is one of the great bulwarks of liberty, and can never be restrained but by despotick governments.

13. That a well-regulated militia, composed of the body of the people trained to arms, is the proper, natural and safe defense of a free State; that standing armies in time of peace should be avoided as dangerous to liberty; and that in all cases the military should be under strict subordination to, and governed by, the civil power.

14. That the people have a right to uniform government; and, therefore, that no government separate from, or independent of the Government of Virginia, ought to be erected or established within the limits thereof.

15. That no free government, or the blessings of liberty, can be preserved to any people, but by firm adherence to justice, moderation, temperance, frugality and virtue, and by frequent recurrence to fundamental principles.

16. That religion, or the duty which we owe to our Creator, and the manner of discharging it, can be directed only by reason and conviction, not by force or violence; and therefore all men are equally entitled to the free exercise of religion, according to the dictates of conscience; and that it is the mutual duty of all to practice Christian forbearance, love and charity towards each other.

Appendix II

DECLARATION OF INDEPENDENCE

July 4, 1776

When in the Course of human events, it becomes necessary for one people to dissolve the political bonds which have connected them with another, and to assume among the Powers of the earth, the separate and equal station to which the Laws of Nature and of Nature's Gold entitle them, a decent respect to the opinions of mankind requires that they should declare the causes which impel them to the separation.

We hold these truths to be self-evident, that all men are created equal, that they are endowed by their Creator with certain unalienable Rights, that among these are Life, Liberty and the pursuit of Happiness. That to secure these rights, Governments are instituted among Men, deriving their just powers from the consent of the governed. That whenever any Form of Government becomes destructive to these ends, it is the Right of the People to alter or to abolish it, and to institute new Government, laying its foundation on such principles and organizing its powers in such form, as to them shall seem most likely to effect their Safety and Happiness. Prudence, indeed, will dictate that Governments long established should not be changed for light and transient causes; and accordingly all experience hath shown, that mankind are more disposed to suffer, while evils are sufferable, than to right themselves by abolishing the forms to which they are accustomed. But when a long train of abuses and usurpations, pursuing invariably the same Object evinces a design to reduce them under absolute Despotism, it is their right, it is their duty, to throw off such Government, and to provide new Guards for their future security. Such has been the patient sufferance of these Colonies; and such is now the necessity which constrains them to alter their former Systems of Government. The history of the present King of Great Britain is a history of repeated injuries and usurpations, all having in direct object the establishment of an absolute Tyranny over these States. To prove this, let Facts be submitted to a candid world.

He has refused his Assent to Laws, the most wholesome and necessary for the public good.

He has forbidden his Governors to pass Laws of immediate and pressing importance, unless suspended in their operation till his

Assent should be obtained; and when so suspended, he has utterly neglected to attend to them.

He has refused to pass other Laws for the accommodation of large districts of people, unless those people would relinquish the right of Representation in the Legislature, a right inestimable to them and formidable to tyrants only.

He has called together legislative bodies at places unusual, uncomfortable, and distant from the depository of their Public Records, for the sole purpose of fatiguing them into compliance with his measures.

He has dissolved Representative Houses repeatedly, for opposing with manly firmness his invasions on the rights of the people.

He has refused for a long time, after such dissolutions, to cause others to be elected; whereby the Legislative Powers, incapable of Annihilation, have returned to the People at large for their exercise; the State remaining in the meantime exposed to all the dangers, of invasion from without, and convulsions within.

He has endeavoured to prevent the population of these States; for that purpose obstructing the Laws of Naturalization of Foreigners; refusing to pass others to encourage their migrations hither, and raising the conditions of new Appropriations of Lands.

He has obstructed the Administration of Justice, by refusing his Assent to Laws for establishing Judiciary Powers.

He has made Judges dependent on his Will alone, for the tenure of their offices, and the amount and payment of their salaries.

He has erected a multitude of New Offices, and sent hither swarms of Officers to harass our people, and beat out their substance.

He has kept among us, in times of peace, Standing Armies, without the Consent of our legislature.

He has affected to render the Military independent of and superior to the Civil Power.

He has combined with others to subject us to a jurisdiction foreign to our constitution, and unacknowledged by our laws; giving his Assent to their Acts of pretended legislation:

For quartering large bodies of armed troops among us:

For protecting them, by a mock Trial, from Punishment for any Murders which they should commit on the Inhabitants of these States:

For cutting off our Trade with all parts of the world:

For imposing Taxes on us without our Consent:

For depriving us in many cases, of the benefits of Trial by Jury:

For transporting us beyond Seas to be tried for pretended offenses:

For abolishing the free System of English Laws in a neighbouring Province, establishing therein an Arbitrary government, and enlarging its Boundaries so as to render it at once an example and fit instrument for introducing the same absolute rule into these Colonies:

For taking away our Charters, abolishing our most valuable Laws and altering fundamentally the Forms of our Governments:

For suspending our own Legislature, and declaring themselves invested with Power to legislate for us in all cases whatsoever.

He has abdicated Government here by declaring us out of his Protection and waging War against us.

He has plundered our seas, ravaged our Coasts, burnt our towns, and destroyed the lives of our people.

He is at this time transporting large armies of foreign mercenaries to complete the works of death, desolation and tyranny, already begun with circumstances of Cruelty & perfidy scarcely paralleled in the most barbarous ages, and totally unworthy the Head of a civilized nation.

He has constrained our fellow Citizens taken Captive on the high Seas to bear Arms against their Country, to become the executioners of their friends and Brethren, or to fall themselves by their Hands.

He has excited domestic insurrections amongst us, and has endeavoured to bring on the inhabitants of our frontiers, the merciless Indian Savages, whose known rule of warfare, is an undistinguished destruction of all ages, sexes and conditions.

In every stage of these Oppressions We have Petitioned for Redress in the most humble terms: Our repeated Petitions have been answered only by repeated injury. A Prince, whose character is thus marked by every act which may define a Tyrant, is unfit to be the ruler of a free People.

Nor have We been wanting in attention to our British brethren. We have warned them from time to time of attempts by their legislature to extend an unwarrantable jurisdiction over us. We have reminded them of the circumstances of our emigration and settlement here. We have appealed to their native justice and magnanimity, and we have conjured them by the ties of our common kindred to disavow these usurpations, which would inevitably interrupt our connections and correspondence. They too have been deaf to the voice of justice and of consanguinity We must, therefore, acquiesce in the necessity, which denounces our Separation, and hold them, as we hold the rest of mankind, Enemies in War, in Peace Friends.

We, therefore, the Representatives of the United States of America, in General Congress, Assembled, appealing to the Supreme Judge of the world for the rectitude of our intentions, do, in the Name, and by Authority of the good People of these Colonies, solemnly publish and declare, That these United Colonies are, and of Right ought to be Free and Independent States; that they are Absolved from all Allegiance to the British Crown, and that all political connection between them and the State of Great Britain, is and ought to be totally dissolved; and that as Free and Independent States, they have full Power to levy War, conclude Peace, contract Alliances, establish Commerce, and to do all other Acts and Things which Independent States may of right do. And for the support of this Declaration, with a firm reliance on the protection of Divine Providence, we mutually pledge to each other our Lives, our Fortunes, and our sacred Honor.

Appendix III

DÉCLARATION DES DROITS DE L'HOMME ET DU CITOYEN, AUGUST, 1789

The representatives of the people of France, formed into a National Assembly, considering that ignorance, neglect or contempt of human rights, are the sole causes of public misfortunes and corruptions of government, have resolved to set forth in a solemn declaration, these *natural, sacred and inalienable rights: that this declaration being* constantly present in the minds of the members of the community, they may be kept ever attentive of their rights and their duties; that the acts of the legislative and executive powers of government, being capable of being at all times compared with the end of political institutions, may be more respected; and also, that the future claims of citizens, being directed by simple and incontestable principles, may always tend to the maintenance of the Constitution and the general happiness

For these reasons the National Assembly recognizes and declares, in the presence of the Supreme Being, and with the hope of his blessing and favour, the following sacred rights of men and citizens:

ARTICLE 1. Men are born and remain free and equal in respect of their rights. Civil distinctions, therefore, may be founded only on *public utility.*

ARTICLE 2. The end of all political association is the preservation of the natural and imprescriptible rights of man. These rights are liberty, property, security, and resistance of oppression.

ARTICLE 3. The source of all sovereignty resides essentially in the nation. No individual and no body of men is entitled to exercise any authority which is not expressly derived from it.

ARTICLE 4. Liberty consists in being able to do whatever does not injure another. Thus, the exercise of the natural rights of each man has no other limits than those that are necessary to secure the free exercise of the same rights by other members of the society. These limits may be determined only by the law.

ARTICLE 5. The law ought to prohibit only actions hurtful to the society. What is not prohibited by law may not be hindered, and no one may be compelled to do that which the law does not require.

ARTICLE 6. Law is the expression of the will of the community. All citizens have a right to co-operate, either personally or through their representatives, in making it. It should be the same for all, whether it protects or punishes. All citizens, being equal in its sight, are equally eligible to all public honours, places and employments, according to their abilities, and without any other distinction than that created by their virtues and talents.

ARTICLE 7. No man may be accused, arrested or detained except in cases determined by law and according to the forms prescribed by law. All who solicit, promote, execute, or cause to be executed arbitrary decrees ought to be punished; but every citizen called upon, or apprehended by virtue of the law ought immediately to obey: he makes himself culpable by resistance.

ARTICLE 8. The law ought to impose only those penalties that are strictly and clearly necessary; and no one may be punished except under a law established and promulgated before the offence, and legally applied.

ARTICLE 9. Every man being presumed innocent until he has been convicted, should it be deemed necessary to arrest a man, all violence towards him beyond what is indispensable to apprehend him should be strictly repressed by the law.

ARTICLE 10. No man should be molested on account of his opinions, not even on account of his religious opinions, so long as his expression of them does not disturb the public order established by law.

ARTICLE 11. The free expression of thought and opinion is one of the most precious rights of man; every citizen may speak, write and publish freely, provided that he is responsible for the abuse of this liberty in cases determined by law.

ARTICLE 12. A public force is necessary to secure the rights of men and of citizens; this force is, consequently, instituted for the benefit of all and not for the particular advantage of those to whom it is entrusted.

ARTICLE 13. A common contribution is necessary for the maintenance of this force and for meeting the expenses of government; it should be levied equally on all citizens, in proportion to their means.

ARTICLE 14. All citizens have a right, either personally or by their representatives, to establish the need for the public contribution, to vote it freely, to appropriate it, to determine its amount, its mode of assessment, its collection and its duration.

ARTICLE 15. The community has a right to demand of every public servant an account of his administration.

ARTICLE 16. Every society in which the security of rights is not assured nor the separation of the powers of government established, lacks a constitution.

ARTICLE 17. Property being an inviolable and sacred right, no man may be deprived of his possessions, except in cases of evident and urgent public necessity established by law, and on condition of a just and previously determined indemnity.

Appendix IV

THE STATUTE OF WESTMINSTER, 1931

An Act to give effect to certain resolutions passed by Imperial Conferences held in the years 1926 and 1930. (22 Geo. 5, c. 4) (11 Dec. 1931).

Whereas the delegates of His Majesty's Governments in the United Kingdom, the Dominion of Canada, the Commonwealth of Australia, the Dominion of New Zealand, the Union of South Africa, the Irish Free State and Newfoundland, at Imperial Conferences holden at Westminster in the years of our Lord nineteen hundred and twenty-six and nineteen hundred and thirty did concur in making the declarations and resolutions set forth in the Reports of the said Conferences:

And whereas it is meet and proper to set out by way of preamble to this Act that, inasmuch as the Crown is the symbol of the free association of the members of the British Commonwealth of Nations, and as they are united by a common allegiance to the Crown, it would be in accord with the established constitutional position of all the members of the Commonwealth in relation to one another that any alteration in the law touching the Succession to the Throne or the Royal Style and Titles shall hereafter require the assent as well of the Parliaments of all the Dominions as of the Parliament of the United Kingdom:

And whereas it is in accord with the established constitutional position that no law hereafter made by the Parliament of the United Kingdom shall extend to any of the said Dominions as part of the law of that Dominion otherwise than at the request and with the consent of that Dominion:

And whereas it is necessary for the ratifying, confirming and establishing of certain of the said declarations and resolutions of the said Conferences that a law be made and enacted in due form by authority of the Parliament of the United Kingdom:

And whereas the Dominion of Canada, the Commonwealth of Australia, the Dominion of New Zealand, the Union of South Africa, the Irish Free State and Newfoundland have severally requested and consented to the submission of a measure to the Parliament of the United Kingdom for making such provision with regard to the matters aforesaid as is hereafter in this Act contained:

Now, therefore, be it enacted by the King's most Excellent Majesty by and with the advice and consent of the Lords Spiritual and Temporal, and Commons, in this present Parliament assembled, and by the authority of the same, as follows:—

1. In this Act the expression "Dominion" means any of the following Dominions, that is to say, the Dominion of Canada, the Commonwealth of Australia, the Dominion of New Zealand, the Union of South Africa, the Irish Free State and Newfoundland.

2. (1) The Colonial Laws Validity Act, 1865, shall not apply to any law made after the commencement of this Act by the Parliament of a Dominion.

(2) No law and no provision of any law made after the commencement of this Act by the Parliament of a Dominion shall be void or inoperative on the ground that it is repugnant to the law of England, or to the provisions of any existing or future Act of Parliament of the United Kingdom, or to any order, rule or regulation made under any such Act, and the powers of the Parliament of a Dominion shall include the power to repeal or amend any such Act, order, rule or regulation in so far as the same is part of the law of the Dominion.

3. It is hereby declared and enacted that the Parliament of a Dominion has full power to make laws having extra-territorial operation.

4. No Act of Parliament of the United Kingdom passed after the commencement of this Act shall extend, or be deemed to extend, to a Dominion as part of the law of that Dominion, unless it is expressly declared in that Act that that Dominion has requested, and consented to the enactment thereof.

5. Without prejudice to the generality of the foregoing provisions of this Act, sections seven hundred and thirty-five and seven hundred and thirty-six of the Merchant Shipping Act, 1894, shall be construed as though reference therein to the Legislature of a British possession did not include reference to the Parliament of a Dominion.

6. Without prejudice to the generality of the foregoing provisions of this Act, section four of the Colonial Courts of Admiralty Act, 1890 (which requires certain laws to be reserved for the signification of His Majesty's pleasure or to contain a suspending clause), and so much of section seven of that Act as requires the approval of His Majesty in Council to any rules of Court for regulating the practices and procedure of a Colonial Court of Admiralty, shall cease to have effect in any Dominion as from the commencement of this Act.

7. (1) Nothing in this Act shall be deemed to apply to the repeal, amendment or alteration of the British North America Acts, 1867 to 1930, or any order, rule or regulation made thereunder.

(2) The provisions of section two of this Act shall extend to laws made by any of the Provinces of Canada and to the powers of the legislatures of such Provinces.

(3) The powers conferred by this Act upon the Parliament of Canada or upon the legislatures of the Provinces shall be restricted to the enactment of laws in relation to matters within the competence of the Parliament of Canada or of any of the legislatures of the Provinces respectively.

8. Nothing in this Act shall be deemed to confer any power to repeal or alter the Constitution or the Constitution Act of the Commonwealth of Australia or the Constitution Act of the Dominion of New Zealand otherwise than in accordance with the law existing before the commencement of this Act.

9. (1) Nothing in this Act shall be deemed to authorize the Parliament of the Commonwealth of Australia to make laws on any matter within the authority of the States of Australia, not being a matter within the authority of the Parliament or Government of the Commonwealth of Australia.

(2) Nothing in this Act shall be deemed to require the concurrence of the Parliament or Government of the Commonwealth of Australia in any law made by the Parliament of the United Kingdom with respect to any matter within the authority of the States of Australia, not being a matter within the authority of the Parliament or Government of the Commonwealth of Australia, in any case where it would have been in accordance with the constitutional practice existing before the commencement of this Act that the Parliament of the United Kingdom should make that law without such concurrence.

(3) In the application of this Act to the Commonwealth of Australia the request and consent referred to in section four shall mean the request and consent of the Parliament and Government of the Commonwealth.

10. (1) None of the following sections of this Act, that is to say, sections two, three, four, five and six, shall extend to a Dominion to which this section applies as part of the law of that Dominion unless that section is adopted by the Parliament of the Dominion, and any Act of that Parliament

adopting any section of this Act may provide that the adoption shall have effect either from the commencement of this Act or from such later date as is specified in the adopting Act.

(2) The Parliament of any such Dominion as aforesaid may at any time revoke the adoption of any section referred to in subsection (1) of this section.

(3) The Dominions to which this section applies are the Commonwealth of Australia, the Dominion of New Zealand and Newfoundland.

11. Notwithstanding anything in the Intepretation Act, 1889, the expression "Colony," shall not, in any Act of the Parliament of the United Kingdom passed after the commencement of this Act, include a Dominion or any Province or State forming part of a Dominion.

12. This Act may be cited as the Statute of Westminster, 1931.

Appendix V

DECLARATION OF THE IRISH REPUBLIC

JANUARY 21, 1919

Whereas the Irish people is a free people;

And whereas for seven hundred years the Irish people has never ceased to repudiate and has repeatedly protested in arms against foreign usurpation;

And whereas English rule in this country is and always has been, based upon force and fraud, and maintained by military occupation against the declared will of the people;

And whereas the Irish Republic was proclaimed in Dublin on Easter Monday, 1916, by the Irish Republican Army, acting on behalf of the Irish people;

And whereas the Irish people is resolved to secure and maintain its complete independence in order to promote the common weal, to re-establish justice, to provide for future defence, to insure peace at home and good will with all nations, and to constitute a national policy based upon the people's will, with equal right and equal opportunity for every citizen;

And whereas at the threshold of a new era in history, the Irish electorate has in the general election of December, 1918, seized the first occasion to declare by an overwhelming majority its firm allegiance to the Irish Republic;

Now, therefore, we, the elected representatives of the ancient people, in National Parliament assembled, do, in the name of the Irish nation, ratify the establishment of the Irish Republic, and pledge ourselves and our people to make this declaration effective by every means at our command.

To ordain that the elected representatives of the Irish people alone have power to make laws binding on the people of Ireland, and that the Irish Parliament is the only Parliament to which the people will give its allegiance.

We solemnly declare foreign government in Ireland to be an invasion of our national right, which we will never tolerate, and we demand the evacuation of our country by the English garrison.

We claim for our national independence the recognition and support of every free nation of the world, and we proclaim that independence to be a condition precedent to international peace hereafter.

In the name of the Irish people, we humbly commit our destiny to Almighty God, Who gave our forefathers the courage and determination to persevere through centuries of ruthless tyranny, and strong in the justice of our cause which they have handed down to us, we ask His divine blessing on this, the last stage of the struggle which we have pledged ourselves to carry through to freedom.

Appendix VI

CONSTITUTION (BASIC LAW) OF THE UNION OF SOVIET SOCIALIST REPUBLICS, 1936

Social Organization

ARTICLE 1. The Union of Soviet Socialist Republics is a Socialist State of workers and peasants.

ARTICLE 4. The economic foundation of the U.S.S.R. consists in the socialist system of economy and socialist ownership of the implements and means of production, firmly established as a result of the liquidation of the capitalist system of economy, the abolition of private ownership of the instruments and means of production, and the abolition of exploitation of man by man.

ARTICLE 5. Socialist ownership in the U.S.S.R. has either the form of State ownership (public property) or the form of co-operative and collective farm ownership (property of individual collective farms, property of co-operative associations).

ARTICLE 9. Alongside the socialist system of economy, which is the dominant form of economy in the U.S.S.R., the law allows small private economy of individual peasants and handicraftsmen based on individual labour and excluding the exploitation of the labour of others.

ARTICLE 10. The personal ownership by citizens of their income from work and savings, home and auxiliary household economy, of objects of domestic and household economy as well as objects of personal use and comfort are protected by law.

State Organization

ARTICLE 13. The Union of Soviet Socialist Republics is a federal State, formed on the basis of the voluntary association of the Soviet Socialist Republics with equal rights.

ARTICLE 14. The jurisdiction of the Union of Soviet Socialist Republics, as represented by its supreme organs of power and organs of State administration, extends to:—

(a) Representation of the Union in international relations, conclusion and ratification of treaties with other States.

(*b*) Questions of war and peace.
(*c*) Admission of new republics into the U.S.S.R.
(*d*) Control of the observance of the Constitution of the U.S.S.R. and ensuring conformity of the Constitutions of the Union republics with the Constitution of the U.S.S.R.
(*e*) Approval of alterations of boundaries between Union republics.
(*f*) Organization of the defence of the U.S.S.R. and the direction of all the armed forces of the U.S.S.R.
(*g*) Foreign trade on the basis of the State monopoly.
(*h*) Protection of State security.
(*i*) Establishment of the national economic plans of the U.S.S.R.
(*j*) Approval of the unified State budget of the U.S.S.R. as well as the taxes and revenues entering into the U.S.S.R., Union republic and local budgets.
(*k*) Administration of banks, industrial and agricultural establishments as well as trading enterprises of all-Union importance.
(*l*) Administration of transport and means of communication.
(*m*) Direction of the monetary and credit system.
(*n*) Organization of the State insurance of property.
(*o*) Contracting and granting of loans.
(*p*) Establishment of the fundamental principles for the use of land as well as the exploitation of deposits, forests and waters.
(*q*) Establishment of the fundamental principles in the field of education and protection of public health.
(*r*) Organization of a unified system of national economic accounting.
(*s*) Establishment of basic labour laws.
(*t*) Legislation on judicature and legal procedure, criminal and civil codes.
(*u*) Laws on citizenship of the Union, laws on the rights of foreigners.
(*v*) Passing all-Union amnesty acts.

Basic Rights and Obligations of Citizens

ARTICLE 118. Citizens of the U.S.S.R. have the right to work—the right to receive guaranteed work with payment for their work in accordance with its quantity and quality.

The right to work is ensured by the socialist organization of national economy, the steady growth of the productive forces of Soviet society, the absence of economic crises, and the abolition of unemployment.

ARTICLE 122. Women in the U.S.S.R. are accorded equal rights with men in all fields of economic, State, cultural, social and political life.

The possibility of realizing these rights of women is ensured by affording women equally with men the right to work, payment for work, rest, social insurance and education, State protection of the interests of mother and child, granting pregnancy leave with pay, and the provision of a wide network of maternity homes, nurseries and kindergartens.

ARTICLE 123. The equality of the rights of citizens of the U.S.S.R., irrespective of their nationality or race, in all fields of economic, State, cultural, social and political life, is an irrevocable law.

Any direct or indirect restriction of these rights, or conversely the establishment of direct or indirect privileges for citizens on account of the race or nationality to which they belong, as well as any propagation of racial or national exceptionalism or hatred and contempt, is punishable by law.

ARTICLE 124. To ensure to citizens freedom of conscience the church in the U.S.S.R. is separated from the State and the school from the church. Freedom to perform religious rites and freedom of anti-religious propaganda is recognized for all citizens.

ARTICLE 125. In accordance with the interest of the toilers, for the purpose of strengthening the socialist system, the citizens of the U.S.S.R. are guaranteed:—

(*a*) Freedom of speech.
(*b*) Freedom of the Press.
(*c*) Freedom of assembly and meetings.
(*d*) Freedom of street processions and demonstrations.

These rights of the citizens are ensured by placing at the disposal of the toilers and their organizations printing presses, supplies of paper, public buildings, streets, means of communication and other material conditions necessary for their realization.

ARTICLE 126. In accordance with the interests of the toilers and for the purpose of developing the organizational self-expression and political activity of the masses of the people, citizens of the U.S.S.R. are ensured the right of combining in public organizations: trade unions, co-operative associations, youth organizations, sport and defence organizations, cultural, technical and scientific societies, and for the most active and conscientious citizens from the ranks of the working-class and other strata of the toilers of uniting in the Communist Party of the U.S.S.R., which is the vanguard of the toilers in their struggle for strengthening and developing the socialist system and which represents the leading nucleus of all organizations of the toilers, both public and State.

Appendix VII

EXTRACTS FROM THE PROGRAMME OF THE TURKISH REPUBLICAN PARTY

Endorsed by the Fourth Grand Congress of the Party, May, 1935

Introduction

The fundamental ideas that constitute the basis of the Programme of the Republican Party of the People are evident in the acts and realizations which have taken place from the beginning of our Revolution until to-day.

On the other hand, the main ideas have been formulated in the general principles of the Statutes of the Party, adopted also by the Grand Congress of the Party in 1927, as well as in the Declaration published on the occasion of the elections to the Grand National Assembly in 1931.

The main lines of our intentions, not only for a few years, but for the future as well, are here put together in a compact form. All of these principles which are the fundamentals of the Party constitute Kemalism.

Principles:

Turkey is a nationalist, populist (i.e. dependent upon popular sovereignty), State socialist, secular, and revolutionary Republic.

The form of administration of the Turkish nation is based on the principle of the unity of power. There is only one Sovereignty, and it belongs to the nation without restriction or condition.

The Grand National Assembly exercises the right of sovereignty in the name of the nation. The legislative authority and the executive power are embodied in the Grand National Assembly. The Assembly exercises its legislative power itself. It leaves its executive authority to the President of the Republic, elected from among its members, and to the Council of Ministers appointed by him. The courts in Turkey are independent

The Essential Characteristics of the Republican Party of the People

The source of Will and Sovereignty is the Nation. The Party considers it an important principle that this Will and Sovereignty be used to regulate the proper fulfilment of the mutual duties of the citizen to the State and of the State to the citizen.

We consider the individuals who accept an absolute equality before the Law, and who recognize no privileges for any individual, family, class, or community, to be of the people and for the people (populist).

It is one of our main principles to consider the people of the Turkish Republic, not as composed of different classes, but as a community divided into various professions according to the requirements of the division of labour for the individual and social life of the Turkish people.

The farmers, handicraftsmen, labourers and workmen, people exercising free professions, industrialists, merchants, and public servants are the main groups of work constituting the Turkish community. The functioning of each of these groups is essential to the life and happiness of the others and of the community. . . .

The Party considers it a principle to have the laws, regulations, and methods in the administration of the State prepared and applied in conformity with the needs of the world and on the basis of the fundamentals and methods provided for modern civilization by Science and Technique.

As the conception of religion is a matter of conscience, the Party considers it to be one of the chief factors of the success of our nation in contemporary progress, to separate ideas of religion from politics, and from the affairs of the world and of the State.

Appendix VIII

EXTRACTS FROM THE WEIMAR CONSTITUTION, PASSED BY THE NATIONAL ASSEMBLY, AUGUST 11, 1919

Preamble:

The German people, united in every respect and inspired by the determination to restore and confirm the Reich in freedom and justice, to serve peace at home and abroad, and to further social progress, has given itself this Constitution.

The Frame of the Constitution

(Art. 1) The German Reich is a Republic. The political power emanates from the people. (Art. 17) Every State must have a republican Constitution (*freistaatliche Verfassung*). The representative body must be elected by universal, equal, direct and secret suffrage of all German citizens of either sex, according to the principles of proportional representation. The State government must have the confidence of the people's representatives.

(Art. 20) The Reichstag shall be composed of the representatives of the German people. (Art. 22) The deputies shall be elected by the universal, equal, direct and secret suffrage of all men and women over twenty years of age, according to the principle of proportional representation. *(Art. 48) If a State fails to carry out the duties imposed upon* it by the national Constitution or national laws, the President of the Reich may compel performance with the aid of armed force.

Fundamental Rights and Duties

(Art. 109) All Germans are equal before the law. Men and women have in principle the same civil rights and duties. Privileges or discriminations in public law, based upon birth or rank, are abolished.

(Art. 114) Liberty of the person is inviolable. A restriction upon, or deprivation of, personal liberty, may not be imposed by public authority except by law. (Art. 118) Every German has the right within the limits of the general laws to express his opinion freely. This right must not be affected by any conditions arising out of his work or employment, and no one shall discriminate against him if he makes use of such right. (Art. 123) All Germans have the right to assemble peaceably and unarmed without notification or special permission. (Art. 124) All Germans have the right to form societies or associations for purposes not prohibited by the criminal code. This right may not be limited by preventive regulations.

(Art. 135) All inhabitants of the Reich shall enjoy complete liberty of belief and conscience. The peaceful exercise of religious worship shall be guaranteed by the Constitution and is under the protection of the State. (Art. 136) Civil and political rights and duties shall be neither conditioned upon, nor restricted by, the exercise of religious freedom. The enjoyment of civil and political rights as well as eligibility to public office shall be independent of religious belief.

(Art. 151) The organization of economic life must conform to the principles of justice to the end that all may be guaranteed a decent standard of living. (Art. 153) Property shall be guaranteed by the Constitution. Its nature and limits shall be prescribed by law.

(Art. 165) Workers and employees shall be called upon to co-operate in common with employers, and on an equal footing, in the regulation of salaries and working conditions as well as in the entire field of the economic development of the forces of production. The organization on both sides and their agreements shall be recognized.

Workers and employees shall, for the purpose of looking after their economic and social interests, be given legal representation in Factory Workers' Councils, as well as in District Workers' Councils organized on the basis of economic areas and in a Workers' Council of the Reich.

District Workers' Councils and the Workers' Council of the Reich shall meet with the representatives of employers and other interested population groups as District Economic Councils and as an Economic Council of the Reich (*Reichswirtschaftsrat*) for the purpose of performing economic functions and for co-operation in the execution of the laws of socialization. District Economic Councils and the Economic Council of the Reich shall be constituted so that all important economic groups shall be represented therein proportionately to their economic and social importance.

The National Ministry shall, before proposing drafts of politico-social and politico-economic bills of fundamental importance, submit them to the Economic Council of the Reich for consideration. The Economic Council of the Reich shall itself have the right to initiate drafts of such bills. If the National Ministry fails to assent, it shall nevertheless present the draft to the Reichstag accompanied by an expression of its views. The Economic Council of the Reich may designate one of its members to appear before the Reichstag on behalf of the proposal.

Powers of control of administration may be conferred upon Workers' Economic Councils within the spheres assigned to them.

The regulation of the development and functions of Workers' and Economic Councils, as well as their relations with other administratively autonomous social bodies, shall be exclusively a matter of the Reich.

Appendix IX

EXTRACTS FROM THE CONSTITUTION OF THE SPANISH REPUBLIC, PROCLAIMED ON DECEMBER 9, 1931, BY THE CONSTITUENT CORTES

Spain, by Right of Its Sovereignty, and represented by the Constitutional Cortes, decrees and sanctions this Constitution:

(Art. 1) Spain is a democratic republic of workers of all classes which is organized as a régime of liberty and justice. The powers of all its organs emanate from the people. The Republic constitutes an integral State compatible with the autonomy of municipalities and regions. . . .

Rights and Duties of Spaniards

(Art. 2) All Spaniards are equal before the law. (Art. 25) Race, descent, sex, social class, wealth, political ideas or religious beliefs shall not be considered the basis of privilege in public law. The State shall not recognize distinctions or titles of nobility.

(Art. 3) The Spanish State has no official religion. (Art. 27) Freedom of conscience and the right to profess and practise freely any religion are guaranteed in Spanish territory, provided public morals are safeguarded. . . . All denominations may observe their rites privately. Public celebration of the rites of a sect in each case must be authorized by the Government. No one shall be compelled to declare officially his religious beliefs. (Art. 26) All religious denominations shall be considered as associations subject to special laws. The State, the regions, the provinces and the municipalities shall not maintain or favour or financially aid the Churches and the religious associations and institutions.

(Art. 33) Every person is free to choose his profession. Liberty of industry and commerce is recognized, except for limitations that the law may impose for social and economic reasons of general interest. (Art. 39) Spaniards shall have the right freely to form associations and syndicates for the diverse purposes of life in conformity with the laws of the State. . . .

(Art. 34) Every person has the right to express freely his ideas and opinions, making use of any means of diffusion without subjecting himself to prior censorship. (Art. 38) The right of peaceable assembly without arms is recognized. A special law shall regulate the right of outdoor meetings and parades. (Art. 36) Citizens of both sexes over the age of 23 years shall have equal voting rights in accordance with the laws.

Economy and Culture

(Art. 44) All the wealth of the country regardless of its ownership is subordinate to the interests of national economy and it affects the maintenance of public obligations in accordance with the Constitution and the laws. The ownership of all types of property may be the object of forced expropriation in the interest of social welfare by means of an adequate indemnification, unless a law approved by an absolute majority of the Cortes shall make contrary disposition. The Socialization of property may be carried out under the same conditions. Public services and enterprises which affect the common interest may be rationalized in such cases as social necessity may require. The law permits the State to participate in the development and co-ordination of industries and enterprises should this be required in the regulation of production and the interests of national economy. In no case shall property be confiscated.

(Art. 45) All the artistic and historical wealth of the country, regardless of ownership, constitutes the cultural treasure of the nation, and it shall be under the guardianship of the State, which shall have the power to forbid its exportation and transference and to decree the legal expropriations which may be deemed proper for its preservation. ... (Art. 46) ... The Republic shall assure each worker the conditions necessary for suitable existence. Social legislation shall regulate: question of health, accident, unemployment, old age, disability, and death insurance; the labour of women and the young, and especially the protection of maternity; the number of hours of work and the minimum income of individuals and families; yearly vacations with pay; the condition of the Spanish worker in foreign countries; co-operative societies and associations; the economic and legal relation of the factors which integrate production; the participation of workers in the administration, direction, and benefits of enterprises and everything that affect the welfare of the workers.

(Art. 47) The Republic shall protect the farmer and to this end shall legislate, among other matters, concerning such family patrimony as is non-mortgageable and exempted from all kinds of taxes, agricultural loans, indemnification for loss of crops, co-operatives for production and consumption, weather bureaus, schools of practical agriculture, experimental stations for agriculture and cattle raising, irrigation, and rural roads.

(Art. 48) ... The primary school shall be free and compulsory. ... Teaching shall be laical; it shall use work as the centre of its methodological activity, and it shall be inspired by ideals of human solidarity...

The Cortes

(Art. 51) The legislative power resides in the people and is exercised by means of the Cortes. (Art. 52) The Cortes is composed of representatives elected by equal, direct and secret universal suffrage. (Art. 53) All citizens over twenty-three years of age without distinction as to sex or civil status shall be eligible for membership provided that they fulfil the conditions fixed by the electoral law. . . .

(Art. 66) By means of the "referendum" the people may decide upon the laws passed by the Cortes. This may be accomplished by a petition signed by fifteen per cent of the electoral body. The Constitution and its complementary laws, the ratification of international agreements registered in the League of Nations, the regional statutes and the tributary laws shall not be subject to such action. The people shall, likewise, exercising the right of initiative, present to the Cortes the proposal of a law whenever this should be demanded by at least fifteen per cent of the electors. A special law shall regulate the proceedings and guarantees of the "referendum" and popular initiative.

Amendments of the Constitution

(Art. 121) A Court of Constitutional Guarantees is established with jurisdiction over the entire territory of the Republic. . . .

(Art. 125) The Constitution may be amended: (*a*) on proposal of the Government; (*b*) on proposal of one-fourth of the members of Parliament. In either of these cases the proposal shall indicate concretely the article or articles that are to be suppressed, amended or added to. It shall follow the procedure specified by a law, and the vote for the reform shall require two-thirds of the Deputies, in the exercise of their office, during the first four years of the life of the Constitution and an absolute majority thereafter. Once the necessity for reform is agreed upon, the Cortes shall be automatically dissolved and a new election shall be held within sixty days. The Cortes thus elected, functioning as a Constituent Assembly, shall decide upon the proposed amendment and it shall act then as the ordinary Cortes.

Temporary Disposition

The present Constituent Assembly shall elect by secret vote the first President of the Republic. For his election it shall require an absolute majority of the votes of the members in the exercise of their office. If none of the candidates shall obtain an absolute majority of votes, a new vote shall proceed, and the candidate who obtains the majority of votes shall be proclaimed elected.

Appendix X

THE DECLARATION OF INDEPENDENCE AT THE PLENARY SESSION OF THE CONGRESS AT LAHORE, 1939

"We believe that it is the inalienable right of the Indian people, as of any other people, to have freedom and to enjoy the fruits of their toil and have the necessities of life so that they may have full opportunities of growth. We believe also that if any government deprives a people of these rights and oppresses them, the people have a further right to alter it or abolish it. The British Government in India has not only deprived the Indian people of their freedom but has based itself on the exploitation of the masses, and has ruined India economically, politically, culturally and spiritually. We believe, therefore, that India must sever the British connection and attain *Purna Swaraj* or Complete Independence.

"India has been ruined economically. The revenue derived from our people is out of all proportion to our income. Our average income is 7 pice (less than 2½d.) per day, and of the heavy taxes we pay, 20 per cent are raised from the land revenue derived from the peasantry, and 3 per cent from the salt tax which falls most heavily on the poor.

"Village industries such as hand-spinning have been destroyed, leaving the peasantry idle for at least four months in the year and dulling their intellect for want of handicrafts; and nothing has been substituted, as in other countries, for the crafts thus destroyed.

"Customs and currency have been so manipulated as to heap further burdens on the peasantry. The British manufactured goods constitute the bulk of our imports. Customs duties betray clear partiality for British manufactures, and revenues from them is used not to lessen the burden on the masses but for sustaining a highly extravagant administration. Still more arbitrary has been the manipulation of the exchange ratio, which has resulted in millions being drained away from the country.

"Politically, India's status has never been so reduced as under the British régime. No reforms have given real political power to the people. The tallest of us have to bend before foreign authority. The rights of free expression of opinion and free association have been denied to us, and many of our countrymen are compelled to live in exile abroad and cannot return to their homes. All administrative talent is killed, and the masses have to be satisfied with petty village offices and clerkships.

"Culturally, the system of education has torn us from our moorings and our training has made us hug the very chains that bind us.

"Spiritually, compulsory disarmament has made us unmanly, and the presence of an alien army of occupation, employed with deadly effect to crush in us the spirit of existence, has made us think that we cannot look after ourselves or put up a defence against foreign aggression, or even defend our homes and families from the attack of thieves, robbers and miscreants.

"We hold it to be a crime against man and God to submit any longer to a rule that has caused this fourfold disaster to our country. We recognize, however, that the most effective way of gaining our freedom is not through violence. We will therefore prepare ourselves by withdrawing, so far as we can, all voluntary association from the British Government, and will prepare for Civil Disobedience, including non-payment of taxes. We are convinced that if we can but withdraw our voluntary help and stop payment of taxes without doing violence even under provocation, the end of this inhuman rule is assured. We therefore hereby solemnly resolve to carry out the Congress instructions issued from time to time for the purpose of establishing *Purna Swaraj*."

INDEX